A THEOLOGY OF THE THIRD ARTICLE

A THEOLOGY OF THE THIRD ARTICLE

KARL BARTH AND THE SPIRIT OF THE WORD

AARON T. SMITH

Fortress Press
Minneapolis

A THEOLOGY OF THE THIRD ARTICLE

Karl Barth and the Spirit of the Word

Cover image: The Pentecost/Scala/Art Resources, NY

Cover design: Laurie Ingram

Library of Congress Cataloging-in-Publication Data

Print ISBN: 978-1-4514-6471-9

eBook ISBN: 978-1-4514-6957-8

The paper used in this publication meets the minimum requirements of American National Standard for Information Sciences — Permanence of Paper for Printed Library Materials, ANSI Z329.48-1984.

Manufactured in the U.S.A.

This book was produced using PressBooks.com, and PDF rendering was done by PrinceXML.

For Ralph

CONTENTS

Acknowledgments

This book has been several years in the making. I first saw the need for it as a doctoral student at Marquette University and made an initial pass at its argument in my dissertation.[1] Few elements of that work remain; the structure of the whole has been changed, two chapters have been replaced entirely, and two others have been thoroughly rewritten. Only chapter 3 endures in a form that can be likened to its previous self, yet even here a final subsection has been added, which places Einstein's thought more thematically in conversation with Barth's.

Many of these changes have come from my own inability to leave the line of inquiry alone. Trusted advisors directed me to the others. The late Ralph Del Colle (d. July 2012) was an especially dear mentor whose work on Spirit-Christology exercised noteworthy influence, clarifying ideas and leading me to conclusions both convergent and divergent with his.[2] My debt to Bruce McCormack is substantial. McCormack has not only guided me with patience through the intricacies of his work, which show up here, but also forborne conversations about the use I would make of it. Markus Wriedt, Julian Hills, and Fr. Phil Rossi each gave helpful recommendations at the dissertation's defense concerning everything from style and tone to the theo-logic of Protestantism to the philosophy of ontological actualism. All of these recommendations have found their way into this book in some form.

I am grateful to students at Colorado Christian University who have taken my seminar, "Readings in Karl Barth," where together we have investigated several of the writings that feature prominently in the following pages. Also, students in Systematic Theology I and II have graciously endured my effort to apply the findings presented here by structuring the order and logic of the classes around the Spirit. (How is Lessing's ditch crossed? By God being so much God as to be this God again – *God* in and with what is not God, God in and with our space-time, God in and with *us!*)

---

1. Aaron T. Smith, "Inverberation—The Idiom of 'God among Us': Karl Barth's Filial-Pneumatology as the Basic Structure of Theology" (Ph. D. diss., Marquette University, 2009).

2. See Ralph Del Colle, *Christ and the Spirit: Spirit-Christology in Trinitarian Perspective* (Oxford: Oxford University Press, 1994).

Much of the research for the project was conducted while in receipt of a *Stipendium* from the *Johannes a Lasco Bibliothek* in Emden, Germany. I must thank my wife, Dawn, who selflessly put her own career plans on hold in order to allow the move "across the pond." I also must thank Prof. Dr. Herman Selderhuis and the *a Lasco* board for their generosity. The exceptional resources, which the library has collected and maintained, enabled me to work at a higher level than would have been possible otherwise. Given the guidance and material assistance that I have received, whatever shortcomings remain in the following pages surely stem from my own limitations.

Introduction

Christian theology thinks and speaks of God in terms of Jesus Christ. But what exactly does it mean to think and speak of God in terms of Jesus Christ? If Christian theology is to be decidedly *Christian* thought and speech, then it has to be more than religion, piety, or social justice. It has to be the reiteration of Jesus Christ himself—his life, ministry, death, and resurrection—in contemporary thoughts and words. If Jesus is anything less or other than the content of our thinking and form, the material of our speaking and method, then we cannot avoid constructing "God" according to some preconceived pattern in religious imagination, for which Jesus merely supplies the color and texture.

Christian faith, in other words, is not prior religious sentiment to which Jesus gives meaning and direction, or prior ethical impulses to which he provides an avenue of action. It is just the opposite. Christian faith is belief in Jesus as the revelation of God, as the condition by which belief in God is real and possible; it is thus the critical interrogation of all religious sentiment, and the life-act from which all ethical impulses are cultivated.

For Christian knowledge and confession, there is no God behind or prior to this one, Christ Jesus, no religion that is not subsumed into this life and no ethics that is not derived from it. Everything that we would think and say of God in eternity and in time, God in himself and for us, is given in the historical event of his being God-with-us, Immanuel.

I begin with these delimiting observations because this is a book about a topic commonly pursued with little delimitation, namely, the Holy Spirit. More exactly, it is a book about how to think and speak of the Holy Spirit as the center of further thought and speech of God. It is an extended prologue to a theology of the Third Article of the ancient creed of Nicaea (325 c.e.) and more fully, Nicaea-Constantinople (381 c.e.), the first of which confesses the existence of God's Spirit, and the second of which more fully acknowledges the divinity of the Spirit, along with the church and the life to come.[1] It is dedicated

---

1. On the rules of faith deriving from the first and second ecumenical councils of Nicaea and Nicaea-Constantinople, see for starters Henry Bettenson and Chris Maunder, eds., *Documents of the Christian Church*, 4th ed. (Oxford: Oxford University Press, 2011), 26–28; J. N. D. Kelly, *Early Christian Doctrines*, 5th ed. (New York: Harper & Row, 1978), 223–79.

to the premise that to think and speak of God even as Spirit, we must do so in terms of Jesus Christ, when "in terms of" indicates both a material and a methodological rule. *The only Spirit known and confessed by Christian theology is Spirit of the enfleshed Word.*

To do theology in terms of the Holy Spirit is to think and speak of God being God a third time. It is to think and speak of God being God again, as God always has been, but here and now, specifically in the terms of God's engagement with the creature, in the event of being engaged by God as a creature. There is no basis on which we might think and speak of God being God except the event in which he *is* God-with-us.

To be even more exact, then, this is a book about how to think and speak about God in terms of the Holy Spirit, arguing necessarily from within its own operation of faith, that is, clunky and suspicious as it may initially sound, *as* thought and speech given in and shaped after encounter with God being God *for us*. It can only show that we must think and speak of the Spirit in terms of Christ Jesus *by* thinking and speaking in terms of Christ Jesus. It does not linearly deduce that Christ is the exclusive basis and norm of thought and speech of the Spirit, for that would already mean that Christ is *not* its exclusive basis and norm, that it might work from a given ground or manner of deduction at least for a while, until it "found" God in Christ. It recognizes that the theologian does not find anything that has not first found it, that she is thrown into this hermeneutical spiral: one can only move to God from within God's movement to her in the incarnate Word. One can think of the Spirit only from within the divine address according to which the Spirit is known (but also of course, by whom there is the divine address!).

Those familiar with the last century of Christian theological reflection will notice that this line of thinking closely resembles that of the Swiss master, Karl Barth. In fact, this book makes its case by following Barth, teasing its defining features out of Barth's work and showing their necessary interconnection. It demonstrates that Barth had to think the way he did, and so must we—from Christ outward—lest the Holy Spirit be subsumed under the human spirit.

In this regard, the work also functions as a kind of summary defense of Barth against his critics, who maintain that he left little room for thinking and speaking of the Holy Spirit. Perhaps the most well known of such critics is Lutheran theologian Robert W. Jenson.

It is not entirely accurate to call Jenson a "critic" of Barth, for the majority of his work on Barth is approving,[2] and his own constructive efforts have clearly taken much from Barth.[3] Still, Jenson has publicly critiqued Barth for an alleged tendency to avoid a fully agential account of the Spirit, and to operate by lengthy turns with a "binitarian" rather than "trinitarian" logic.

In his brief but dense article "You Wonder Where the Spirit Went,"[4] Jenson "nit-picks" Barth's use of the Trinity as a dogmatic locus.[5] As is typical of Western trinitarian theologians, says Jenson, Barth conceives of God's three-in-oneness in a way that provides no resources for conceiving of the Persons as "parties of divine action."[6] And it would seem necessary to understand the Father, Son, and Spirit as discrete parties or self-directing agents if one is to *use* their respective activity to make other doctrinal claims, as Barth tries to do—to contend, for example, that maleness and femaleness reflect the Father–Son interplay of command and reception.[7] Barth would need to show how each of

---

2. See, for example, Robert W. Jenson, *Alpha and Omega: A Study in the Theology of Karl Barth* (New York: Thomas Nelson, 1963).

3. See, for example, Robert W. Jenson, *Systematic Theology*, 2 vols. (New York: Oxford University Press, 1997–99).

4. Robert W. Jenson, "You Wonder Where the Spirit Went," *Pro Ecclesia* 2, no. 3 (1993): 296–304.

5. Ibid, 297. Jenson identifies three modes of trinitarian thinking in Barth's work: as the identity of God, as a technical doctrine, and as a construct that one might use to think of other doctrines. It is only the last that Jenson "nit-picks" (his term) as lending itself to neglect of the Spirit.

6. Jenson, "You Wonder," 299.

7. "Male and female being is the prototype of all I and Thou, of all individuality in which man and man differ from and yet belong to each other," writes Barth in *Church Dogmatics*, III.4, ed. G. W. Bromiley and T. F. Torrance (London: T&T Clark, 2004), 150; subsequent citations in this book follow the conventional abbreviation, CD, followed by volume and part numbers, then page number. This individuality in belonging, or diversity in unity, is, for Barth, grounded in God's own life and characteristic of our being made in "the image of God" (Gen. 1:26-27): "That God created man as male and female, and therefore as His image and likeness . . . is something that can never lead to a neutral It . . . . but rather [founds] an inward, essential and lasting order of being as He and She, valid for all time and also for eternity" (CD III.4, 158). Because humanity is created per se as male and female, "they stand in a sequence. It is in this that man has his allotted place and woman hers" (CD III.4, 169). There is an order proper to male and female as humankind bears God's image. "A precedes B, and B follows A. Order means succession. . . . It means super- and sub-ordination" (CD III.4, 169). However, the language of "command and reception," or "super-ordination and subordination" should be taken neither to indicate a form of ontological deficiency in the Godhead nor to justify, on such a basis, male–female hierarchy in humanity. "When it is a question of the true order which God the Creator has established, succession, and therefore precedence and following, super- and sub-ordination, does not mean an inner inequality between those who stand in this succession and are subject to this order" (CD III.4, 170). That is because obedience is as proper to God's God-ness in the mode of his being the Son as command is of the Father; the former is not in any way a lesser sort of being, divine or creaturely. For more on this see CD IV.1, 199–210; see also Kevin Giles, "Barth and Subordinationism," *Scottish Journal of Theology* 64, no. 3 (2011): 327–46.

the Persons is constituted in or determined by such respective agential qualities if he is to apply those qualities to human social entities.

But rather than thinking of the Trinity in a way that allows for understanding the Persons as individual parties, Barth notoriously considers God as a singular being eternally existing in three *modes* (*Seinsweise*), where "being" (*Sein*) is not a substantialist über-quality, but an adverbial manner of existence (specifically, a unique and active Lordship). God is God in being Lord three times differently. In this, Barth reflects a Western emphasis on God's oneness,[8] and for all his creativity, Jenson argues, he cannot avoid slavishly repeating the failure latent in this emphasis of not thinking robustly of distinct centers of action in God. Thus, his doctrine of the Trinity does not justify the use that he tries to make of it.

This quintessential Western failure is a bigger problem in Barth's theology than in other thinkers "just on account of his achievements."[9] Because Barth succeeds in making the full scope of salvation history real in the life of God, God's triunity functions as a kind of calculus according to which God's life in relation to the creature, as well as the origin, nature, and goal of creation, is reckoned. So Jenson concludes, "in Barth's theology, Western trinitarianism's common difficulty in conceiving the Spirit's specific immanent initiative in God must become a difficulty in conceiving the Spirit's entire salvation-historical initiative."[10]

8. "A Western emphasis on God's oneness" is a somewhat casual association of two phenomena: a historical development in dogma emerging during the patristic era, above all in St. Augustine, which formulates its conception of triune God on the basis of a philosophical pre-commitment to the unity of "nature" (over against an Eastern/Cappadocian model deriving from distinct activities), and a more general tendency reflected among Catholic and Protestant dogmaticians across Christian history to emphasize the essential unity of the one God. Théodore de Régnon is credited with laying out the defining parameters of the first phenomenon; see *Études de théologie positive sur la Sainte Trinité* (Paris: Victor Retaux, 1892–98). Insofar as Jenson's critique is, at bottom, a critique of a basically Augustinian conceptual pattern (at least roughly following de Régnon's outline), then it is already refuted by Michel René Barnes and Lewis Ayres, each of whom has shown that de Régnon's construct fails to do justice to Augustine's actual dogmatic development and conclusions. See Barnes, "De Régnon Reconsidered," *Augustinian Studies* 26, no. 2 (1995): 51–79; Ayres, *Nicaea and Its Legacy: An Approach to Fourth Century Trinitarian Theology* (Oxford: Oxford University Press, 2004), 366–67; Ayres, *Augustine and the Trinity* (Cambridge: Cambridge University Press, 2010). Yet insofar as Jenson's concerns are directed toward the second phenomenon, a recurrent tendency in Catholic and Protestant dogmatics to give only superficial treatment to the Persons' distinctive activities vis-à-vis the constitution of God's God-ness, this especially with respect to the Spirit (so that one is left without adequate resources to think of "God" pneumatocentrically), then it continues to bear weight and must be addressed.

9. Jenson, "You Wonder," 299.

10. Ibid., 300.

Barth shares in the shortcoming of failing to account for the actuality not only of the Persons generally but above all of the Spirit. Since Augustine, the tendency has been to think of the Spirit as the "principle of peace" between the Father and the Son, making the Father and Son to be defined agents and the Spirit to be an undefined agency. The Father and Son have their Personhood in standing opposite one another—again in Barth, in a dynamic, salvation-historical way such that the Son has his Son-ship or filiation in humanly living the obedience to the Father that the creature does not, and in fully becoming sin for us, taking upon himself the judgment of the Father that is due us. It is not clear, in turn, how the Spirit is a self-determinative contributor to the triune life of God:

> Precisely in that the inner-trinitarian relations do gloriously become concrete and alive in Barth, so that the Father and the Son *confront* one another, the actuality of a *vinculum* between the two parties Father and Son must be their I-thou relation itself. Thus the very reality of the Spirit excludes his appearance as a party in the triune actuality.[11]

God is actually triune God in the eternal event of self-election wherein the Father and Son stand in a concrete, salvation-historical relationship to one another, leaving the Spirit only to be the impersonal relation or mutuality between the First and Second Persons. We might say that the Spirit actualizes the Father–Son history; he is not an actuality with the Father and Son in history. "When does the Spirit disappear from Barth's pages," Jenson asks? "Whenever he would appear as someone rather than something. We miss the Spirit at precisely those points where the Bible or catechism have taught us to expect him to appear as someone *with* capacities, rather than as sheer capacity."[12]

Jenson is surely right to raise the conundrum, not unique to Barth, as to how the Holy Spirit can be known as the power of God without, by that very knowledge, denying self-determinative actuality in full correspondence to the self-determinative actuality of the Father and Son. I put the matter this way—in view of the *knowledge* of God—because it strikes me that this is the fulcrum, the point to which Jenson's analysis leads yet also at which it comes up short, thus

11. Ibid., 301.
12. Ibid., 304.

the point at which Barth's thought concerning the Spirit is comprehended in its full viability.

Absent from Jenson's otherwise incisive analysis, perhaps just due to its limited scope but conspicuous all the same, is the central Barthian motif of *revelation*. Granting potential shortcomings attending the method, it is nevertheless important that Barth derives his doctrine of the Trinity from a question concerning *who* it is that reveals, *what* is revealed, and *how*.[13] He does so because he realizes that one really cannot properly inquire of God without having first been met by God; one cannot presume adequate, operative "equipment," if you will, by which one forms even the very question of God. Apart from the prior fact of revelation, one knows neither the triune God nor her place within the salvation-historical life of God, so that she might summon the thoughts and words by which "God" becomes a proper object of investigation.

Precisely in self-determined triunity, God is so "wholly other," so qualitatively distinct from humanity that humanity stands comprehensively in need of God's Word if God is to be known. Yet in speaking to us, in telling us who God is and who we are in relation, God must remain *God*—utterly distinct and transcendent even in familiarity and proximity. If "God" is to mean anything more than *glorified humanity*, Barth reasons, then he must not be inhibited either by himself, unable by virtue of his eternal distinctness to come to time and familiarity, or by us, unable by virtue of our temporal commonness to be Lord among us. He must moment-by-moment remain the incomparable Lord even as he exists in ordinary flesh and language.

For Barth, then, the being of God, his very triune existence is an active *way* of being; it is, namely, the dialectical reality of overcoming the boundary that separates deity and humanity exactly in the event that he makes that boundary to be real and perceived. There is no God or God-ness (way of being "God") outside of this active happening.

13. Or, the doctrine of the Trinity is the doctrine of God as "revelation," "revealer," and "being revealed"; see Barth, CD I.1, 304–33. Concerning potential shortcomings of Barth's trinitarian derivation in CD I.1, see Bruce McCormack, "The Doctrine of the Trinity after Barth: An Attempt to Reconstruct Barth's Doctrine in the Light of His Later Christology," in *Trinitarian Theology after Barth*, ed. Myk Habets and Phillip Tolliday, Princeton Theological Monograph Series 148 (Eugene, Ore.: Pickwick, 2011), 87–118. McCormack argues that the abstractedness characterizing Barth's concept of divine Lordship, trading as it does upon undefined notions of power, which guides his early triune discourse, would have to be revised in light of the concrete, human submission of the Son in his mature Christology.

That means that there is no God outside of the event in which God makes himself known, the event of revelation. Barth expects us to think and speak of God entirely within this event. And in doing so, there is in fact meaningful opportunity to think and speak of the Holy Spirit as full actuality or "party" in the life of God. To be precise, it is possible within the framework of revelation to think and speak of the Spirit as both the power of God and a center of power, as both the principle of divine love and self-determinative iteration of that love in salvation history.

I argue that the Spirit is God a third time, subsisting in ontological unity with the Father and Son, yet distinctly his own Person in that he is the contemporaneity of the revelation event in which God has his existence. The Spirit self-determinatively repeats the (ontologically decisive) will of God to be God-with-us by reiterating the life-act in which God is in fact with us. The Spirit is contemporary instantiation of the Incarnation, or, the parallel life-act of *Inverberation*.

To *verberate* means "to strike so as to produce a sound."[14] The object struck can be an instrument, as in percussion. But the meaning I would highlight is the etymological act of producing sound waves: air struck by vocal muscling, which generates an object for hearing. When I say that in and as the Spirit God is inverberate I mean that he continues to generate a real object for ocular and auditory ingestion by placing himself before us in the reading and proclaiming of Scripture. As these human words throttle space-time, the Spirit mediates correspondence between them and the eternal Word. The beating rhythm of Spirit-Word is God's truth, which objectivity shapes us as subjects. The Spirit-shaped event is not something that, as such, can only be "perceived" by a mystical sixth sense, if we close off our natural senses and wait to be enraptured in inexpressibilities. Rather, God makes *himself* perceptible in and by our senses, in and by speech and its ocular and auditory partaking.

In and through this coordinated object of sensation we are translated subjects, we receive the "eyes and ears" of faith and recognize that we cannot fix this occurrence as spoken, seen, and heard. We recognize that it is faith itself that enables us to speak, see, and hear truthfully. Our tongue, eyes, and ears are ratified *and* rebuffed moment by moment in the event of God among us. Wording, seeing, and hearing *God,* they are muted, blinded, and deafened, "for no one may see me and live" (Exod. 33:20b). The dialectic of this No and Yes, of God having his life in the unique freedom to be both against sin and for us,

---

14. *Oxford English Dictionary*. With *inverberation* I am trying to evoke an etymological association with *verbum*, as in *verbum dei*.

uniquely in judgment and salvation, to be God in the incarnate Word again today in unqualified continuity with, yet real distinction from, his way of being God there and then, is the life and work of the Holy Spirit.

The Holy Spirit is *Spirit of the Word*. He is not a free-floating second revelation of God alongside or at variance with Christ, but the ongoing reality of God in his historical revelation as that revelation takes place in the idiomatic thoughts and words (*verba*) of Christ's proclamation today.

The desire, however catechetically inspired and ecumenically minded, to think and speak of the Spirit as a party of action in the Godhead does not grant license to ideate in abstraction from God's self-determinative act of revelation, of speaking to us but as God, of assuming flesh but as the eternal Lord. The Spirit, too, is this very self-determination. He is God in active generation and assumption of ongoing, contextualized human words bearing witness to the revelation event of the Word's enfleshing. This *act* of assumption must be understood in terms of the Word's assuming flesh, so that again we are not thinking and speaking of God in any way other than his thought and speech directed to us. And the *content* of the act, the actual, collective ideas and words assumed, must be neither more nor less than formal witness to God's own thought and speech, to Jesus Christ.

The Spirit is Spirit, then, in the event of the *church*—the where and when of gospel proclamation—in a manner parallel to the way that the Word is Word in the specific flesh of Jesus of Nazareth (and not flesh or humanity in general). The Word assumed *this* flesh, and the Spirit assumes witness to *this* logically prior assumption.

Jenson rightly calls attention to the intimate connection between the Personhood of the Spirit and the actuality of the people of God. He suggests that Barth's failure to understand the Spirit as a distinct center of action in God corresponds to his failure to think concretely and extensively enough about the church. "Perhaps the final reason for the whole web of Spirit-avoidance in the *Kirchliche Dogmatik* is avoidance of the church."[15] "Spirit-avoidance" is a misleading caricature, as is the curious corollary that Barth somehow avoids the church in his massive *Church Dogmatics*. (Is this not a work for the church and, in many respects, about the church inasmuch as it is about the God who only is known as Lord over these people, Father of these children?) But Jenson is correct to locate the salvation-historical life and work of the Spirit in and with those being "called out" to faith in Christ. I will show that Barth in fact points us in just this direction.

15. Jenson, "You Wonder," 302.

As Spirit of the Word, the Spirit is agentially objectified in the act and content of the church's proclamation of the gospel, in which act and content the *ecclesia* itself comes into being. Proclamation of Christ means holistic obedience to Christ, the embodied, visible, secondarily determinative life-act of receiving and attentively declaring him, declaring and attentively receiving him in thoughts, words, and kinetic activities shaped after the testimony of the prophets and apostles.

Jenson indicates that this is the direction Barth ought to have taken:

> For if the Pentecostal creation of a structured continuing community were identified as the "objectivity" of the gospel's truth *pro nobis*, then this community itself, in its structured temporal and spatial extension, would be seen as the *Bedingung der Möglichkeit* of faith. Or again, if the Community between the Father and the Son were himself an agent of their love, immanently and economically, then the church, as the community inspirited by the Agent, would be the active *mediatrix* of faith.[16]

I contend that this is the direction Barth *did* take, albeit perhaps incipiently in a penultimate phase of his work (yet already with greater refinement than Jenson's critique affords), thus that the Spirit is not nearly so absent from his pages as it might seem. On the contrary, Barth gives ample resources for thinking and speaking of the Spirit precisely as a Western Protestant theologian committed to the decisiveness of the Word.

Barth perceives, especially in a period of work stretching from the mid-1920s to the late 1930s, that at the heart of the Reformation construal of the church is not its imperceptibility but its event-character. The church is a being in becoming, which corresponds directly to the actuality of God's own being in Christ Jesus. The church happens in the happening of obedience to Christ, thus it is an entirely visible enterprise, an organism of the gospel's objectivity with space-time extension. But unlike Jenson, whose ecumenical interests leave him dissatisfied with an ecclesiology that does not locate faith's "condition of possibility" in the church, Barth retains the Reformation emphasis on the active operation of God in the event of faith rather than on the (all too human) church.

16. Ibid., 303.

The *Bedingung der Möglichkeit* of faith is not the community per se, but the condition of the community's possibility, for the community is neither more nor less than beings in every time and place who are receiving and coming to faith. It is neither more nor less than those who have met Christ Jesus again, in this context, and have responded again, in ways appropriate to this context. The Spirit is the power of this happening, as well as the origin and goal. He is the authority of the witness confronting these persons in this place, its force and effect, as well as the inspiriting source and illuminating end of this witness. He is therefore identified with the community of faith, but indirectly, as the Son was indirectly identified with the flesh of Jesus.

In short, Barth is able to think and speak of the Spirit in a way that his critics do not allow, as the divine agency *and* agent. But he can do so *only* by remaining true to the insight, flashing once more upon the scene during the Reformation, that God is the *living* God. God has his being actualistically, in the life-act of the incarnate Word here and now just as he did there and then, in 1–30 C.E.

If we are to follow Barth, then we think and speak of the Spirit not only as an agency in service to the Word but also as a party in the Godhead known and confessed in terms of the Word. We seek the Spirit in truth when we seek him in the same self-determinative will of God to be-with-us that we encounter in Christ Jesus, in continuing encounter with the reality of Christ Jesus as Lord in our time and place *and* in reiteration of the real dialectic that is Christ Jesus. The Spirit is Spirit of the Word when and where Christ is made to be Lord here and now, in the event of actual thought and speech that are captive to him, *and* thus in the generation and assumption of that thought and speech as the revelation of God. The Spirit is Spirit of the Word in the event of the church, when "church" is the collective happening of faith in Christ extending across space-time, hence occurring again as a structured reality in this space-time.

I make this argument over five chapters. Chapter 1 demonstrates that at the core of Barth's understanding of God, as an understanding forged in response to the subjectivity of modern Protestant liberalism, is the objectivity of God's life-act in the enfleshed Word. This objectivity must remain in force in any account of God, for it is characteristic of God as he makes himself known, which is to say, as he *is* in the event of revelation. We cannot circumvent divine objectivity without also circumventing divine revelation, and in this, the determinative event of God *being God*. Thus, when we turn to the Spirit, to the event of God being God *in* human being, we cannot lose the objectivity of God. Divine subjectivity remains shaped after divine objectivity, after God's uniqueness in Christ Jesus; God is God in Christ even when and where he is God in us.

Barth states the same basic conviction concerning the subject-determining objectivity of God in terms of "reality" and "possibility." Chapter 2 shows that the reality of God is given shape and structure in Christ, such that reality external to him (the life-act of the creature) and all possibility (that and what God might be and that and what creation might be) are critically delimited by Christ. The revelation of God in the Christ-event is determinative of God and of all being relative to God. If we are to do theology in terms of the Spirit, then, we must do it in terms of the event of revelation in which the definition and determination of divine and human reality take place.

Indeed, the possibility of such thought and speech must itself be grounded in the movement of this revelation, given in and with it, for there is no reality outside of this event according to which true thought and speech of God can happen. The happening of revelation must be generative, and it must be reiterated here and now; the dialectic of God's assuming creaturely modalities without forfeiting his deity in so doing, but in fact, having his deity just in the freedom for this act of assumption, must be a continuing reality in the Spirit. The Spirit must have his life and work *in* contemporary *verberation* of witness to Christ if authentic thought and speech of God are even to be *possible*.

But if God is objective reality, such that all creaturely reality and subjective possibility are contingent upon his being God in Christ, of the Spirit of God having his life and work in the act of making Christ authoritatively manifest here and now, then God is no aloof entity in some kind of metaphysical stasis.[17] Chapter 3 contends that God is God in coming to space-time, in fact, in taking

17. So far as I can tell, the argument that I am making in this book runs parallel to that made recently by Kevin W. Hector in *Theology without Metaphysics: God, Language, and the Spirit of Recognition*, Current Issues in Theology 8 (Cambridge: Cambridge University Press, 2011). Hector argues for a "non-essentialist" account of language, in which concepts obtain meaning as they "link up with a chain of precedents that carries on the normative commitment implicit in an initial act of picking-out, in such a way that one inherits . . . that commitment" (p. 38). The concept of God, for instance, becomes an intelligible concept insofar as it is takes place within a normative pattern of discursive commitments, which are implied in the primitive act of selecting this particular "God-language"; then and only then can it be inherited and passed along. In such an account, the Spirit of Christ is the agency of normative commitment. He is recognized, or perhaps better, re-cognized in intersubjective patterns of thought and behavior stemming from Christ through his disciples. At times, Hector is still able to speak of "the Spirit" as an entity, which commandeers language, and thus in at least quasi-metaphysical terms. For instance, he can say that "the Spirit conforms one's beliefs to Christ" (p. 39), when it would seem more consistent with his own argument to formulate this more like, "the Spirit's life is in the act of conforming one's beliefs to Christ," or more strongly, "the Spirit just is the conforming of one's beliefs to Christ." There is no knowledge, no concept, "spirit," external to this life-act. But this is a nit-picky observation on my part, and one that Hector may be able to answer with more expansive explanation (to call *Theology without Metaphysics* dense would be a terrific understatement). In any event, I take his main point to be

up the constitutive features of space-time in order to make himself known in them and thus remaking them in each instant of his revelation to be adequate to him. It shows that this way of thinking and speaking of God (this Spirit-centered thought and speech patterned after Christ) is entirely viable relative to the modern understanding of space-time articulated by Albert Einstein.

God has his being in coming to space-time; humanity has its being in contemporary response, correspondence, to this coming. Just as God takes temporality to himself in Christ, so does he create the condition of possibility for us to be his children in this temporality, in the life-act of obedience to him, which co-determines our history as *time for God*. Chapter 4 returns to the constructs of *reality* and *possibility* in order to show that the event of God being God a third time entails the continued restructuring of human existence in the lived happening of the *church*. The church is the first fruit of space-time obedience to the Word through which the inverberate opposition of God to all non-being, darkness, and death is made manifest to the world.

To think and speak of God in terms of the Spirit as the Spirit of Christ Jesus, then, is to think and speak of God in his self-determination to be God in refusal of every force of opposition to him, in the revelation and cultivation of obedience to his definitive Lordship. Chapter 5 argues that the Spirit is the contemporary instantiation of obedience to God made real and revealed in Christ Jesus as the Subject and Object of the primal decision in which, for Barth, God is God. He is the Spirit of divine Self-election to the humiliation of servitude, damnation, and death, on the one side, and in and through this, to the exaltation of rule, salvation, and resurrection, on the other.

Lakewood, CO
August, 2013

correct, namely, that we can think and speak of the Spirit only in the event of re-cognizing the normative patterns of thought and speech given in Christ Jesus.

1

The Spirit of Objectivity and Subjectivity

What I object to is the disappearance of the object. In art, as in theology, it is the object that counts, not the subject.
-Karl Barth[1]

Karl Barth was born in 1886 in Basel, Switzerland, into a tradition of Reformed Protestant ministry. His father and both grandfathers were pastors in Basel. In keeping with the family's legacy, Karl undertook theological studies at the universities of Bern, Berlin, Tübingen, and Marburg, completing his formal education in 1909. He intended to study for a doctorate under his beloved Marburg professor, Wilhelm Herrmann, but that never materialized. In fact, he never earned an advanced degree.[2] Instead, like his father and grandfathers, Barth entered parish ministry. He served for two years as assistant pastor of a German-speaking Reformed congregation in Geneva, then for ten years as pastor of a mostly working-class congregation in Safenwil.

Barth's time in the parish helped him to clarify certain convictions about the Christian message, which later gave him a distinctive voice in the academy. He learned above all that the liberal tradition he had enthusiastically embraced in theology (Herrmann), history (Adolf von Harnack), social theory (Leonhard Ragaz and Herrmann Kutter), and exegesis (Adolf Jülicher) did not address the existential crisis that he found parishioners to bring with them to church. Barth discovered that the questions that really animated his parishioners, that made

1. Karl Barth, cited by John T. Elson, "Witness to an Ancient Truth," Time, April 20, 1962, 65.

2. He was, however, awarded eleven honorary doctorates; see Barth, *Letters 1961–1968,* ed. Jürgen Fangmeier and Hinrich Stoevesandt, trans. Geoffrey W. Bromiley (Grand Rapids: Eerdmans, 1981), 259. See also Barth, *Final Testimonies,* ed. Eberhard Busch, trans. Geoffrey W. Bromiley (Grand Rapids: Eerdmans, 1977), 23: "That's *all* I am," Barth replied to an interviewer asking why he was listed only as an honorary doctor. "It's the way it was. I was not aiming at an academic career. I wanted to be a pastor."

them come to church in the first place, concerned the fact and nature of God's existence and their nature and destiny relative to him. They did not primarily concern ethical directives. It was not enough, therefore, to treat their faith as one expression of a universal religious consciousness (even if the highest), from which one could distill timeless principles of moral living. It was not enough to cultivate ethical social values modeled after the "historical Jesus."

It is not that Jesus' historical life is irrelevant. Rather, as most pastors do, Barth learned that people handle moral living well enough on their own. "Obviously the people have *no* real need of *our* observations upon morality and culture," he reflected.[3] Laypersons are capable of modeling a life of charity and personal discipline around the life, ministry, death, and resurrection of Jesus without the historical-critical insights of the liberal pastor. What they really wanted, and needed, was someone to speak to the *horizon of mortality*. Barth found that his education and approach to ministry more or less domesticated this existential need. It offered almost nothing to the demanding, in fact impossible task actually confronting the minister: to address the everlasting reality facing humanity beyond death.[4]

Faced with the insufferable pastoral challenge to speak of the eternal beyond rather than ephemeral morality, of the life of God before and above the life of humanity, Barth began to rethink the very nature of preaching and theology. How could it be possible to speak of God if not in terms of pious affections? What is "God" if not the basis and goal of human devotional ideals, of a manner of being that transcends brutish survivalism and self-interest in pursuit of higher consciousness and purpose? What can the content of "God" be—to what can the term give expression—apart from realization of superlative states of being and doing: the Ground of Existence, the Ultimate, the *Summum Bonum*? What can the Christian know of deity except as realization of a purified humanity?

Barth was on the cusp of realizing that the heart of the Christian message is not insight into "the divine within" or some "numinous potency" but an objectively distinct Being who makes himself susceptible to temporal experience *without sacrificing his eternal nature and identity* in doing so. The

---

3. Barth, "The Word of God and the Task of the Ministry," in *The Word of God and the Word of Man* (1928; Gloucester, Mass.: Peter Smith, 1978), 188.

4. "Why . . . did the theologians I knew seek to represent the minister's perplexity, if they touched upon it at all, as a condition superable and sufferable, instead of *understanding* it at all costs, instead of facing it—and thereby perhaps discovering in it, in its very insuperableness and insufferableness, the real theme of theology?" Barth, "The Need and Promise of Christian Preaching," in *The Word of God and the Word of Man*, 102.

essence of God's revelation in Jesus of Nazareth is that God is sensibly perceived as a phenomenon in space-time, yet as Lord (Maker, Redeemer, Sustainer) of space-time. In short, Barth was on his way to moving the content of theological discourse, indeed all speech of God, away from subjective principles and goods toward God's inimitable *revelation*. *In* human being and doing, God remains distinguishably *God*.

"It was Thurneysen who in private once whispered the keyword to me, half aloud: what we need for preaching, instruction and pastoral care is a 'wholly other' theological foundation."[5] Thinking together with his longtime friend, Eduard Thurneysen, Barth began to ground Christian thought and practice in God's external address to humanity rather than internal religious enthusiasm. He began to understand that this was the quintessence of Christian Scripture—revelation of the God who is not mere discharge of "spiritual" potential latent within the human, but "wholly other." He thus reread the Bible with an entirely new appreciation for its content.

The textual proving ground, so to speak, for Barth's emerging conviction that the Bible contains an objective Word to humanity, which interrogates and in fact condemns human principles and goods as non-divine idolatry, rather than mystically astute human words about divinity, was the Apostle Paul's Letter to the Romans. In 1916 Barth began to write a commentary on Romans, the eventual success of which would catapult him to academic recognition.[6] He was awarded an honorary professorship in Reformed theology at the University of Göttingen subsequent to publication of that commentary (the first edition appeared in 1919 and the rewritten second edition in 1922). From Göttingen (1921–1925) Barth became Professor of Dogmatics and New Testament Exegesis in Münster (1925–1930), then Professor of Systematic Theology in Bonn (1930–1935). In 1935, having refused to make the newly required oath of allegiance to the German *Führer*, Barth was suspended from teaching in the German university. He accepted an invitation to a chair in the theological faculty in his hometown of Basel, where he taught until his retirement in 1962, and wrote and lectured thereafter until his death in 1968.

In the preface to the second edition of his Romans commentary, Barth indicated his central thematic concern. "If I have a system," he wrote, "it is limited to a recognition of what Kierkegaard called the 'infinite qualitative

5. Barth, "Nachwort," in *Schleiermacher-Auswahl: mit einem Nachwort von Karl Barth* (Gütersloh: Gütersloher Verlagshaus Mohn, 1980), 294. The next sentence continues: "[The way] onward from Schleiermacher obviously went no farther."

6. For fuller treatment of this history, see Busch, *Karl Barth: His Life from Letters and Autobiographical Texts*, trans. John Bowden (Grand Rapids: Eerdmans, 1994), 92–125.

distinction' between time and eternity, and to my regarding this as possessing negative as well as positive significance: 'God is in heaven, and thou art on earth.'[7] Extolling Paul's judgment about the final spuriousness of natural revelation (Rom. 1:18-32), the immutability of *divine* faithfulness *in opposition to* very mutable *human* faithfulness (Romans 3), the relationship of "pot" to "potter" (Romans 9:19-24), and so on, Barth argued that when it comes to knowledge of God, fallen humanity cannot rely on pious inclinations, transcendent awareness, or inductive inferences sourced in piety or principles of self-transcendence. Before God's reality these are all subject to inconsistency and error. Paul teaches that we have no reliable basis in ourselves to perceive God or comprehend God's works. Restricted to nature and reason, we manufacture idols. That is the negative significance of the "infinite qualitative distinction" between God and humankind.

Thus, we must receive knowledge entirely from a source external to ourselves. God is God in revealing to humanity the ontological barrier between deity and humanity. The positive significance of recognizing humanity's utter differentiation from God is that it necessarily places us in a posture of receptivity. If we cannot look inward, then we must turn outward to hear from God. In the ongoing event of his self-revelation, God establishes both our need and his supply. He both shows us our incapacity for him and overcomes it.

Barth contended that if we would speak rightly of God—and in this, perceive creation rightly and reason rightly—then everything we would know and speak of God and his relationship to space-time must come from God. God alone *as God* is the source of our knowledge and speech. Barth's criticism of liberal theology can be summarized as relentless demonstration of its untoward tendency to liquefy the essential difference between eternity and time, to create an inappropriately fluid account of divine and human being. As he famously quipped, one does not speak of God by speaking loudly of man.[8] One either speaks of God *by God*, that is, by constructive reiteration of God's own speech under the tutelage and power of God's ongoing act, or one evacuates the term "God" of meaning and significance.

7. Barth, *The Epistle to the Romans*, trans. Edwin C. Hoskyns (London and New York: Oxford University Press, 1968), 10. The final phrase is a reference to Ecclesiastes 5:2.

8. "With all due respect to the genius shown in his work, I can *not* consider Schleiermacher a good teacher in the realm of theology because, so far as I can see, he is disastrously dim-sighted in regard to the fact that man as man is not only in *need* but beyond all hope of saving himself; that the whole of so-called religion, not the least the Christian religion, *shares* in this need; and that one can *not* speak of God simply by speaking of man in a loud voice" (Barth, "Word of God," 195–96).

The onset of World War I supplied Barth with the historical proving ground for his conviction that God is not humanity and that humanity has no intrinsic ability to ascertain, let alone attain, divinity. He was scandalized to find that nearly all of his liberal professors publicly supported Kaiser Wilhelm II's war effort.[9] Barth recognized that it was ultimately the ready association of human ideals with divine qualities that enabled them to readily embrace bellicose nationalism. The will of God was presumed to be unfolding in, indeed guiding the movement of history. Individuals transcended bondage to brute survivalism as they sacrificed personal realization in service to social and political transformation, ultimately accomplished in the triumph of the nation-state. In this, the collective sociopolitical good of the German people became the theater of the numinous, the context in which persons took part in a higher way of being.

Manifestly absent in this way of thinking, Barth observed, was a God free enough to criticize cultural agendas. Liberal theology left no resources for self-critique in that it located the life and power of God in the fulfillment of idiosyncratic human goods. Now patriotism, collective achievement, and racial purity were endowed with divine significance and made relevant to salvation. *Blut und Ehre* not for *Vaterland*, but Heilig *Vaterland*!

Barth diagnosed the critical failure to be liberalism's assumption of a capacity for ultimacy, transcendence, and various other expressions of "divinity" within human being and doing. It could not see the ways that all human potential and activity, however exercised and intended (that is, even in service to inspiring public ends), are tainted with sin and shortsightedness and can hardly be, of themselves, means of personal realization or salvation. Again in historical context, transferring human fulfillment into belligerent accomplishment of the ideals of any nation-state is simply *immoral*. It fails to hear the *wholly other* God's "No!" Against this, Barth took a definite theological posture, which endured throughout his life's work. He asserted the distinctiveness of God as the necessary starting point of all thought and speech about the deity. God faces us objectively, not as the sum total of human ideals or the projected negation of human failings.

---

9. On August 1, 1914, ninety-three German intellectuals issued a statement endorsing the German war policy. Barth saw that almost all of his former professors had signed the statement. "[My teachers] seemed to have been hopelessly compromised by what I regarded as their failure in the face of the ideology of war. . . . A whole world of exegesis, ethics, dogmatics and preaching, which I had hitherto held to be essentially trustworthy, was shaken to the foundations" (Barth, *Fakultätsalbum der Evangelisch-theologischen Fakultät Münster* [1927], and "Rückblick," in *Das Wort sie sollen lassen stahn: Festschrift für Albert Schädelin,* ed. Hans Dürr et al. [Bern: H. Lang, 1950], 4; cited in Busch, *Karl Barth,* 81).

Yet this objectivity (God standing distinctively before humankind) constitutes human subjectivity (living thought, word, and action) in its very happening. God could not be objective God if he did not make himself known as such. If he did not take up our perceptual apparatus and enable us to see and hear him just in his complete differentiation from all other objects of perception and from our acts of perceiving in themselves, then how could we ever know of him as anything other than an aggrandized version of ourselves? God is God in revealing to humanity the ontological barrier between deity and humanity *and so crossing the barrier.*

When God actually stands before humanity in Jesus Christ, he changes human being and doing. Coincident with his condemnation of sinful thoughts, words, and acts in Christ, God re-creates these modes of our being. He makes and maintains conditions according to which he is truthfully known and spoken. He generates *faith.* He speaks a clear "Yes!" in the echo of his "No!" He brings true salvation in the wake of judgment. The way that Barth formulated the particulars of this dialectical situation changed over the years, but as a description of his thought, "real dialectic"—that is, the event of eternal God coming to temporal humankind but as eternal God and thus with full ontological determination as to his being and ours—remained central.

Our opening chapter demonstrates that the real dialectic of God coming to humanity in Christ is so ingredient to Barth's thinking that one cannot conduct any sort of Spirit-centered theology in abstraction from it if one is to appreciate the gains that Barth achieved relative to liberal theology. One cannot abandon dialectic as if it was merely a methodological presupposition. One cannot uncritically turn to a synthesis of eternity and time, God and humanity. One cannot imbed the Spirit in creation, religion, piety, ultimacy, or any other category of human existence.

Moreover, one does not *need* to make such moves as if the Spirit was otherwise absent from Barth's christocentric thinking. This chapter also shows that there is a substantive pneumatological undercurrent flowing together with and even guiding his more overtly christological conclusions.[10] One can draw out and build on Barth's own "pneumatocentric dialectic."

Finally, as these introductory remarks have indicated, the matter at hand reaches well beyond Karl Barth and a right understanding of his thought. Dialectic so understood is central to Barth's understanding of the Christian God for good reason: it derives directly from a series of commitments fundamental to Christian faith, namely, the nature of the human predicament and the character of grace. In and as Jesus Christ, humanity encounters a God who is *Lord*, the Maker who brings all things to be in and through his Word. In this, it encounters creation utterly dependent on God, contingent on the exercise of an incomparable creative power. From first to last, indeed from all eternity the abundance of limitless self-defining love summons beings into existence out of nothingness. Yet the creature's absolute dependence on the Creator is not

---

10. I would qualify Busch's claim that in advocating a theology of the Third Article the late Barth "was thinking of a theology which, unlike his own, was not written from the dominant perspective of christology but from that of pneumatology" (Busch, *Karl Barth*, 494). My concern is with the phrase, "unlike his own." If this is taken to mean that Barth wished for a new generation of theologians to "begin again at the beginning," as he often liked to say, rethinking every doctrinal statement in terms of the work and Person of the Holy Spirit in exactly the same way he had done with the work and Person of Christ Jesus, then that is to the good. If, on the other hand, it is taken to mean that Third Article theology ought to be undertaken as a formal and material alternative to Barth's Second Article approach, then that is to the bad. There is no Christology that is not also Pneumatology. One simply cannot understand the Word, particularly as the center of dogmatic reflection in the light of which Christian thought takes defining shape and substance, apart from the living action and distinct identity of the Spirit. There is no Word ontologically or epistemologically independent of the Spirit, certainly none that Barth speculatively posited as the ground of theological activity. Conversely, there is no Spirit independent of the Word, certainly none that Barth now speculatively advocates as some new dogmatic norm and guide. There is no Pneumatology that is not also Christology. Busch is reflecting Barth's concession that the "neo-Protestant" impulse, which led to treating the human subject as source and norm of dogmatics, "has a legitimate place within the doctrine of the Holy Spirit" (Barth, CD I.2, 368). Thus, Busch concludes that when envisioning a theology of the Third Article, Barth intended one "in which the concerns of the theology of the eighteenth and nineteenth centuries were not so much repeated and continued as understood and developed further" (Busch, *Karl Barth*, 494). But Barth nevertheless insisted that *genuine* human being (and, correspondingly, theology that places humanity within its central theme), is given in Christ. "Human self-determination, and therefore the life of the children of God, is posited under the predominant determination of revelation" (Barth, CD I.2, 368). The actualistic event of human being can function at the center of theological reflection, but only insofar as it is understood in terms of the determination of all being in the event of the Christ. Only insofar as human existence is the event of coming to be before God understood within the life and activity of the God-human does it obtain any significance for Third Article theology. Pneumatology, if it is really to be *Christian* Pneumatology (and not neo-Protestant speculative anthropology), takes its structure and material significance from Christology.

enough to keep it from rebellion. The space and time opened up by God to be the vicinity and order of loving union with the creature affords the illusion of self-realization, of assuming God's charity rather than gratefully receiving it, and constructing from this false flash a life lived independently of the Creator.

But God refuses to be stymied by sin. He does not allow our contrived agendas to have the last word. He remains who he is in spite of who we might make him, ourselves, our people, our environment, our cosmos. He is the God of grace and as such he makes himself present to fallen creation. He shows himself as he is, the God of yesterday, today, and tomorrow, the self-consistent "he who is" whether we would have him or not, hence he who will have us in spite of our rebellion. Thus, the human predicament is that we have no basis for independent existence, yet we seek it. God's grace is that he wills from all eternity to grant us existence before him, which willing is not undone by our infidelity.

The very logic of God being eternal God just in the event of his coming to humanity, then, is basic to Christian faith. It is as central to our knowing and speaking here and now—contemporaneous encounter with the Spirit—as it was to the knowledge and speech of the prophetic and apostolic witness to Jesus, for there is no Christian God spiritually or biblically except the One who is bent on reviling sin and loving creation. Pneumatology can only be constructive reiteration of biblical Christology.

For this reason, we lead with Barth's exegesis of the prologue to the Gospel of John, one of the most profound New Testament statements concerning the nature of Christ. Barth helps us to see the essentially pneumatic core to John's logic. Specifically, we start with John 1:18.

Why the final verse and not the first? First, materially, this verse concisely expresses the dialectical circumstance that we have been addressing. In that no one has perceived God, God makes *himself* known *as God*; this, moment by moment in the event of self-exegesis in Christ Jesus.

Second, formally, it should become clear as we proceed that knowledge and speech of God in terms of Spirit are entirely dynamic—they are know*ing* and speak*ing*. There is nothing static about this kind of theology. Any conclusions that we draw dogmatically are characterized by encounter, event, happening. In God's coming to humankind, *we* think and speak; indeed, our thinking and speaking are part and parcel of God's coming, coordinated in content and form with the flesh of Jesus. Inverberation is thus not a circular sort of dialectic where we simply go back and forth and never progress. It is, rather, a spiraling affair. John 1:18 sets the interpretive parameters for the rest of the prologue, which we will consider in the ensuing chapters. When we conclude with v. 17 in chapter 5, the reader may then reconsider v. 18 from a "higher" vantage point, poised, it is hoped, to experience the very motion assessed throughout.

BARTH'S EXEGESIS OF JOHN 1:18

THEON OUDEIS HEŌRAKEN PŌPOTE

No one has seen God at any time;[11]

"What is meant by *theon oudeis heōraken pōpote*? Precisely what is said. . . . God's essence is not seen."[12] If we are to get a handle on Barth's Spirit-centered thought, then we must be willing to risk the proverbial thousand repetitions in order to say this one thing: no one has seen God. Barth's pneumato-logic, his thinking and speaking of the Spirit, shoots up from christological negation of all human thought and speech. If we are to set ourselves down the right path in this first chapter, then we must perceive the significance of this "No!"

In fact, we must allow the force of this "No" to meet our own thinking and speaking, *or we have not perceived its significance.* The christological negation cannot be a mere datum of knowledge for us, only a descriptor of a peculiar kind of thought and speech apart from us. Rather, it must function for us, too, lest we make an exception in favor of our own thinking and speaking as being theologically competent.

Now, I have to acknowledge that it is difficult to demonstrate his conviction that this "No" must meet us from strict exposition of Barth's exegesis, because Barth does not try to describe this pneumatic happening. He assumes it as the condition of his exegesis. His writing operates on its basis, as

---

11. *Translations are from the New American Standard Bible (NASB).*

12. Barth, *Witness to the Word: A Commentary on John 1. Lectures at Münster in 1925 and at Bonn in 1933,* ed. Walther Fürst, trans. Geoffrey W. Bromiley (Grand Rapids: Eerdmans, 1986), 126. Barth never completed his exegesis of John's Gospel; his lectures only cover through chapter 8. With the typescript of the 1933 series serving as default text (amended with the earlier material where it made better sense), the lectures were published posthumously in 1976. See Barth, *Erklärung des Johannes-Evangeliums (Kapitel 1–8). Vorlesung Münster Wintersemester 1925/1926, wiederholt in Bonn, Sommersemester 1933,* Gesamtausgabe 9 (Zurich: Theologischer Verlag, 1976).

thinking and speaking that exist only in the light of what has come to them and therefore as having no other content. They can repeat only what they have learned as their basis, substance, and goal. I can demonstrate this way of thinking and speaking only by relating what Barth has written and then drawing attention to the Pneumatology implicit therein.

To be as straightforward as possible at this point: Barth does not merely exegete the biblical text as a word addressed to him. It is again that, too. But it is such a Word as to involve Barth as exegete in the address, to refuse him, like all exegetes, perception of its subject on the one side even as it reveals that subject (the living God) to them on the other, and more, as it involves their labor, their own thinking and speaking, their exegesis, in that revelation. *Noēsis* of the divine derives entirely from the event ontology of God's self-determinative engagement with humanity, his being God in and with us. God is *God* in the event that he is *Immanuel*—the *event* that takes place as he is actively known and confessed to be Immanuel, what I am calling "Inverberation," or the contemporaneous manifestation of God in *verba* of the christological negation through which God makes himself to be and to be known as he is.

Back to the verse at hand. When I say that Barth's own thinking and speaking assume the christological negation of human thought and speech, I mean that he includes himself as being among those who do not see God:

> It should be noted that the perfect *heōraken* . . . has here present or supratemporal significance, so that it is not part of a narrative but is presenting a universal fact. The whole statement, with its full content, applies also to those who hear and believe and proclaim the gospel. The second statement does not say that he has enabled us to see or perceive God. It is still true that no one ever sees God.[13]

John's declaration is a supratemporal declaration. It involves us, too. This is indicated by the continuing effect of the perfect verb form. The fundamental situation is not altered by a temporal locus after Christ; our inability to see God is not undone by the fact that "one has made him known," as we will discuss shortly. Rather, in God's being made known in Christ, we encounter him as unknown.

13. Barth, *Witness to the Word*, 127.

We encounter him this way. All humans are included in the christological negation. In the Spirit, we are *made* absolutely dependent on God, moment by moment *set* before him. The dependency of which the father of liberal theology, Friedrich Schleiermacher (1768–1834), spoke so powerfully is rendered actualistic by Barth; it happens contemporaneously not in feeling (*Gefühl*) or piety (*Frömmigkeit*) or any other human modality statically conceived, but in God's self-determinative activity of making himself known as he is.

Dependency is not an implanted seed of the divine within us, which blossoms to full-grown divinity with the water of religion. There is no such point of contact with God, only God's coming to us and making a point of contact, which as such is no point at all, no place, entity, or happening that can be taken for granted as just there for us, but only the intersection of eternity with time that God brings about moment-by-moment in and of himself. There simply is no ladder outside of us in nature or internal to us in reason, will, or religious consciousness by which we may ascend to heaven.

In regard to the actualistic dependency established by God in the form of apostolic testimony to Christ confronting us today, Barth, in exegeting John 1:18, makes reference to his earlier exegesis of Romans 1:20. That is because Romans 1:20 seems to stand in tension with John 1:18 as Barth reads it. Romans 1:18–32 represent one of Scripture's most renowned statements on so-called natural revelation, the idea that God can in fact be seen, that there are seeds of divinity in creation, which can be watered and can climb upward toward the deity. Verse 20 says, "for since the creation of the world, God's invisible qualities—his eternal power and divine nature—have been clearly seen, being understood from what has been made, so that people are without excuse." Does this verse not suggest, in contrast to Barth's exegesis of John 1:18, that some have seen God's God-ness, at least impressions or vestiges of it in the created world?

In treating Romans 1:20, Barth agrees that God ought to be seen in and through the visible work of creation. "In truth things are such that we are completely able to see the full reality, namely, the invisible being of God, directly in the mirror of the visible."[14] But notice that what we see, if in fact we see *God*, is his *imperceptibility*, his sui generis glory, his complete unlikeness to the finite objects and powers of creation; we see that it is of his essence not to be seen. It is God's *invisible* qualities that are mirrored in the visible.

14. Barth, *Der Römerbrief (Erste Fassung) 1919*, Gesamtausgabe 16 (Zurich: Theologischer Verlag, 1985), 28.

That is how things *ought* to be according to Paul: God ought to be seen, but *as God*. But Paul also indicates that it is not how things are. Humanity does not give God his glory and instead ranges his deity among the visible, as a variation of the visible. Humanity is "without excuse," says Barth, for failing to confess the wholly otherness of God's true being—the incomprehensibility of his eternal life to our temporally conditioned reason and so our need for his revealedness. "Without excuse is our false religiosity, because the works of the Creator speak to our reason of the '*eternal* power' of the invisible God and protest with it in advance against the idol worship through which we make him equal to finite and visible and derived powers."[15]

The human thinks and speaks of God in the same way that it does all other objects—as the conjunction of attributes that it perceives in creation and the projection of categories on to those objects.[16] The creature must *receive* the appropriate constructs for meaningfully arranging God's attributes, but instead it assumes those constructs and ranges the deity's qualities according to cognitive constructs native to it. In this, it creates a god out of both the actualities and possibilities of space-time as it knows and exists spatially-temporally. It is not that true God is space-less and timeless, as we will see in chapter 3, for assuming that would simply be to negate the conditions of our knowledge and call it "eternity." The problem is rather the projective trajectory, which is intuitively operative, to work from the nativity of space-time to "God" rather than the other way around. Working from itself, humanity fabricates an aggrandized version of creaturely being and doing, an idol, and relates to it by supplication, sacrifice, and prayer when of course it has predetermined what the outcomes of these activities can and must be.

---

15. Ibid., 29.

16. Barth (especially in the first edition of his commentary on Romans), appropriates certain insights of modern epistemology, specifically the critical realism of Immanuel Kant. Just as for Kant there is no reality apart from the projection of categories of being onto objects of perception, for Barth there is no creaturely or divine reality apart from the reference frame of perception. "Nothing *is* in itself, everything *is* only insofar as we see, know, think it. Nothing *will be* of itself, but everything that will be, will be through spirit, through reason, through word, through which we see it. Nothing is *there*, which is not first *here*" (*Der Römerbrief 1919*, 28). *Es gibt kein Ding an sich*, "there is no thing in itself," Kant famously taught. All things, as they are, have their being at the nexus of constituent qualities in perception. Knowledge is an event. It is the coincidence or meeting of sense data, on the one hand, and the projection of categories by which those data are meaningfully arranged, on the other. For Kant and, *mutatis mutandis*, for Barth, knowledge entails not just what things are but also what they can be; their defining attributes are placed within a prereflective matrix consisting above all of spatiality and temporality. On Barth's epistemology, see Bruce McCormack, *Karl Barth's Critically Realistic Dialectical Theology: Its Genesis and Development 1909–1936* (Oxford: Oxford University Press, 1997).

Why does humanity do this? Why do we lack the categories to perceive God as he is in creation when we ought to possess them, and so supply our own? We pervert creation's testimony because we exist in sin. Barth's thinking becomes fairly intricate at this stage, but we must continue with him for a bit, for what he exegetes from Romans 1:20 concerning sinful humanity is, once more, integral to his understanding of the firm declaration stated in John 1:18.

Barth considers human perception of God not on speculative anthropological grounds, not from what the human might have become and known and what God might have been and been known to us if Genesis narrated a different history, but from the sober reality of life east of Eden. "Sin is that by which man as we know him is defined, for we know nothing of sinless men."[17] Humanity faces God in the rebellion represented by Adam and Eve. *Represented* by Adam and Eve—the primeval couple are not to be taken as the origin of sin as if in a chronological sequence from sinlessness to sinfulness, but as the picture of humankind bound for sin and death. "Adam has no existence on the plane of history and of psychological analysis. He exists as the first Adam, as the type of the second Adam who is to come, as the shadow cast by His light."[18] Adam has no independent identity; he is "mankind" (Hebrew *'ādām*) insofar as he is the object of the True Man's redeeming work. Humanity as such is known only in the light of Christ, namely, as repetition of Adam's disobedience, the shadow to which God's light is directed, the unworthy object of God's gloriously extensive affections.

The Genesis account of Adam must be read in light of Paul's "second Adam" (Romans 5; 1 Corinthians 15), in which case it functions as a comprehensive expression of the human condition. Specifically, it shows us as sinners, when "sin" means living in contrast to the righteous way of being revealed in Christ. "Sin is . . . meaningless and incomprehensible except as the negation of the righteousness which is in Christ."[19]

Sin is not mere behavior but holistic negation of the right order of things revealed in Jesus. It is impatience with our mortality before the Immortal, replacement of our remoteness from God with the presumption of proximity, rejection of his otherness in favor of his similarity to us, romanticizing our own way to infinity:

17. Barth, *Epistle to the Romans*, 167.
18. Ibid., 171.
19. Ibid.

Sin is robbing of God: a robbery which becomes apparent in our arrogant endeavor to cross the line of death by which we are bounded (i. 18, 19); in our drunken blurring of the distance which separates us from God; in our forgetfulness of His invisibility; in our investing of men with the form of God, and of God with the form of man; and in our devotion to some romantic infinity, some 'No-God' of this world, which we have created for ourselves.[20]

Sin is perpetual criminal offense, unjustified reversal of life and death, the relationship in which we stand with God, visibility and invisibility, human and divine being, time and eternity. It is robbing God of his due majesty and glory by placing ourselves first and him second.[21]

In short, God has established his glory and majesty, his inherent invisibility in the created order, but in sin the creature perverts that order and renders God visible, made after creation rather than the other way around. In his revelation, God restores the right order of things; he makes himself invisible in his visibility. He shows himself as he is in relation to us as we are, sinners in need of his gracious revelation.

But why should we be beset by sin? Would our condition not be God's "fault," so to speak, if we are made by him to see him but are not able to do so?

Barth allows that the theoretical possibility of sin, of idolatry, is given in the character of the world as God has made and sustains it, but the culpability or guilt of sin is ours in each place and moment that we exercise the capacities given by God to form the world after us. Sin is originally ours in the event-

---

20. Ibid., 168.

21. "Sin is the act of man in which he ignores and offends the divine majesty. Sin is, therefore, disobedience" (Barth, CD IV.1, 414). Barth's fullest discussion of sin takes place across three part-volumes of the *Dogmatics*: CD IV.1 §60, IV.2 §65, and IV.3.1 §70. Each treats human "pride," "sloth," and "falsehood," respectively. As a general summary, Barth contends that sin can be understood only in terms of the reconciling work of Jesus Christ, as its persistent contrast (see esp. CD IV.1 358–413). As disobedience, sin is "the human action that does not correspond to the divine action in Jesus Christ but contradicts it" (CD IV.1, 215). It is a way of being opposed to the God who has his life in upholding communion with his creature. It is, as such, a possibility opened up by God's creation of vicinities and sequences of being, thinking, and doing external to himself, of granting creaturely freedom. "Man proves himself to be a liar in whose thinking, speech, and conduct his liberation by and for the free God transforms itself into an attempt to claim God by and for himself" (CD IV.3.1, 368). God's liberating work is perverted by humanity into the moment-by-moment lie by which it claims God; as if it could, humanity reverses the right knowledge of God, placing itself in the position to think and speak and act as lord over God.

ontology of our existence, in the pre-conscious instinct to think everything, including God, from a center in ourselves.

Barth presents an interesting take on "original sin." He retains the Augustinian emphasis on the ontological quality of sin, construing it as a condition endemic to all humanity. "Sin is power—sovereign power. . . . By it men are controlled."[22] Sin is no mere behavior or infelicitous choice. It is an inheritance more basic than action and volition. But Barth does not think of this human inheritance as a static characteristic emerging at a definite point on the timeline of human ancestry, which is then passed down biologically or socially or what have you. On the contrary, it is "an especial relationship of men to God."[23] Sin is a disordering of the right existence between Creator and creature. It is breaking the essential bond of fellowship with God.

Thus sin, for Barth, is the actualistic contradiction of existence in rebellion against grace, which defines all of humankind, for we have our *being* in this *act*. Concretely, God creates the faculties for authentic relationship—above all perception and volition. God does not create automatons but genuinely conscious and willing creatures intended to return his knowledge and love. It is in such perceiving and willing that we enjoy secondary co-determination: we reckon the world and our place in it honestly or in self-serving deception as we instantiate an intimate closeness or cold remoteness relative to God and each other. In the latter, we drag the world into sin and nothingness:

> There has come into being a *cosmos* which, because we no longer know God, is not Creation. . . . It is a world in which things move toward independence, a world of things existing powerfully in their own right, a world of principalities and powers and thrones and dominions. Like men, the world is imprisoned. As their world, it unwillingly participates in the perversity of men and shares their damaged relationship with God.[24]

Sin is moment-by-moment exercise of the faculties with which we were endowed by God, faculties by which we are to exist in authentic relationship with God, to construct a world of autonomous self-rule, a world independent of

22. Barth, *Epistle to the Romans*, 167.
23. Ibid.
24. Ibid., 169.

God in which we act as lord over him and each other. Once more, this exercise is basic to the full range of human existence.

That does not make sin and its guilt a reality only when a person reaches an age of conscious and volitional accountability, for that would be to suggest that before this age there is such a thing as unaccountable humanity, a way of being opposite God without God, such that the relationship in which we exist with God and its negation by sin take place at some eventual stage of being and not in the core of our being. No, there are no faculties of knowing and willing that are not given and sustained by God from the beginning in his Word, and thus only a truly baseless rebellion all along the line. We cannot explain sin as original to us except by acknowledging that it is an opportunism at every stage of life, an ever-ready impulse to self-priority. "Sin is the characteristic mark of human nature as such; it is not a lapse or a series of lapses in a man's life; it is the Fall that occurred with the emergence of human life. Sin occurs before it has taken concrete form consciously or unconsciously in this or that man, and it is powerful before it takes control of his will or disposition."[25]

Adrift in the vacuous throes of sin, the human needs to be shown her problem if she is to see and desire its solution. There is no foothold otherwise, no cleft in the rock on which to stay the fall into nothingness. God must overcome every instinct of the darkness to its own priority. "In this world [of sin], which is our world, the true life is invisible, unknown, and impossible. . . . The only glory of the Creator which remains is that by which this independent validity [of the human and its objects of perception] is limited. . . . The only possibility of perceiving the glory of God is that perception which operates sub specie mortis."[26] Only from the perspective of our negation is God to be seen as he is—only in the light of our death is God the true source and meaning of life.

If God is to remain *God* before sinful human being and doing, he must judge sin that ensnares (en-frames) us and, in us, our world. He cannot simply stand at the end of our religious intuitions as their outcome, but must condemn the very impulse to place him there. He must definitively reject our misshapen idolatrousness if he is actually to be our God, if he is actually to relate to us as we need him to, if he is to put an end to our relentless self-compromise. Salvation comes through damnation; grace through judgment; gospel through the law. God's "No" is the precondition of his "Yes." "The wrath of God [Rom. 1:18-19] . . . which comes to expression in the ruinous condition in which we see the world today (5:12; 8:19-20), is not fate (*Schicksal*) but bitter necessity."[27]

25. Ibid., 173.
26. Ibid., 169.
27. Barth, *Der Römerbrief (Erste Fassung)*, 29.

The desertion unto death and frustration in which creation convulses (Rom. 5:12; 8:19-20) is the "bitter necessity" of humanity's fallen, in fact falling state of being.

Death is the required outcome of human infidelity to its source of being, the ultimate relativizing of our baseless existence. "Living without sharing in life, men are defined as mortal; loosed from primary existence, they are non-existent; in their wild unrelatedness and absoluteness and independence, they are relative."[28] Yet in this way, death is the final reminder of our dependency on God. It is the door through which humanity must pass to resurrection, the gateway to life, if we may use that expression.

Death, from which no human is exempted, is at once God's rejection of human infidelity and victorious assertion of his deity. It is damnation of our sin, which damnation is the means of reconciliation with God. God shows us the non-being to which our instinct to reject his priority leads—in the revelation of his life he shows us death—and in this showing and death's realization among humankind, he reestablishes his priority to us, or, our dependency on him for life. "Death never occurs but it calls attention to our participation in the Life of God and to that relationship of His with us which is not broken by sin."[29] Death is both God's judgment against us and the condition of his judgment for us, both his refusal of our rebellion and through that refusal the reestablishment of our life in him—his declaration that he is not subject to the world and its lords as we have made them, therefore neither shall we be.[30]

As indicated, Barth appeals to this exegesis of Romans from 1919 and 1922 when in 1925 he turns to John 1:18. "It strangely contradicts John's Gospel, and the rest of the New Testament [e.g., 1 Tim. 6:16]," he writes, "if, with most exegetes, we take Rom. 1:20 to refer to seeing the invisible God and not to perceiving his invisibility, the mystery of his hiddenness in the works of creation."[31] Barth finds no other way of reconciling John's thought with Paul's than by stressing invisible rather than qualities in Romans 1:20. Creation shows humanity a glory that cannot be ranged by sense—it signifies, indeed, but what it signifies is inscrutability, the "mystery of his hiddenness." It conducts us to humble confession that we have no means of understanding the God upon whose work our perceptual apparatus is entirely contingent. It teaches that every god of creation's glory, every notion of deity bubbled up from within

28. Barth, Epistle to the Romans, 170.
29. Ibid.
30. On Barth's twofold account of death, see Epistle to the Romans, 166–72.
31. Barth, Witness to the Word, 126.

or worshiped in the stars, leads to idolatry and death, that if God is to be God then knowledge of God is God's to impart and not ours to construct.

Barth reads in *oudeis heōraken* a Johannine rejection of all forms of seeing God. "What we do not have, whether as *horan* or *theōrein* or *theasthai*, is the seeing of him who, or that which, is here called *theos*. No one sees God."[32] John's community decisively cuts the connection between creaturely perception and divine knowledge. Humanity does not locate God in visions natural or beatific, in empirical deduction or gnostic insight, in personal experience or mystical intuition. The way of sense is shut, including sixth sense.

No one, ever! With these few words, John 1:18 summarily restates a consistent theme of Christian Scripture: there is no point of reference from humanity to God, no bridge from time to eternity, no stairway from earth to heaven. Eden's gate is closed and kept (Gen. 3:23-24). The city with a tower to heaven is scuttled and its builders scattered (Gen. 11:8-9). Mediums and spiritists are forbidden and discredited (Lev. 19:31). Religious festivals and solemn assemblies are despised (Amos 5:21-22). "God is in heaven and you are on earth (Eccl. 5:2)!"

There is no equivalence or reversal here. Barth's exegetical logic, then, merely reflects an essential canonical conviction:

> Because we are human we can none of us see God's face. Not even those who are prophets. . . ! One has to say that we have here an essential theological determination of humanity. . . . This essential determination of humanity in relation to God, great though the distinctions may be in detail, distinctions of service within this relation, sets them all in principle on the same level. No matter what they become, or how wonderfully God may use them, or how much or how little . . . they are able or manage to grasp of him, one thing is certain, namely, that none of them, in general or in particular, finally sees or knows or understands anything of God, of the essence or substance or being of God, of his *theiotēs*.[33]

32. Ibid.
33. Ibid., 128–29.

MONOGENĒS THEOS HO ŌN EIS TON KOLPON TOU PATROS EKEINOS EXĒGĒSATO.

> *The only begotten God who is in the bosom*
> *of the Father, he has explained him.*

Once again, the force of the christological negation to which the prophets and apostles testify must become real to us (or else it is not *God* with which we have to do in theological thinking and speaking today but an adaptation of ourselves). We must hear it as directed to us, too, so that it structures our self-perception and our perception of the world, so that we genuinely think and speak the definitive boundary between heaven and earth, between God and ourselves and the creation at large.

In other words, we must find our words within the words of the prophets and apostles who first perceived the negation. For it was in fact that very perception which qualified them to be prophets and apostles, which made them to be witnesses to the Word of God. If we are to think and speak of the Holy Spirit, then we must do so as the event in which the christological boundary between heaven and earth becomes real to us in the language of prophetic and apostolic testimony to Christ, that is, as the event in which our reality is overcome by the reality of God established in Christ by the Scriptures, as the event in which we become *secondary witnesses.*

Throughout his exegesis of John, Barth describes the modality of witness in the actualistic terms of God's activity in Christ. As God in Christ makes himself known as unknown, his eternal glory is unveiled in the veil of flesh, suffering, and death, so also witness is only always un-witness, the revelation of *God* by a *human* in *human* words. "On earth [John] bears no halo by which we know that he is an apostle as we know a king on his throne. To see him as an apostle we need the same illumination that he needed and received in order to be an apostle. He does not proclaim God without God, nor may he be known as one who proclaims God without God."[34]

What qualifies the evangelist to speak of God is God, his illumination to right understanding of the right relation between God and creature. What qualifies us to recognize the authority of the evangelist and the truth of his message is the same illumination. We must be made to think in the same terms:

34. Ibid., 6.

> We have to speak, not of quality, nor of the qualified nature, but of the qualifying of his word, not of being but of an action. . . . That the Gospel really comes to us in that original and inescapable way is not proper to it as a kind of natural or magical force that may be perceived and experienced in the power of the reader, and displayed and made efficacious in the power of the preacher or exegete. The Gospel comes to us with the promise that God himself will confess it.[35]

Barth's reasoning obviously is structured here by an essential pneumato-logic: he assumes that the living activity of God by which the apostle is an apostle continues here and now in the reading, exegesis, and preaching of the apostolic testimony. If it did not, then there would be no *apostolic* testimony; there would be no authoritative witness to God if the thought and speech of that witness did not become authentic thought and speech again, if that witness did not generate further witnesses.

Apostolic testimony is authoritative witness to God only if it operates by God's continuing power. "It is not self-evident that this should happen. It is in the balances, no, it depends on God's good pleasure whether it does so or not."[36] It cannot be self-evident that the Bible is the Word of God. It can only be the Word of God if God in fact speaks in and through it according to his good pleasure—if he *speaks*, present tense, in and through it. Revelation is only revelation in and with revealedness, for it is only in and through the latter that the prophets and apostles themselves think and speak as anything other than blind human guides.[37]

And it is only in and through the same action of God today, among us, that these witnesses come to be who they are, prophets and apostles of *God*. "The point of our action as hearers and expositors of the Gospel stands or falls with God's action through the instrument with which we have to do."[38] God speaks *to us* in and through the speaking of the prophets and apostles, making us to be witnesses of their truth, committed advocates of the same message that he spoke

---

35. Ibid., 6-7.

36. Ibid., 7

37. Again, nothing in their nature makes them anything but blind human guides. "The apostles do not speak to us as such unless it is ever and again given to them to do so by God. . . . This giving is an event, an action, the action of God in the strictest sense of the term" (Barth, *Witness to the Word,* 7).

38. Ibid.

to them. This action is decisive in the same way for us as it was for them or there is no sense among us that it was ever decisive for them!

In traditional theological language, Barth does not differentiate in an overly rigid way between *inspiration* and *faith*; as the second presupposes the first, so does the first presuppose the second. There is no act of God upon John the evangelist that is not coordinate with, indeed of the same character as, his action upon John's readers and hearers down to today. "Our starting point is that the Gospel at once addresses to us a demand for faith that we can neither miss nor avoid. . . . But what is faith if not the illumination without which we cannot perceive the light of scripture? And what is this illumination if not the inscrutable and uncontrollable work of God upon us for which we can only pray?"[39]

One more time: the event-ontology of witness, including scriptural witness, derives from the fact that in it we encounter the Word of God in fully *human* words. The witnesses are not themselves gods or in any way capable of God. If it is not the other way around, that God is capable of them, then neither is there sense in the term "God" nor is there any content for these claims about God (outside the lives of the witnesses themselves), nor would there be any reason for us to consider these claims. But we consider these claims because by the Spirit we, too, encounter this capacity of God for humanity, this self derived power and authority of "God" to have his being as *God-with-us*. It is the life and action of the Spirit to overcome our reality with God's, to be the self-determinative capacity of God for us.

Yet as Barth indicated, this encounter in which the Spirit has his life and action is given its substance and shape by the subject of the claims made by the prophets and apostles; it comes "through the instrument with which we have to do." It is not an undefined capacity of God for humanity, a vague power of "spirit" that we experience, but concrete readiness of God for Man in Christ Jesus. Precisely in his uniqueness, his total differentiation from the witness to him, he is the shape and substance of witness.

Christ must be differentiated from his witness—this, according to his witness—in order to be its content and form; he must establish the boundary between God and us, being first and foremost God's confrontation with humanity's idolatrous constructions. Christ does not make God known as a human would make him known, but as God makes himself known. That is the significance of *monogenēs theos ho ōn eis ton kolpon tou patros ekeinos exēgēsato*.

39. Ibid., 7–8.

"The *monogenēs* . . . is a stronger form of the term 'son' and expresses the uniqueness with which an only son is related to his father, is close to him, knows him, and is his representative and heir. Everything that this conclusion to the prologue has to say converges on this uniqueness."[40] What makes Jesus to be the revelation of God is that as to his natures he is, while human, fully the Son of the Father. He is the eternal Word of the Father; the *logos ensarkos*, yes, but the *logos tou patros*.

Christ is the "exegesis" of the Father only because as to his being and identity he is "in the bosom of the Father," one with him. It is this unity, not his unity with us, that qualifies him to reveal God. "The solidarity [with humanity] is broken and removed by the fact that *he*, the *Logos*, became flesh. While standing among others, he really stands over against them."[41] It is just this standing-over-against-us-while-being-with-us, this drawing inside our realm of the boundary between heaven and earth, this break among creatures between Creator and creature, this refusal of flesh and history in flesh and history, this confrontation with human thought and speech in human thought and speech, which makes up the content and shape of the message of God in Christ Jesus. It is a real dialectic that is repeated, no, re-verberated in the witness to Christ Jesus.

It is not some prophetic genius that makes a prophet to be a spokesperson of God. The true prophets—Barth mentions Moses, whom God allowed to see his "backside" (Exod. 33:18-23)—all recognized their inadequacy for the task. They all understood that *nothing* in their human knowing or being made them able to speak for God, but that only God can speak for God. They all recognized that their need, their condition of being, was given in and with their promise—the Word of God—and that this Word, not the cultivation of religion or development of special sensitivity to the so-called supernatural, was the sum total of their task. It is, again, simply this recognition, understood in the light of Christ as an action and not a quality of being, that makes them prophets of God:

> The full concreteness of the situation on Sinai between Moses and Yahweh has been brought to light by the fact that the Word became flesh. Where Moses reminds all of us of our *human* essence, so that we have to stand alongside all others, this one, who stands and goes as man among us, stands at the side of *God*. . . . Here revelation is

40. Ibid., 129.
41. Ibid.

not received and passed on as with Moses, and as is proper for human beings. Here, as the presupposition of all such receiving and passing on . . . revelation is *given*, as is proper for God.[42]

We stand with Moses, or Moses, great as he was, stands with us. Christ Jesus, meek as he was among us, stands with God. It is this situation, this essential relationship, in which we must again find ourselves. We must find our need again in this promise, the promise of God to be-with-us in Christ Jesus. He, this Word of God, must become our task, the basis and goal of our thought and speech of God. It is exactly this finding and becoming, becoming and finding, that together are the life and action of the Spirit of the Word.

BARTH'S 1922 LECTURES ON THE NATURE AND TASK OF PREACHING AND THEOLOGY

The revelation of God in Christ Jesus according to the witness of the prophets and apostles amounts to a living confrontation between God and humanity, or more exactly, to establishment of the factual relation in which God is God and humanity his dependent creature in confrontation with the reverse relation set up artificially by sin. And if this is in fact to be a *living* confrontation, the actual establishment of a relation *here and now* as it was there and then in 1–30 C.E., then it is a pneumatological event. It takes place in and by the Holy Spirit.

Indeed, if the Holy Spirit is one with this God, the God who has his being in christological confrontation with the world of sin, then the Spirit has his life and identity just in reverberation of this event. He is God inverberate, we must say, subsisting in a manner or way of being that is parallel to God's incarnate way of being in Christ Jesus. He comes to be personally determined in the onto-epistemic event that God's reality overcomes ours. He is agentially objectified as the Third Person of triune God in that he reiterates a third time God's distinct essence as God-for-us: the God who creates and reconciles is again the God who will make that creative and reconciling work to stand against the destructive patterns of sin today, who will forever be redemptively present to creation.

The Spirit is the Spirit—we only know "spirit" as such—in the place and moment that we know the Christ. We only know the Spirit in the place and moment that we encounter the right relation of things established by God in Christ. We only know him in terms of the actualistic dependency into which

42. Ibid., 129–30.

he sets us relative to God by making Christ to be the determination of reality today as ever.

In 1922, three years before giving the lectures that would substantially comprise his commentary on John, Barth gave two other addresses in which we can perceive his basic pneumato-logic, and which are therefore worth consideration here. These are "The Need and Promise of Christian Proclamation," and "The Word of God as the Task of the Ministry." Both addresses describe the character of authentic thought and speech of God in terms of the event in which humanity is made by God to recognize the infinite and qualitative break between it and God, which must be and is overcome by God. It is not only that God establishes the break and overcomes it, but also the recognition of this action (as in fact repetition of the action), which comprehensively constitutes the *revelation* in which God wills to be God.

"The Need and Promise of Christian Proclamation" was offered on July 25, 1922, before a meeting of Reformed pastors in Schulpforte. It was given in response to an invitation for Barth to introduce his theology, as it had been formulated in the recently published second edition of his commentary on Romans.[43] But Barth resisted the label of "my theology," not feeling that he could yet be considered one of "the great creators of theological programs and systems."[44] Such reticence owed to the fact that by 1922 Barth had not tried to construct a theological system. His Romans text, while comprehensive in scope and broadly received, was but "a marginal note" on other concepts, programs, and agendas.[45] If anything, it amounted to a single point, "and that not, as one might demand as the least qualification of a true theology, a *stand*point, but rather a *mathematical* point upon which one cannot stand—a *view*point merely."[46]

The single point that constituted Barth's thought in his Romans commentary, as noted, is that there is an infinite and qualitative difference between God and humanity, which difference comprises the central message of the biblical text and which must become real for the reader of that text for it to be understood. The Bible must be read not simply as a collection of human experiences of the divine, but as the revelation of God *as God*. We who read and interpret Scripture should not breezily presume to locate our religious instincts therein, as if it was merely a collection of such instincts authored by particularly

43. "Not und Verheissung der Christlichen Verkündigung," in *Vorträge und kleinere Arbeiten 1922–1925*, Gesamtausgabe 19 (Zurich: Theologischer Verlag, 1990), 65.

44. Ibid., 67.

45. Ibid.

46. Barth, "Need and Promise," 97–98.

wise and pious souls. On the contrary, "the commentator must be possessed of a wider intelligence than that which moves within the boundaries of his own natural appreciation. . . . When an investigation is rightly conducted, boulders composed of fortuitous or incidental or merely historical conceptions ought to disappear almost entirely. The Word ought to be exposed in the words."[47]

The exegete orients to Christian Scripture with a readiness to hear its message on its own terms; not without the historical-critical tools of context, authorial intent, and so on, but also not satisfied with the yield of those tools as the final word. In this word, one hears an objectively Other voice, the Word for which this word stands.

In this regard, Barth construes the work of exegesis (and engagement with the biblical text more generally) as an encounter or event. It is, of course, a kind of lab work—linguistic analysis, historical study, documentary evaluation. But it is also a meeting between two worlds, between the realm and life of God, on the one side, and the realm and life of humanity, on the other. The message of Christian Scripture is that this God is God in the event that he makes himself to be God-with-us, in fact to meet us in our history as he met the prophets and apostles in theirs; this, as the condition of perceiving the truth of their words (precisely as his being-with-them was the singular condition of their perception, too!).

To explore this actualistic situation further in Schulpforte, Barth turned to the problem of the sermon:

47. Barth, *Epistle to the Romans*, 8. Barth's prefaces to the six editions of this work have been the subject of analysis, which highlights Barth's interpretive convictions vis-à-vis the biblical text and their importance for the discipline of theology; see Richard E. Burnett, *Karl Barth's Theological Exegesis: The Hermeneutical Principles of the Römerbrief Period* (Grand Rapids: Eerdmans, 2004). Barth's disagreement with his former professors concerning the nature of theological studies is encapsulated in the preface to the second edition. "My complaint is that recent commentators confine themselves to an interpretation of the text which seems to me to be no commentary at all, but merely the first step towards a commentary. Recent commentaries contain no more than a reconstruction of the text, a rendering of the Greek words and phrases by their precise equivalents, a number of additional notes in which archaeological and philological material is gathered together, and a more or less plausible arrangement of the subject-matter in such a manner that it may be made historically and psychologically intelligible from the standpoint of pure pragmatism" (*Epistle to the Romans*, 6). For further introduction into Barth's perspective relative to that of his liberal teachers, see his open letter exchange with Adolf von Harnack, "Text of the Barth–Harnack Correspondence of 1923," in Martin Rumscheidt, *Revelation and Theology: An Analysis of the Barth–Harnack Correspondence of 1923,* Monograph Supplements to the Scottish Journal of Theology (Cambridge: Cambridge University Press, 1972).

> I am . . . ever harder put upon by the specific *pastor's* problem
> of the *sermon*, I have attempted . . . to find my way between the
> problematic of human life on the one hand and the content of the
> Bible on the other. To the *human*, indeed I as pastor should speak in
> the outrageous contradiction (*unerhörten Widerspruch*) of their lives,
> but speak of nothing less than the outrageous message (*unerhörten
> Botschaft*) of the *Bible*.[48]

The confrontation between God and humanity becomes a living reality
each week anew in the work of the pastor composing a sermon. The pastor is
set in the meeting of these two worlds; she participates in the human condition,
on the one hand, and encounters God's construal of and answer to that
predicament, on the other. Moreover, she is compelled in her station to publicly
locate the human contradiction in Scripture's diagnosis of that contradiction, to
think and speak of it in the terms of this "outrageous" Word (rather than of her
own piety or religious insight). This situation is instructive for theology[49] as a
discipline in that the theologian is also tasked with thinking and speaking in her
particular situation of God's address according to the biblical witness.[50] I will
return to that matter momentarily.[51]

48. "Not und Verheissung," 70.

49. As indicated, Barth's turn to the "strange world within the Bible" famously characterized his break
with the liberal theological tradition, and while he hardly gave up his Swiss socialism in making this turn,
it gave way to the Bible as the defining orientation of parish ministry and theological study. On Barth's
move from strong interest in religious socialism to his Tambach lecture, where he critiques all attempts to
subsume the church under political and social agendas, see Busch, *Karl Barth*, 82–116. For Barth's own
appraisal of the significance of his turn to the Bible, see Barth, "The Strange New World within the
Bible," in Barth, *Word of God and the Word of Man*, 28–50.

50. Thomas Schlegel has pointed up the significance of the pastor's situation in proclaiming the gospel
as arguably the major tributary in Barth's early concept of "theology." He shows that the same
"impossible necessity" confronting the pastor in the church—namely, the utter *necessity* of speaking of
God according to his full authority, immortality, and divinity in the light of our contingency, mortality,
and humanity, and the utter *impossibility* of speaking thus—confronts the theologian. It is out of the
critical, dialectical condition of answering God's revelation on its own terms, and yet as a human whose
capacity for those terms is judged as deficient by them, that both preaching and theology spring. See
Schlegel, "Theologie als unmögliche Notwendigkeit: der Theologiebegriff Karl Barths in seiner Genese
(1914–1932)" (Th. D. diss., Friedrich-Schiller University Jena, 2005), esp. 108–37.

51. The best study I have found on the close relationship between preaching and theology in Barth is
Axel Denecke, *Gotteswort als Menschenwort: Karl Barths Predigtpraxis – Quelle seiner Theologie* (Hannover:
Lutherisches Verlagshaus, 1989). Denecke shows that "in Karl Barth's theological work 'preaching and

The sermon is instructive for Barth because of its existential poignancy. "On Sunday morning when the bells ring to call the congregation and minister to church, there is in the air an *expectancy* that something great, crucial, and even momentous is to *happen*."[52] It is not, of course, that everyone feels or is equally conscious of this anticipation, but that does not alter the fact that "expectancy is inherent in the whole situation."[53]

The sermon is wreathed in readiness. For what? Not merely for edification, entertainment, or instruction, Barth says, but to hear and confess that "God *is* present. The whole situation witnesses, cries, simply shouts of it, even when in minister or people there arises questioning, wretchedness, or despair."[54] It is to hear and interrogate the biblical claim that God is in fact present even in the midst of doubting and wretched humanity that people come to church and the minister climbs the pulpit.

Barth stresses that it is not to hear a mere repetition of the sort of transcendental "presence" one experiences in "a blossoming cherry tree, Beethoven's ninth symphony, the state, or even our own honest daily work."[55] If the sermon were merely about such things, then "why the superfluous appurtenances? Why the unique features here, if they do not point to a unique, specific, bolder meaning of 'God is present?'"[56]

theology' move so close together that both concepts often become interchangeable" (p. 22). Preaching is the "source," "mirror," and "immediate result of theological work," but especially the first (pp. 24–25). That is because the sermon "brings the subject matter of theology [the Word of God in Jesus Christ] to its clearest and most immediate expression" (p. 24). Theology hears and identifies the Incarnation as the Word of God in which it, too, must operate, in the sermon. "It is exactly a sign of the sovereignty of God and of his free grace . . . that through the incarnation of the Word of God in Jesus Christ the human word—that of Paul, of Karl Barth, of every preacher—is elevated and enabled to bear the free, sovereign, independent Word of God. In its externalization (*Entäusserung*) in the world God's Word binds itself to the words of the preacher and enjoins itself to the preacher. That is the human counterpart to the corporeality (*Leiblichkeit*) of the Word of God in this World" (p. 113). This dialectical occurrence of God's Word in human words following from the Incarnation is irreducibly spiritual. "The giving and sending of the Holy Spirit are the dual criteria in preaching and theology, which—beyond all human possibilities—honors the promise of the identity between human words and God's Word" (p. 148). Denecke's study is clearly in agreement with the construal of Barth's theology offered here in that the dialectical method of Barth's pneumatocentric thought is grounded in the nature of the Incarnation in proclamation.

52. Barth, "Need and Promise," 104.

53. Ibid.

54. Ibid., 106–7.

55. Ibid., 107.

56. Ibid.

The sermon is distinct from other alleged encounters with the divine in that in it the character of God's presence is a problem before it is a solution, a question before it is an answer. "God is present, which is doubtless given, in a way, in all of these things [cherry tree, Beethoven, etc.]—the content of truth in them, their witness to a meaning in life—has evidently become a question, become the great riddle of existence."[57] In the sermon, the human encounters God not at or as the highest rung on the ladder of her being, but as the great question about her being. From what and to what and about what is she?

At least, this is the essence of the sermon in specifically *Protestant* worship, that is, in a form of worship that derives entirely from the Bible. Instead of having to reckon with this book and its attendant confrontation week in and out, how much easier it would be to return to, indeed how much "nostalgia" (*Heimweh*) the pastor occasionally feels for the Roman Mass. In the sacrament, "the way from God to man and man to God is so clear, lucid, and ordered."[58] It is as if there is a stabilized bridge between heaven and earth, which as such might be treated as a channel from earth to heaven. Our pious impulses are left intact and affirmed, not rejected, infused with medicinal aid and rendered useful as conduits of the transcendent.

But "the Reformation took away everything incidental and cruelly left us the Bible alone."[59] Barth construes the Reformers' divestiture of sacramentalism to be "cruel" because it leaves us with a text whose message relentlessly judges us as sinners. It is persistent in showing us our alienation from God as a situation we bring about but cannot correct; indeed, it is the moment-by-moment activity of our self-transcendent imagination that causes the alienation. In this, Barth construes the Bible as "weird" or uncomfortable (*unheimlich*):

> The Bible is weird to us because it brings a new, great (greatest!), powerful *expectation* into the church's situation, from the *other* side. The congregation primarily *brings* into the church the great *question* of human life and *searches* for an answer, while conversely the Bible *brings* primarily an *answer*. And what does the Bible *search* for? The *question* after this answer that questioning *people* would understand, seek, and find—this answer as such, exactly as answer to the corresponding question.[60]

57. Ibid.
58. "Not und Verheissung," 80.
59. Ibid., 81.
60. Ibid., 83–84.

The Bible brings an entirely distinct set of expectations, judging our queries to be inadequate anthropomorphisms and at once asking the question that we would ask, but properly. We bring our questions to church. We operate within the perceptual framework of *ādām* and inquire after God according to the possibilities allowed by that framework. In the sermon we are confronted with *God's* answer. His answer does not take up our sinful questions but reframes them. We come seeking God; he comes teaching us how to seek. His answer to our questions at once intensifies and reformulates them, making them the actual questions we should be asking.

We find that "from the first all of our questions were preparation and practice, and now the question is first asked, whether we ask in *earnest*, whether we really would ask after God."[61] Barth understands all of humanity's "little questions" to be taken up in the "great question" of Jesus Christ on the cross, "My God, my God, why have you forsaken me?"[62] If we really are to ask *after* God, then we must hear our existential longings expressed on God's lips. We must hear that we are on the far side of the moon, so to speak, relative to the Creator of all things. We must hear that God is not humanity writ infinite. We must hear that our sinful presumptuousness to assume an easy correlation between humanity and God instantiates the ruinous condition of our world, the cold abandon of God's forsakenness.

Once more, in the proclamation of the Bible, there is (or at least ought to be—Barth is well aware that in his day as in ours the Protestant sermon has devolved into something considerably different from what the Reformers intended) an intensification and reconfiguration of the existential questions with which the parishioner comes to church:

> To suffer in the Bible means to suffer because of *God*; to sin, to sin against *God*; to doubt, to doubt of *God*; to perish, to perish at the hand of *God*. In other words, that painful awareness of the boundary of mortality which man acquires with more or less certainty in life's rise and fall becomes, in the Bible, the order of the God of holiness; it is the message of the *cross*, and from it, in this life, there is no escape.[63]

In the sermon, humanity's existential concern about mortality is for the first time seen in its full weight—as an eternal and moral problem, the death of a sinful

---

61. Ibid., 85.
62. Ibid., 85–86.
63. Barth, "Need and Promise," 119.

creature before a holy God. It is a *theologia crucis* and not a *theologia gloriae* with which we are confronted in Scripture.

Yet of course, the message of the cross is also a message of *grace*—indeed, it is this more loudly than it is a word of condemnation. God speaks across the divide. He comes to humanity. He takes the cold abandon of sinful humankind and gives it his own voice. God lives God-forsakenness and in so doing shows us that he is not against us but for us.

Our expectation that we can come to church prepared to interrogate the deity is met with God's "No." But our questioning is affirmed in the answer. "*This* No is likewise Yes. *This* judgment is grace. *This* condemnation is forgiveness. *This* death is life. *This* hell is heaven. *This* terrifying God is the loving father, who gathers his forsaken Son in his arms."[64] The rejection of our asking is simultaneously acceptance, *in God's terms*. He asks as we ought to, but do not, in fact cannot. We encounter God as God; not as we would seek and find him, but as he would be sought and found, as both the specific rejection and specific acceptance of our inquiring. As the self-giving object of our inquiry, God determines our manner of asking after him. Otherwise put, "the *answer* is *primary*. There would be no question if there was no answer. In order for the answer really to *be answer* to the human, it must meet him as question. God is the fullness of the Yes; in order for us to *understand* him as *God*, we must go through his No."[65]

We do not ask, Where is God?, as if we stand outside a linear progression of eternity and time watching The Eternal behave as we naturally expect—alone, then creating the world, then relating to us as we assume proper of deity, then mysteriously vanishing when things really get desperate—so that we might rightly demand, "Where are you *now*, when I need you!?" Rather, in the light of Christ, we see that our questions are properly formulated by thought structured after God, by being in the middle of his life and action, not before and outside of it.

Where is God? Shaped after the cross, this question is no longer a sinful manifestation of constricted expectations thrust onto deity but a sincere statement of faith along the lines of Psalm 22. It expresses our thrownness into abandonment, but in hope and not despair, looking for God to bear this burden with us. We acknowledge that his existence is not aloof, in uncaring detachment from us, as one whose will amounts to inexplicable mystery since

---

64. "Not und Verheissung," 86.
65. Ibid., 87.

he only here and there visits us with his presence, and rarely when we need him, but instead, he *is* God-with-us.

We intuit a God who simply intervenes in space-time as we know and shape it, but if we are honest with ourselves—and of ourselves, this kind of honesty is impossible to achieve—then we really want a God who is captive to our schematics neither of intervention nor space-time. We need a God who first says "No" to us, who makes himself absent to the ways we naturally frame our needs and put them upon him. (Even at our most magnanimous, we cannot perceive the ways that at least some of our interests, passions, and loves are zero-sum. And we have lost *all* ability to account for the full range of consequences stemming from millennia of dark thoughts, words, and actions—a world populated by genetic mutations and neurological heritages toward selfish perversions, ours and others—within which we simply find ourselves thrown. In such a world, *no one* is innocent.) We need a God who thus frames human need on humanity's behalf, precisely in meeting that need.

Such a God is both our need and our *promise*—a God who comes to us in the midst of our hopeless condition and frees us from it, who shares his freedom with us and enables us to think and speak according to a new horizon—to live toward redemption in the midst of tragedy, life in the midst of death. Our promise is in a God who with his "No" says just as definitively, and more loudly, "Yes" to us. Our promise is in a God whose absence is the precondition of his presence, but which absence we perceive only because he chooses to have his being in the merciful act of coming to us.

We learn from Christ that true God-ness is in the act of the Creator coming to the tragedy that creation at large has become and making himself real amidst the long-evolved impulses to sin and evil and their attendant consequences without ceasing to be creation's Lord. Without ceasing to be who he is, and without annihilating us, necessarily in both, the God of Calvary sets his face to the redemption of all things:

> Dogs surround me,
> a pack of villains encircles me;
> they pierce my hands and my feet.
> All my bones are on display;
> people stare and gloat over me.
> They divide my clothes among them
> and cast lots for my garment.
> But you, Lord, do not be far from me.

> You are my strength; come quickly to help me.
> Deliver me from the sword,
> my precious life from the power of the dogs.
> (Ps. 22:16-20)

At Calvary, humanity's misfortune, doubt, despair, and even death are thrust on God. The very things about which we would question, God himself expresses, existentially, in Jesus Christ. There and then, as that question is made real before us by the Holy Spirit, we perceive God as our answer. In the sermonic event in which we recognize our questions asked and addressed by him in Christ, God reveals the full character and measure of our crisis and presents himself as its solution.

We see, then, in Barth's lecture to the ministers at Schulpforte the kind of Spirit-centered thinking that guides his later exegetical reflections on the Gospel of John. The sermonic event is but repetition of the Christ-event in which God is God. It is reiteration of God's confrontation with the world of sin, to which the prophets and apostles bore witness. It can be this reiteration, indeed, a form of divine testimony itself, only insofar as it is *exclusively* grounded in their testimony; that is, only insofar as it refuses any other content and structure, any alternative account of divine presence or "spirituality," including sacramental spirituality.

The sermon is simply the moment when again God establishes humanity's need in its true form and meets that need. It is the happening when the minister himself is judged and forgiven by Scripture, which judgment and forgiveness he feels and knows and is made to accept, and as such turns and speaks to the congregation. It is thus the event in which God acts as he has always acted: in refusal of chaos, darkness, and death and therefore in creating, reconciling, and redeeming life.

The proclamation of Scripture becomes the proclamation of the Word of God, participating in the character of Scripture itself. It has to be thought of as God's en-wording or Inverberation, construed in the very terms of the Son's Incarnation. It is the contemporaneous happening of God's presence in the sense just described, that is, not just the kind of self-transcendence encountered in a blossoming cherry tree, symphony, and so on, but in actual existential transformation. It is the agential phenomenon of the Spirit of the Word in that it is at once refusal of the minister's thoughts and words and their acceptance, reformulation of the people's questions, remaking of this space-time. It is here and now, in the reading and speaking and hearing of Scripture, that, as Barth put it above, "painful awareness of the boundary of mortality which man acquires with more or less certainty in life's rise and fall becomes . . . the order of God's holiness."

God meets us again today as he always has: not as we would have him but as he will have us. He comes to us not simply as the answer to our questions but as such an answer that reconfigures our questions; as the genuine problem to which he alone is the genuine solution. As noted, Barth applies this logical structure derived from the sermon to the nature and task of theology as a discipline:

> Beyond their [the religious scholars'] existence and the existence of all questions that are linked with it, they know a great What? Whereto? Wherefrom? Wherein? which is the minus before the entire bracket, a question, which causes all the already-answered questions within the bracket to be asked anew. They themselves know no answer to give to this question of all questions . . . and thus they thrust us into our strange, special existence, they put us in their pulpits and lecterns that there we should ourselves speak of God, of the answer to this last question.[66]

Theological studies can no more be a detached, antiseptic process of historical-critical research than can exegesis and the sermon. That is because here, like there, such research, while important, is only penultimate. Here, like there, eternity stands as a minus outside the bracket of a mathematical equation, reframing all the terms of human life and all the academic subcategories by which it is understood. There is an ultimate question that meets the scholar's questions in the same way that it does the layperson's: from what and to what and about what am I?

It is only a willingness to address this question that justifies the study of theology. "It is the paradoxical but undeniable truth that as a science like other sciences theology has no right to its place; for it becomes then a wholly unnecessary duplication of disciplines belonging to the other faculties."[67] There is no shortage of scientific fields dedicated to the penultimate questions of

66. "Das Wort Gottes als Aufgabe der Theologie," in *Vorträge und kleinere Arbeiten 1922–1925*, 151–52.
67. Barth, "Word of God," 193.

religious history, psychology, and philosophy. The theologian does well not simply to reduplicate in a poor way the work for which her colleagues are better trained. Her existence is warranted among the sciences to the extent that she is ready to speak to the one thing that they are not, to the one ultimate question that they are not prepared to answer.

"There is an academic need which in the last analysis, as might be inferred, is the same as the general human need we have already described."[68] Just as out of its need the congregation comes to church, so also out of the same need the university "tolerates theology within its walls."[69] The academy is aware that its questions take place within the specter of a larger, all-determinative question, or at least it "has a bad conscience"[70] about this fact. It has a kind of existential uncertainty about its presuppositions, about the full reach of its conclusions, and so it allows theology, "once the mother of the entire university," a continued place "if even with a somewhat sunken head."[71]

Theology, therefore, arises and gains definite structure as an event coordinated with the event of the sermon. As with the minister, so also with the theologian, she ought to speak of God, but as God speaks of himself. Of course, like the pastor, the theologian can*not* speak of God as God speaks of himself! The task is an insuperable one for her, too. She is not the solution:

> The solution of the riddle, the answer to the question, the satisfaction of our need is the absolutely *new* event whereby the impossible becomes *of itself* possible, *death* becomes life, *eternity* time, and *God* man. There is *no* way which leads to this event; there is *no* faculty in man for apprehending it; for the way and the faculty are themselves new, being the revelation and faith, the knowing and being known enjoyed by the new man.[72]

Of himself, God becomes human. *Of himself*, God speaks to life's questions, whether brought by the laity or by the academy. He does this exactly where and when he refuses our self-inflected questions and asks them as we ought. He does this in the event of Christ Jesus, his being God as Man. It is this "absolutely new event," as *absolutely new* (and not summoned up from within us or about us),

68. Ibid., 192.
69. Ibid.
70. Ibid.
71. Barth, "Das Wort Gottes," 157.
72. Barth, "Word of God," 197.

that is at once the minus before the bracket of our questions and their solution. When and where we encounter God as object and not merely a potency of the human subject, we perceive both the end of our seeking and its qualification.

Barth's thesis is that the theologian should moment by moment recognize her "ought" and "cannot" *and give God the glory*. She should confess that no one, she included, can speak the answer to human need, and allow that in just this confession, God may speak:

> Our perplexity is our promise. . . . It may be that the Word, the word of God, which we ourselves never speak, has put on our weakness and unprofitableness so that *our* word *in* its very weakness and unprofitableness has become capable at least of being the mortal frame, the earthen vessel, of the word of God. It may be so, I say; and if it were, we should have reason not so much to speak of our need as to declare and publish the hope and hidden glory of our calling.[73]

Our hope, the only hope worth shouting from the rooftops, is confession that we cannot see God! For in this perplexity is our promise—that he sees and cares for us. The one for whom we have no capacity makes himself (present tense) capable of us. To confess that we cannot see God is paradoxically already to have seen him, specifically as our solution. It is life in the revelation that here and now God is the stairway and not us. And by such living, it may be that we participate as earthen vessels in the proclamation of God's Word to a broader public. It may be that our calling is fulfilled in us by the power of that Word to command an alternative way of being. It may be that where we are nothing but empty vessels passing along what is given to us, the Spirit of God is everything; that as Christ was everything in the there and then of prophetic and apostolic need, he again becomes everything in the moment of our emptiness here and now.

Here, too, we are dealing with a highly pneumatological set of observations. Barth is obviously impressed by the etymological makeup of *theology* as "speech of God." The theologian, like the pastor, speaks of God. But if she is to speak of *God*, then her first word, in keeping with that of the prophets and apostles, is that she cannot speak of God. Thus, theology can only ever be God's own speech in human words. Like Scripture and sermon, it is not religious wisdom, or in this case, scientific insight that makes theological speech true, that qualifies it as God's speech. It is only God who does this.

73. Ibid., 216.

So, theology, too, can only be an event. It has to be the same kind of event that we encounter in Scripture and sermon—the establishment of the boundary between heaven and earth precisely in its crossing, or again, awareness of the minus before the bracket precisely in its solving. We will see in the next chapter that Barth does not, in this, equate theology with Scripture and sermon; it does not become the Word of God. But we must not rush to the distinction. We must first note the relation: theology is an event deriving from and shaped after the same event of God being God-with-us, which formed and shaped these words. It is a work of the Spirit, or, a tertiary instance of Inverberation.

Just as in the sermon the laity is made aware of the real shape and substance of their questions, so also in theology the academy's uneasy conscience receives its full scope and content. The wherefrom? and whereto? of their work receive an answer. It is here, too, a matter of an existential event, of God's coming to be who he is before even the most studied form of human inquiry. It is not just that "God" is placed like a factor in the sequence of that inquiry, but that he actually comes to stand before it as its proper shape and goal, that he actually becomes alive and real to the inquirer in encounter with theological thought and speech. Yet that means, for Barth, that just as God willed to have his existence with humanity in Christ, so does he will again that same existence today, now in this kind of tertiary witness to Christ. It is not just the idea of God or a distinct historical form of the God-concept with which laity and academy are confronted, but the reality of God specifically as the decisive negation and acceptance of their very existence per se.

Barth never lost sight of this dialectical reality. Indeed, the very contemporaneousness of God demands that his being among us take a dialectical shape. God is God in coming to humankind as humanity's judgment and salvation, "No" and "Yes," which is to say, as humanity's all-determinative Lord. The Spirit of God is this divine contemporaneousness. He just is the event in which God is sensed here and now as the Lordship of Christ Jesus. He is the presence and action of Christ in our thinking and speaking today, the ongoing exegesis of God by Christ witnessed in the prophets and apostles, proclaimed in the church, and studied in the academy. In this respect, Barth laid the groundwork for an essentially pneumatocentric theology already in his earliest lecture material. We must, by way of conclusion, step back and assess this claim formally.

Pneumatocentric Theology? Locating Barth's Dream
within the Arc of His Thought

The Spirit, for Barth, is the contemporaneousness of God in the real dialectic of coming to humanity as its Lord, at once rejecting creaturely self-priority and accepting the creature as his own. "Is God, whom his people recognize through his federal revelation and as such the God proclaimed in the world—is he not Spirit across the board (John 4:24; 1 [sic] Cor. 3:17)—therefore is he not the God who in his own freedom, power, wisdom, and love makes himself contemporaneous and relates himself?"[74] The God encountered as God in the world *is* Spirit. The Spirit is not some entity floating behind or above the revelation of God to us, but one with that revelation. He is the Word's freedom, power, wisdom, and love, the condition by which God is seen as unseen. He is, in short, the determinative reality of the Word—its dimension and authority. And God is *recognized* as such. He is perceived precisely in and as Spirit.

In defense of this observation, Barth cites John 4:24, "God is Spirit," together with 2 Corinthians 3:17, "Now the Lord is Spirit, and where the Spirit of the Lord is there is freedom." In this, we note a continuation of the logic of God's subject-determining objectivity, which informs the lectures just discussed. God's very existence as Spirit is in the contemporaneous act of reconstituting our being in the place and moment of his presence, of remaking us as the new man (freeing us from the sin that binds us) in and with his ever-new turning to us. In a recent work on Barth's pneumatology viewed in the context of Western trinitarianism, Travis Ables nicely articulates this characterization:

> We should think of the self-giving act of God as a singular act in Christ, and should not look for a second act in the Spirit. The missions of the trinitarian persons do not necessarily entail distinct redemptive acts in the economy of salvation. Rather, we should look for one act of God in different valences, or modalities: the reception of the act of God is part of that very act itself. . . Pneumatology names something performative: it is not so much a description of the nature of the third hypostasis of the Trinity as it is the discourse that encodes

---

74. "Der sich selbst vergegenwärtigende und applizierende Gott" (Barth, "Nachwort," 311). As for the second biblical reference, Barth cites 1 Cor. 3:17, but this must be a mistake. While this verse does have a spiritual connotation, it is about not destroying God's temple (the body). Second Cor. 3:17 obviously fits his thought better, namely, that the God we know just is the Spirit.

the event of our participation in the Trinity through the work of that hypostasis.[75]

That is, I think, a brilliant way of putting the matter. The Spirit qua Spirit is repetition here and now of the divine performance of redemption, God's self-giving by which there always was and will be life. If only Ables would stop there. Instead, he continues, "we can understand both Augustine and Barth as employing a kind of apophatic trinitarian grammar, oriented around the deification of all our ways of knowing God."[76] That is a bridge too far. Salvation, for Barth, including our experience of it by way of participation in the inner-triune life of God, is not deification in any sense.[77] Such a construal fails to reckon with Barth's studied refusal of constructs that subtly insert divinity or at least a capacity for divinity (easily turned into a *divine* capacity) within the human.[78]

Significantly, Barth penned the observation I cited above late in life, some four decades after the commentaries and lectures we have discussed, which logic

---

75. Travis E. Ables, *Incarnational Realism: Trinity and the Spirit in Augustine and Barth*, T&T Clark Studies in Systematic Theology 21 (London: Bloomsbury T&T Clark, 2013), 12–13.

76. Ibid., 36. Or again, "our participation in Christ is of precisely the same eternal origin and nature as the person of Jesus Christ himself." That is to the good. Yet Ables continues. "But it is *our* response. It is inherent to Pneumatology that it concerns the deification of the human person as agent of its act" (ibid., 187). That is not to the good, at least as a description of a Pneumatology that learns from Barth.

77. One shortcoming of Ables's percipient analysis is that it neglects to locate Barth's thinking consistently within Protestant and, more narrowly, Reformed, rather than Lutheran, theo-logic. (He signals this orientation here and there but programmatically prefers a more philosophical/Hegelian background.) He therefore tends to conflate "participation" and "deification" in a way that Barth does not. For a helpful corrective, see Bruce L. McCormack, "Participation in God, Yes, Deification, No: Two Modern Protestant Responses to an Ancient Question," in *Orthodox and Modern: Studies in the Theology of Karl Barth* (Grand Rapids: Baker Academic, 2008), 235–60. The key issue is that the performative life-act of the Spirit is always *God's* life-act *as distinct from humanity* even when it takes place in and with humanity, so that it is never a matter of humanity transcending itself and becoming God or Godlike in the *knowledge* event; it is always only a matter of God drawing what he is not into himself and thereby constituting that other authentically in the *revelation* event. The two go together, and Ables is right in seeing that, but as I have been demonstrating in this chapter, the order (from God to humanity, revelation to knowledge) is critical and can never be reversed.

78. A second shortcoming of Ables's work is that Barth's break with liberalism is largely neglected when, as I have noted, it is decisive. It is Barth's understanding of the Bible—its character in reflection of its content—to which he turned specifically in contrast to the tradition of modern liberal theology, which forms his own theology as inherently dialectical, and which therefore must continue to guide our understanding of his Pneumatology.

it repeats. He wrote it in a postscript to a text on his intellectual friend and nemesis Schleiermacher. It formed part of a now-infamous speculation:

> What I here and now . . . have casually taken into consideration concerning material clarification of my relationship to Schleiermacher and here and there already indicated among good friends, is the possibility of a theology of the third article, dominating and decisively of the Holy Spirit. Everything to be believed, thought, and said of God the Father and God the Son in understanding the first and second articles would in its essence be demonstrated and clarified through God the Holy Spirit.[79]

This oft-cited and never-developed reflection has provoked speculation by eager students trying to discern what a turn to the Nicene Creed's Third Article would entail. To my knowledge, none has returned to Barth's early writings and constructively traced out their essentially pneumatological trajectory, as I have begun to do.[80] If Barth is considered to be a christocentric thinker, the tendency has been to take this reflection as encouragement to pursue an alternative kind of theology to his own. Apparently seizing on the reference to Schleiermacher, and knowing the younger Barth's criticism of the German pastor-theologian (as attempting to speak of God by speaking loudly of humankind), the natural assumption appears to be that Barth was finally endorsing the correlation of pneumatology and anthropology. He would seem to be moving away from the decisive objectivity of his youth, in which God is self-constituted Other from us who condescends to commune with us, toward understanding God according to human religiosity.[81]

79. Barth, "Nachwort," 310-11.

80. I must here register thanks to one of Barth's own graduate students, who enjoyed more than one occasion to discuss with Barth the idea of Third Article theology while studying with him in Basel. Terrence Tice, eventually an expert on Schleiermacher himself, kindly considered, over an extended lunch meeting in fall 2008, my proposed return to the early Barth as the best means of undertaking pneumatocentric theology. He agreed with my critique of Jürgen Moltmann and others who have used Barth's postscript to oppose his late and early work, then sided with the late Barth and synthetically united the human and divine by way of "spirit" (see fn. 81). Such is inconsistent with Barth's intentions. Tice likewise encouraged my contrary efforts as a promising means of remaining true to Barth, mature and young.

81. Jürgen Moltmann and Wolfhart Pannenberg are the most recognizable figures who, otherwise learning much from Barth, have found it necessary to invoke a more fluid account of the relationship

But in the light of the logic we have been tracing thus far, this has to be a mistake, for Barth's christocentrism is at once pneumato-logical. His thought trades upon the agency of the Spirit at every turn; apart from the event of faith, which is Spirit-inspired and maintained, there is no christocentric point of departure for pastoral or theological thought and speech. And at the same time,

between God and humanity in order to speak meaningfully of the Spirit. See Moltmann, *The Spirit of Life: A Universal Affirmation*, trans. Margaret Kohl (Minneapolis: Fortress, 1992); this work supposes Moltmann's self-described "panentheism" – e.g., Moltmann, *God in Creation: A New Theology of Creation and the Spirit of God*, trans. Margaret Kohl (Minneapolis: Fortress, 1993) – in that it continues to synthetically relate God's reality with the creature's via spirit. See also Pannenberg, *Systematic Theology* vol. 2, trans. Geoffrey W. Bromiley (London: T & T Clark, 2004).

Moltmann complains that Barth too rigidly opposed God's revelation and human experience. He contends that the Holy Spirit "can never be experienced" for Barth because the Spirit simply "places human beings in expectation of the 'Wholly Other'" (*The Spirit of Life*, 7). The Spirit per se is not known by the human because his work is only to reinforce the otherness of God by way of eschatological expectation. In this, "Barth merely replaced the theological immanentism which he complained about by a theological transcendentalism" (ibid.). Moltmann's corrective is to think and speak not of God's transcendence, but of the self-transcendence of humanity. "Because God's Spirit is present in human beings, the human spirit is self-transcendentally aligned towards God" (ibid.)

Pannenberg is subtler and more nuanced than Moltmann even as he similarly gives account of the Spirit by turning to notions of human self-transcendence. On the one hand, he commends Barth for distinguishing between God the Spirit and creaturely reality (*Systematic Theology* 2:190, fn. 48). Yet on the other hand, in express opposition to Barth, he understands the constitution of the creature in terms of a "disposition for divine likeness" (ibid, 228), to be "'eccentric' relative to other things and beings," and to possess a fundamental "openness beyond everything finite," which disposition, eccentricity (standing outside oneself), and openness is "actualized" by the Spirit of God (ibid., 228-29).

It is often said that Barth already was on the way to a more flexible construal of the divine and human S/spirit in that he softened the dialectic of his early work, eventually exchanging it for a consistently analogical method. The opposition between God and humanity, which we have seen characterized his response to liberal Protestantism, gave way to a (happier) unity. This line of thinking generally assumes the veracity of the analysis found in Hans Urs von Balthasar, *The Theology of Karl Barth*, trans. John Drury (New York: Holt, Rinehart and Winston, 1971). My work, by contrast, favors Bruce McCormack's critique of Balthasar's thesis; see McCormack, *Karl Barth's Critically Realistic Dialectical Theology*, 1-28 (with reference to important contributions by Eberhard Jüngel, Ingrid Spieckermann, and Michael Beintker). A recent book, which I find largely to miss the mark, critiques McCormack's critique: see D. Stephen Long, *Saving Karl Barth: Hans Urs von Balthasar's Preoccupation* (Minneapolis: Fortress, 2014). The turn to humanity is *not*, again, the direction that Ables takes in order to think pneumatologically after Barth, which is why on balance I find his work commendable. He, too, sees a robust Pneumatology in Barth as specifically christological Pneumatology over and against anthropocentrism. But, as noted, Ables invites a level of reciprocity between what I would call our shared recognition of Barth's Filial-Pneumatology and an unshared transcendental anthropology by closely associating participation with deification. That is more than a point of contact with Schleiermacher; it threatens to subsume Barth under Schleiermacher.

apart from the exegetical work and Person of Christ, there is no pneumato-centric content upon which one could think and speak of God.

Thus, Barth has to be directing us to a pneumatocentrism materially and methodologically consistent with the content and shape of his christocentrism. Clarification of his relationship to Schleiermacher must entail reconstituting sinful humanity's absolute dependence on God, Schleiermacher's material principle, *but exactly in its distinction from God*, in God's free actuality rather than in any human potency. That is, it must be a part of God's external rejection of humanity's artificial sovereignty, of our self-governing space-time, which takes place in each new confrontation with the reality of Christ Jesus. As Christ reveals humankind's total incapacity for God, he at once becomes the singular condition by which we think and speak and thus are restored to God. Human realization (and the reformation of creation), then, is an event in God primarily and us secondarily; it is the event of God coming to space-time here and now just as he did there and then, in which happening we come to be. True humanity is realized in the event of Christ Jesus, which is to say, it is realized in the ever-prior realization of God himself as God-for-us; this, today as ever. It is realized in the Spirit as Spirit of the Word.

Barth himself warned against confusing a call to Pneumatology with a turn to human religious experience, thereby losing God as the subject-determining object of theology:

> And how my nice dream would be misunderstood if one took it to mean that through a theology of the Holy Spirit the discipline can now proceed "all the same as from the human out!" . . . As if the underlying problematic with Schleiermacher was not that he—brilliant like none before and after him—thought and spoke "from the human!" . . . As if pneumatology were anthropology! As if I, instead of concern for the possibility of a better understanding of Schleiermacher, had dreamed, totally primitively, of a continuation of his own method![82]

Theology does not think and speak from the human to God, but the other way around. Barth was consistent on this. It is never synthetic analysis of deity normed after or sourced in prior analysis of some human capacity. It

---

82. Barth, "Nachwort," 312.

rather deals with God as God and is thus, always, *God*'s Word in *human* words. It is always only reverberation of God's presence among us, an a posteriori confession of Christ Jesus as all-determinative reality. Even centered on the Spirit, our thought and speech of God are always only constructive reiteration of God's thought and speech to us. They are defined by Christ, for he alone exegetes the Father.

When Barth takes into consideration Third Article theology, he means rethinking every doctrinal statement according to the contemporaneous objectivity of God. He means rethinking, for instance, the Creator of the First Article according to the event in which we perceive God's ongoing reshaping of space-time by the Spirit in faith. Chapter 3 of the present work explores this by way of illustration. For now, suffice it to say that all of the conclusions we draw pneumatocentrically are defined by a necessarily christocentric dialectic—God's becoming Man as God and the "No" and "Yes" connected with that, always firing like two pistons, the second louder and more definitive, but never moving without the former.

Although I am not aware of anyone who has brought the pieces together to make this argument, it is worth noting that I am not, at least, the first to identify a pneumatocentric orientation to Barth's early thought, precisely as dialectical and properly objective thought. Bruce McCormack has identified four stages to the genesis and evolution of Barth's thinking. These divide in half along a seismic fault that emerged in 1924. During his final year as honorary professor in Göttingen, Barth "discovered" the ancient doctrine (mid-sixth century) of *an-enhypostasia*—the dialectical confession that the flesh of Jesus has no independent preexistence before the Incarnation but exists *in* the hypostasis or personal entity of the Word—and adopted it as a model for Christology.[83] Before that, Barth understood theology to be ultimately determined in content and therefore shaped by an "eschatological reservation." That is to say, it was determined by the conviction that "God is in heaven and we are on earth," as we saw in his commentaries on Romans and in the lectures above.

All human statements about God stand under a reservation implicit in recognizing the infinite qualitative distinction separating God's existence from our own. Barth learned that everything he would achieve through the time/eternity dialectic—specifically, that in his temporal revelation God remains eternal God—could be maintained by the dialectic between God's veiling and unveiling in the Word. As I have begun to demonstrate, what Barth does in his commentary on John, for example, reflects the same dialectic as in his earlier

---

83. McCormack, *Karl Barth's Critically Realistic Dialectical Theology*, 327 and passim.

work, but now with decisive focus on restoration of the created order (seeing God's imperceptibility) *in Jesus*. Because the flesh that God takes up has no self-subsistent *hypostasis* (personal constitution), but has its existence only in the hypostasis of the *logos*, God's self-revelation in space-time does not constitute his giving himself over to some already-subsisting, temporal medium. In his revelation, God creates and sustains the medium he would assume, establishing its existence in his Word and only there, and as such he remains Lord of the means, manner, substance, and place of his self-giving. Even in his full and total unveiling he remains fully and totally veiled; his divine majesty is made known, but in the flesh of the man from Nazareth.

McCormack further divides each of these two major phases of Barth's development into two others and assigns them a period. From 1915 to 1920, Barth's programmatic eschatology was characteristically "process"; from 1920 to 1924, it became "consistent."[84] From 1924 to 1939, his an-enhypostatic Christology was pneumatocentric. Thereafter it became christocentric.[85] My

84. "Process" and "consistent" are descriptors McCormack employs to distinguish between the type of eschatology at work in Barth's first and second commentaries on the book of Romans, respectively; see esp. *Karl Barth's Critically Realistic Dialectical Theology*, 153–55, 231–33. In the first *Römerbrief*, Barth conceived of the eschatological kingdom as an "organic" entity, alive and growing as it progressively incorporates itself into the events of temporal reality. Informing this view is a two-tiered understanding of "history." Happenings of the phenomenal realm are only quasi- or so-called history; their archetypal counterpart or real history occurs in the hidden realm of God's existence. It is as this latter history breaks into the former, which corresponds to the activities of the true body of Christ breaking into the events of the phenomenal church organization, as this takes place the kingdom of God "comes." In response to the abuses to which this schematic was put in its reception, not the least of which was the move to identify moments of the in-breaking "real" history with various cultural phenomena, Barth revised his eschatology in the second Romans commentary. Here, the organic kingdom was replaced with a stable reality delineating the existences of God and humankind. The eschaton referred to a "wholly other" realm, the realization of which remained entirely future, across the line of death at the boundary of our being. What is critical to see is that in both forms Barth's eschatology remained dialectical. Even in his process phase Barth did not intend that the sphere of God's history should be confused with our own, that as its conquest upon the phenomenal realm takes place God's existence could be ranged among human realities and our knowledge of him could proceed one-sidedly from here to there. To this Barth had to strengthen his "No" and consequently revise his eschatology, making the time/eternity dialectic clearer; *clearer* than, but not different from, his first attempt.

85. See McCormack, *Karl Barth's Critically Realistic Dialectical Theology*, 129–204, 205–324, 325–450, and 451–468, for discussions of each of the four phases of Barth's development. Locating the final progression in the year 1939 reflects an update from the paradigm's originally published form; see McCormack, "Seek God Where He May Be Found: A Response to Edwin Chr. van Driel," *Scottish Journal of Theology* 60, no. 1 (2007): 63–66. On the basis of research contributed by his student Matthias Gockel (*Barth and Schleiermacher on the Doctrine of Election: A Systematic-Theological Comparison* [Oxford: Oxford University Press, 2006]), McCormack revised the timing of the shift that took place between

own approach to Third Article theology undertaken in response to Barth's call most nearly approximates stage 3: *pneumatocentric dialectic grounded in anhypostatic-enhypostatic Christology.*[86]

What makes the approach "pneumatocentric" rather than "christocentric" even as it is ultimately oriented around the doctrine of Christ is temporal locus:

Barth's third and fourth phase. Rather than being fully comprehended at the outset of his work on CD II.1, the christological reframing of election, which represents the material condition needed to catalyze the shift to the fourth phase of Barth's development, did not come full-circle until Barth started work on CD II.2 in 1939. Formerly, McCormack located the turn in 1936, shortly after Barth attended a presentation on election given by Pierre Maury at the Geneva meeting of the International Calvin Congress (see CD II.2, 188–94). Barth himself spoke of that presentation as having decisive significance for his understanding of election, but it took some further reflection by Gockel to show that the significance Barth attached to the lecture was not fully integrated into his thinking for several years. (On Maury, see Barth, "Foreword," in Pierre Maury, *Predestination and Other Papers*, trans. Edwin Hudson [Geneva: Labor et Fides; London: SCM, 1957]. Barth writes of Maury that "his 1936 address at once made a profound impression on me," and when he considered election more fully in the preparation of *Church Dogmatics* he stressed "that [Maury's work] ought to be considered as one of the best contributions made towards the understanding of the problem" [p. 16].) It is important to note, however, that fine-tuning the timing of Barth's move does not at all impact its material elements. For McCormack, "the modification consists only in an adjustment of the timing of the inauguration of the fourth and final phase," and "the difference which this modification of my periodization of Barth's development makes for my paradigm as a whole (i.e. a continuous development after 1915 through four phases) is virtually nil" (p. 65).

86. I am contending that the logic that comes to fuller expression in phase 3 according to McCormack's periodization is latent in the logic of phases 1 and 2. I am arguing that Barth was always pneumatocentric at least anticipatorily, by way of his defining convictions. His christocentrism cannot be played off against his pneumatocentrism. McCormack, so far as I can tell, agrees. He does not differentiate between Barth's third and forth phases by contending for material discontinuity, but in terms of strengthened concentration or emphasis. Although phase 2 is properly theocentric, Barth's God is still the Christian God. To that extent his eschatological dialectic is hardly at odds with his eventual christocentrism: Barth always dealt with the *reality* of God-with-us. Speaking concretely of "Not und Verheissung" and "Das Wort Gottes," I have tried to show (in an introductory way) that Barth's dialectic is consistent with *an-enhypostasia*, because that doctrine's function is to construe the relationship between God's eternal *logos* and spatial-temporal "person." The same is manifestly operative in the dialectic between God's Word and human words. In this sense, the earlier lectures witness the same constitutive dynamic as does work from Barth's late Göttingen, Münster, and Bonn years, and are in effect penultimate to this work. For his part, McCormack concludes especially of the Elgersberg lecture ("Das Wort Gottes") that, "the relation which is here established between the incarnation and the possibility of doing theology ought not to be missed. It is a theme which would assume an ever-increasing importance for Barth. God can indeed take up human words to bear witness to himself, in spite of their inherent inadequacy" (*Karl Barth's Critically Realistic Dialectical Theology*, 312–13). It is the dialectical reality of God's advancement into human trappings, as God, which makes theology irreducibly pneumatocentric, concerned finally with the power of God over our naturally incapable language.

God's self-wording for us *today* in distinction from Palestine ca. 1–30 c.e. By his Spirit, God is as fully and totally known and confessed in Christ now as he was then; he continues to elect his being for us and in so doing continues to actualize a history with us, and this actualistic, self-electing of God really to be among us constitutes the basis, norm, and principal subject matter of theological discourse. At this phase, Barth thought similarly:

> The distinction between Barth's theology in this phase and the next phase . . . is this: although the theoretical ground of Barth's theology in this phase was found in his Christology, his basic orientation . . . was towards the revelation-event which occurs in the here and now on the basis of God's Self-revelation in Christ. He did not try, as he would later, to read all of his doctrines off God's Self-revelation in Christ in the there and then of AD 1–30.[87]

The difference between Christ in his Spirit today and Christ in the flesh then, while heuristically beneficial, is literally artificial. Both are the same God in and as his Word. Jesus tells his disciples that the Spirit "will testify about me. . . . He will not speak on his own; he will speak only what he hears. . . . He will bring glory to me by taking what is mine and making it known to you" (John 15:26b; 16:13b, 14). The knowledge that the Spirit imparts is not of his own Person, but of Christ. So Barth insisted in CD I.1 (written, importantly, during his pnuematocentric phase), that "there is no special and second revelation of the Spirit alongside that of the Son. There are not, then, two . . . Words of God."[88] The revelation of God by his Spirit today is the singular Word not distinct in content from the Word revealed in the flesh of Christ. It is in the same vein that Barth would later (fourth phase) remind that the Spirit is "no other than the presence and action of Jesus Christ himself," and that "the only content of the Holy Spirit is Jesus."[89]

This is not to collapse the Spirit entirely into the Word, as if he is simply the Janus face of a single Person. The Spirit does proceed, from the Son as well as the Father.[90] And since the only basis for distinction in God is the processions (of Son from Father and Spirit from both), we must dialectically affirm, again

87. McCormack, *Karl Barth's Critically Realistic Dialectical Theology*, 328.

88. CD I.1, 474.

89. CD IV.2, 322–23, 654.

90. Precisely because of the way it provides a logical basis for distinction among the Second and Third Persons, I take the *filioque* to be a gain for Western trinitarianism.

with Barth, "that the Holy Spirit is differentiated from the Son or Word of God."[91] Proceeding from the Son, the Spirit stands in a relation of opposition to him and therefore exists entirely and sufficiently as a hypostasis in the Godhead alongside him and the Father.

This is the issue: the fact of the Spirit's differentiation from the Son as to his Person does not constitute a second divine objectivity or a second source of knowledge in the human subject. God makes himself known as God in Christ and nowhere else. That entails acknowledging that God does not suffer in respect of Christ's singular objectivity even when he comes to us as and makes himself known by the Spirit. Here and now, too, we perceive God before us, but as God in Christ, imperceptible in his perceptibility. For, as he is known and spoken of today in the words of Scripture and proclamation, he was known and spoken of then in the flesh. Theology cannot derive from any other basis even when it takes it center from *pneuma*. In the proclamation of Scripture, or in the ongoing testimony to Christ Jesus shaped by the testimony of the prophets and apostles, God is with us no less determinatively than in his ancient incarnate presence, for his contemporaneous identity is the same Jesus.

The Spirit is the Spirit of the Word.[92] To speak of the Spirit per se is to speak of his action relative to the Word; he is the power binding the temporal words of Christian witness to God himself in human faith, as well as the generation and assumption of those words. He is God inverberate. To be a pneumatocentric theologian is therefore to presume Christology.

Hence, in shifting to christocentrism Barth did not become an essentially different type of theologian. The move was not to some distinct platform from the one he had been operating on previously; rather, the shift represented "a further concretization" of the norms he had already been employing.[93] McCormack concludes that Barth's christocentric posture served as "a methodological rule . . . in accordance with which one presupposes a particular understanding of God's Self-revelation in reflecting upon each and every other doctrinal topic, and seeks to interpret those topics in the light of what is already known of Jesus Christ."[94] Barth's christocentric shift represented deeper

---

91. CD I.1, 474.

92. The coincident nature of the Spirit's activity in and with the Word or Son is represented by the doctrine of *perichoresis*. By this doctrine I also point out that in the Spirit's activity for us today we are dealing with God fully and totally, with the Father as well as the Son. For all operations of the deity *ad extra* are one; in and with the Spirit's presence is the perfect presence of God. This reality is further assured by the fact that in dealing with God we are dealing with his single essence. God is maximally one.

93. McCormack, *Karl Barth's Critically Realistic Dialectical Theology*, 454.

commitment to the centrality of Jesus Christ *in history* as the *formal criterion* by which doctrinal statements are constructed, not, once more, a move to an alternative source of human thought and speech.

The challenge, as I have said, is then to think and speak from the contemporary reality of God, but to allow that thought and speech to be structured after the historical reality of Christ Jesus, that is, to establish and develop doctrinal statements after the dialectic of God's subject-determining objectivity. This is, I think, the direction Barth would have us move in pursuit of pneumatocentric theology: modified continuation of an approach he once practiced.

Conclusion

Karl Barth issues a direct challenge to thought and speech of God that derives from within the human subject. This challenge emerged in his early work and was reiterated late in life. We must still hear the roar of this "lion" if we are to appreciate Barth's gains relative to the liberal tradition in which he was trained.[95]

94. Ibid.

95. In 1940, in the first part of his second volume of *Church Dogmatics*, Barth reflected upon what he had argued in his commentary on Romans. Citing his exegesis of Romans 8:24, he wrote, "'Redemption is that which cannot be seen, the inaccessible, the impossible, which confronts us as hope. Can we wish to be anything other and better than men of hope, or anything additional?' Well roared, lion! There is nothing absolutely false in these bold words. I still think that I was right ten times over against those who then passed judgment on them and resisted them. Those who can still hear what was said then by both the religious and worldlings, and especially by the religious worldlings, and especially the most up-to-date among them, cannot but admit that it was necessary to speak in this way" (Barth, CD II.1, 634–35). Barth never wavered in his conviction, galvanized by his exegetical return to the Bible, that it is a mistake to treat God as a human possibility. Human hope is in the impossible and inaccessible God making himself known as such to us, which is to say, making his impossibility and inaccessibility real as part of the event in which he renders himself possible and accessible. True human being, in turn, is finding ourselves to be creatures so addressed, to be cut off from our religious sensibilities and re-rooted in God's turn to us, and in this to be reconstituted in what we might become. It is to find our possibility remade according to God's reality. Barth acknowledged that he had to reformulate this dialectical situation because, as initially stated, it froze God's "God-ness" as a limit construct. It turned his being into "that-against-which" creation stands in each moment without articulating clearly that it is *also* "that-toward-which" creation is moving as the consummation of time. God is not only creation's boundary but also its fulfillment. God is not only the "No" to human thought and speech about him and itself, but also the "Yes." Barth realized that he had to strengthen the substance of God's "Yes" if he was to be true to the futurity of even Paul's eschatological orientation. But in strengthening his construal of God's "Yes" to humanity, Barth hardly intended for us to lose sight of the "No." The "No" is outshouted by the "Yes,"

If God is to be known as God, then he must at once show and overcome our propensity, really *our* propensity, to make "God" in the image of humankind. He must confront us, really *us*, objectively with his Lordship.

This he does in Jesus Christ. He is the objectivity of God confronting our subjective deities, which objectivity restructures our cognitive processes (subjectivity) to perceive divinity and humanity. In Christ, we confess the truth of God as the determination of humankind. We confess that God will be with humanity, but as God, right when and where humanity would act as lord.

God is God in the real dialectic of comprehensive subject-determining objectivity. This is so also of his being God as Spirit. There is no thought and speech of God, including that of the Spirit (or of thought and speech centered on him), which takes place outside of his being God in Christ Jesus. There is no "spiritual" acuity apart from God's revelatory coming in the enfleshed Word. The Spirit has his identity in the work of making this revelation to be reality, in the Exegesis of the Exegete, we might say. The Spirit is the presence and action of Christ. He creates the perceptual apparatus to perceive God in the event of making the knowledge of Christ real and authoritative—of bringing God's coming to humanity to the office of prophet, apostolate, pastorate, and theological chair.

To speak of the Spirit per se is to reiterate the dialectical reality of Christ in the contemporaneity of his presence. It is to construe the Spirit as the full and total presence of God in space-time without losing eternity. It is to perceive God veiled in his unveiling, now not in flesh but in thought and word. It is to confess the determinative reality of God inverberate.

---

not eliminated. The dialectical situation in which God exists relative to us was reformulated by Barth, as McCormack has helped us to see, not abandoned.

2

The Spirit of Reality and Possibility

The bearer of revelation himself lives of the recognition that God is declared to be God by his inadequacy.
–Karl Barth[1]

The central theme of chapter 1 is that God is God in living confrontation with humanity in Christ Jesus. His *being* is an *act*, an act, in fact, that constitutes and determines our being. Barth helped us to see that it is only in and through rejection of the creature's self-contrived way of being in the event of revelation, refusal of the sin according to which we fashion the world and God with reference to our selves, that there can be any true account of "God." But that means that God is *God* in the specific happening of human knowing wherein we are made to know ourselves as secondary, derived beings. God is God not just in showing himself as an idea or datum to a creation that cannot receive him, but in making himself received as the condition of creation; he is God in the event that he gives *faith* and is therefore God only as God-with-us. This is, once more, a living, actual event in the here and now as it was in the there and then of the prophets and apostles.

It is only in existential experience of their complete inadequacy for and thus dependency on God, deriving from his complete adequacy for and turn to them, that the prophets and apostles think and speak of God *as prophets and apostles*, and that we, in turn, think and speak after them. God is "God" and creation is "creation" in the where and when of this sovereign happening; in the place and moment that chaotic darkness and every idolatrous impulse of the human entity inclined to that darkness is arrested and, in their stead, the true God becomes the basis and goal of existence.

---

1. Barth, *The Epistle to the Romans*, trans. Edwin C. Hoskins (London and New York: Oxford University Press, 1968), 80.

Only when humanity's questions are reformulated after this unanticipated answer, which comes in the form of the all-determinative question, "My God, my God, why have you forsaken me?" is *God* perceived and *humanity* realized. Here is chaotic darkness in the form of God-abandonment, humanity's crisis in its full scope and depth, but as something that God himself knows, authenticates, and therefore overcomes. Here, and only here, only in this place where he is not here, only where he is God-with-us but *God*-with-us, where his presence is encountered but not as that of a blossoming cherry tree, is God, God and Man, Man.

This pneumato-logic guides Barth's thinking especially during the third phase of his development. This chapter further argues my thesis that the insights characteristic of this period (which, again, can be found in works on the cusp of this time frame as well, such as "The Need and Promise of Christian Proclamation" and, "The Word of God as the Task of Theology") offer robust resources for a theology of the Third Article. God is God a third time today as he has always been, in the ontic-epistemic nexus of faith, which is to say, in the event that he is *known* as the condition of all *being*, which *knowing* is decisive for his *being* and ours.

God is God when and where a boundary is set between heaven and earth, but which is crossed by God in the setting, and as such, only as such, earth comes to be what it is—the theater of the Creator's Lordship. Reality—who and what God is, and who and what all things willed by God to exist outside of him are—is thus an event. It is the place and moment that God exercises his sovereign right, the unique authority by which he determines his own existence, to stand over and against another as its Creator, Reconciler, and Redeemer. Possibility—who and what God might be, and who and what all things willed by God to exist outside of him might be—is correlatively an event. It is the establishment of a freedom by God to exist for the creature and the creature to exist for him without dissolving either the sovereignty of God over the creature or the creature's dependency on him. Reality and possibility take place in revelation/revealedness, or in the Word by the Spirit.

BARTH'S EXEGESIS OF JOHN 1:1-5

EN ARCHĒ ĒN HO LOGOS, KAI HO LOGOS ĒN PROS TON THEON,
KAI THEOS ĒN HO LOGOS.

> *In the beginning was the Word, and the*
> *Word was with God, and the Word was*
> *God.*

The event in which reality and possibility are established, in which God's being as God is given and received and in which, in turn, creation is willed, initiated, and sustained, is the single event of God's Word. God and his world are so not only in an eternal decision and act but also in the repetition of that act in history, the continuing execution of God's will and act in the Incarnation *and*, as Barth's comments on the Gospel of John have helped us to see, in the life and work of the Spirit today understood in terms of the Incarnation, or in the agential identity of Inverberation.

John shows that God's revelation is not auxiliary to God's existence, not a secondary predicate but the very quality of God's God-ness. What is true of God is true of his Word. What makes God of God is made known by the Word, and the content of this knowledge, God's deity, is also the content of the Word. To that end, Barth places emphasis on the *archē* of *en archē ēn ho logos.* "*What* was in the beginning, namely the Word and not something else, is not the point here. Instead, something is being said about the Word. It was already *in the beginning.*"[2] The *logos* is mentioned at the outset of John's Gospel *not* as a given referent, for which the reader has a ready-to-hand understanding, but as a term that receives meaning by its being located *en archē.*

The evangelist is not yet concerned with defining or identifying the Word, but with describing it on the basis of its realm of existence. He is not assuming material substance signified by the term *logos* (deriving from, say, Hellenistic philosophy). Instead, he is emptying the *logos* of all preconceptions and reloading it, as it were. Specifically, he is contending that the Word is not a creature in space-time, but stands before and above space-time. He is associating the Word with God and God with the Word. "The Logos was in,

---

2. Barth, *Witness to the Word: A Commentary on John 1. Lectures at Münster in 1925 and at Bonn in 1933*, ed. Walther Fürst, trans. Geoffrey W. Bromiley (Grand Rapids: Eerdmans, 1986), 19.

with, before, and above the totality of the created world. There is no space in this world that is not limited by it. There is no possibility of evading or escaping it; no more than of evading or escaping God himself. That 'the Logos was in the beginning' means that he is as God. Only God, the Creator himself, was 'in the beginning.'"[3]

John's turn to primordial eternity entails that there is no interval between God and this Second existing *with* him. "The Word was not apart from or alongside God. The Word was 'with God.' It belonged to him."[4] Deploying the preposition *with* to describe the Word's relation to God should not incline us to think of the Word as an "It" external to God, cohabiting the places and cycles of his realm of being as a nondescript, preexistent alternative, substitute, or even complement to God. *With* rather evokes association, union, belonging. The existence that we call "eternal" can only be continuous with the existence that we confess as "God." It can only be the place, motion, and occasion of his being and living. Thus, being "in the beginning," the Word is proper to God, for he is the only agent and agency of this designation.

That means that the Word stands relative to creation as its Creator, as that upon which every nano-instant and nano-object utterly depend. "Being after the manner of God, [the Word] stood and essentially stands beyond the line that is drawn by the beginning of all things."[5] If we would understand Creator and creation, we most crucially must understand the relation posited between them in the Word.[6] God has his being and creation its being in the event that a line is drawn demarcating that which is proper to God and that which is proper to creatureliness. But again, this line is drawn only in the place and moment (space-time) that the Word is spoken. Creation, then, is given in and with revelation/revealedness, or the space-time event in which the knowledge of God takes place by God. This is pneumatocentric theology characterized by an an-enhypostatic account of the incarnate Christ.

In reading John this way, creative though it is, Barth stands with the historic Christian faith against Philo and all Neoplatonic conjecture about a

---

3. Ibid.

4. Ibid., 20.

5. Ibid., 21.

6. Barth does not obliterate all means of differentiation in God by so closely associating the Word with God. The thrice-repeated use of the definite article individuates the Word. Barth conceives of the Word as "a second He who is distinct from the first but who partakes of the same nature and is thus identical in nature." Barth interprets John 1:1 confessionally, speaking of the Word "in the mode of the eternal Son [who] shares the same nature with the person of the Father in the same dignity and perfection. One must admit that the verse makes sense when it is read thus, with the eyes of what has been called orthodoxy since Nicea" (Barth, *Witness to the Word,* 22).

second realm of existence, which is not coterminous with God's own but subsists somewhere between his primordial self-existence and the cosmos he creates. Barth contends that *archē* cannot be an intermediary realm, which John now calls up as the proper home of the Word:

> We turn, not to Philo or the Mandeans, but exclusively to John himself. That is to say, we rule out intrinsically possible meanings whereby the Logos is essentially and primarily a principle, whether in epistemology or in the metaphysical explanation of the world, e.g., as the supreme idea along the lines of Neoplatonism, as creative and ruling cosmic reason along the lines of Stoicism, or as the power of spirit mediating between God and the material world along the lines of Philo. . . . [By contrast], this is the Johannine Logos: the Logos as the principle of revelation, not of being, as that which challenges all that is and all being by the divine address that is directed to humanity from person to person.[7]

We do not think of the Word in terms of a given concept of knowing or being, say, of an epistemological principle that orders communication of truth along a hierarchical series of interconnected ideas, or metaphysical speculation about the emanation of material being through an intermediary agent. The Word is not the first in such a series, not some mere messenger who conveys the truth, but Truth itself; not a third-party entity existing between Creator and creature, but the Creator himself.

But he is this "as the principle of revelation, not of being." The Word is the condition of divine reality not by participation in a given ontological quality called "deity," but in the challenge given to all such qualities in the event of *this* deity. He is that address in and by which God is differentiated *as God*, an address that, as Barth indicated in the quote above, "is directed to humanity from person to person." However tautological it may initially seem, we have to say that precisely in the human proclamation of the Word addressed by God to humankind, God is God and humanity is humanity. Reality, and all things that might be within the limitations of the real, all possibility, is coordinately given in the unity of God with his Word, of the Creator with his Revelation.

7. Barth, *Witness to the Word*, 24–25.

If we do not force metaphysics upon John and deal strictly with the presentation before us, then the Word's reality is structured relative to the same "beginning" as God's. In this case, *archē* refers not primarily to a point in chronological sequence (from eternity to time, from the divine calendar to creaturely *chronos*). John is not saying "long ago and far away." Rather, "the beginning" first and foremost refers to the repetition of God's being as a being that turns outside itself, *in which repetition,* only "then" and "there," the creation of the world takes place. Applied to eternal God, "the beginning" must be a reference to God's initiative, his power and concrete decision to bring something into existence now alongside himself and relate to it. John must be saying something like, "in God's self-determination externally."

But such confession obviously entails God's Lordship over himself. God is not captive to a *static* eternity. Instead, he freely exercises his being to bring existence distinct from himself into being and live in relation to it. "In the beginning" is thus above all a characterization, a declaration of the event and quality of God's becoming. Barth understands John to be teaching this characterization in light of the Word. "The word is the unassuming but incomparably true form in which people simply impart themselves, no more and no less, to others. By the Word God, too, imparts himself to us."[8] In this sense only is it proper to confess with the Athanasians that there is no "time" in which God is without his Word. At the very impulse, freedom, and act of God's coming to be relative to what he is not, at the very impulse, freedom, and act of God to be so much God as to share his existence with creation, God is *God*, which is to say, the Word is with and as God.[9]

---

8. Ibid., 26.

9. On understanding "the beginning" according to an Einsteinian concept of "time," see Douglas Estes, *The Temporal Mechanics of the Fourth Gospel: A Theory of Hermeneutical Relativity in the Gospel of John,* Biblical Interpretation Series 92 (Leiden: Brill, 2008); see esp. pp. 106–13.

HOUTOS ĒN EN ARCHĒ PROS TON THEON.

> He (this one) was in the beginning with
> God.

"This verse receives what might be called perfunctory treatment from almost all expositors. The commentaries tell us that it recapitulates, concentrates, confirms, and repeats. v. 1. This obviously means that they can make neither head nor tail of it."[10] Barth observes that in the flow of the evangelist's presentation, John 1:2 is pleonastic. It adds nothing materially to v. 1. Yet unlike most modern expositors who, unable to make anything noteworthy of the verse, typically dismiss it as a later insertion, Barth treats its material redundancy as having formal significance. The interruption forces the reader's attention forward, to think of the referent to the *logos* that John has thus far to name, to see that "in the whole of vv. 1-18 the author obviously has Jesus Christ in view."[11]

For Barth, the *houtos ēn* of v. 2 not only looks back to the antecedent *logos* of v. 1 but also points forward to another *houtos ēn* spoken of by the Baptist in v. 15.[12] It furthermore anticipates the bookend *ekeinos* of v. 18. That is significant because it encircles John's prologue as witness to Christ around Christ himself, grounding the legitimacy of this witness in the authority of Christ's own self-witness. "*Ekeinos, he* is the *monogenēs,* God by nature, who is in the bosom of the Father. He, *this ekeinos,* definitively establishes the validity of the *houtos ēn* of vv. 1 and 2, the validity of the witness of John, both the Baptist and the Evangelist."[13] The truth of all statements made about God, including the thought and speech of John the Baptist and John the Evangelist, is grounded in God's own thought and speech, in Jesus' exegesis of the Father. As this one/ that one, he is, to anticipate another Johannine expression, the alpha and omega

---

10. Barth, *Witness to the Word,* 27.

11. Ibid., 28.

12. See ibid.: "Why should the *houtos ēn* merely refer back to *ho logos?* Can it not also point forward in some way? Is it arbitrary to hunt around in the prologue and to argue that another highly significant *houtos ēn* occurs in v. 15, in the saying of the Baptist, in which *houtos ēn,* although the name is not mentioned, undoubtedly refers to Jesus?"

13. Ibid., 131–32.

(Rev. 1:8; 21:6; 22:13) of all that God is and we are, precisely as being the beginning and end of the revelation event.[14]

The revelation event in which God is God and creation is creation is not an undefined word from the beyond but the life-act of the man Jesus. It is in him that reality and possibility are structured. When and where he, *this one*, stands in the center of our thought and speech, then and there do we encounter true deity and humanity. The life and work of the Spirit, then, cannot be abstracted from this thought and speech, but is obviously assumed by Barth to take place in this thought and speech as the basis and structure of its happening here and now, as its source and interpretive framework, its in-spiration and illumination.

PANTA DI' AUTOU EGENETO, KAI CHŌRIS AUTOU
EGENETO OUDE HEN HO GEGONEN.

> *All things came into being through Him,*
> *and apart from Him nothing came into*
> *being that has come into being.*

One reason to conclude that v. 2, although pleonastic, is integral to the evangelist's presentation is that repetitious restatement features prominently throughout John. We have another instance of it already in v. 3. It is not enough simply to say that through the Word all things were created (*panta di' autou egeneto*), but John repeats the same idea in the negative, "without him not one thing came into being" (*chōris autou egeneto oude hen*), and punctuates the latter thought with the additional phrase, "which has come into being" (*ho gegonen*).

---

14. In keeping with Barth's insight, it is worth noting that *houtos/ekeinos* represents a "special idiom" of ancient Greek. Its employ expresses the contrast between proximate and remote, and between familiar to the point of contempt and aloof to the point of praise. See H. G. Liddell and R. Scott, *A Greek-English Lexicon,* revised and augmented by H. S. Jones, 9th ed. with revised supplement (Oxford: Clarendon, 1940), 505–6, s.v. *ekeinos,* 1275–76, s.v. *houtos.* The structure generally occurs when *houtos/ekeinos* "refer to two things before mentioned . . . in time, place, or thought" (p. 505), as is the case here in John 1. Framed by this idiom, the prologue of John encompasses all being and doing within the reality of the Word. The construct makes God in the Word simultaneously near to creation and distant from it, or as we have seen, at once absent in his presence.

In fact, this construction is so awkward that it has vexed interpreters and commentators for about as long as the Gospel of John has been read. Should we move *ho gegonen* to the next verse, perhaps, since it adds nothing materially to v. 3? Many church fathers read it that way, and it would make for more rhythmic construction. Space here does not afford opportunity to review the massive history of commentary and debate on this matter (thank God!). For his part, Barth briefly rehearses the main arguments for each perspective and then concludes, for two reasons, that it is best to keep *ho gegonen* as part of v. 3. First,

> for the internal reason that the ending with *oude hen*, i.e., the meaning that it [*ho gegonen*] gives to v. 4, namely that which came into being was or is life in the Logos—in other words, cosmogonic speculation in natural philosophy . . . acquires a breadth and significance and orientation which it cannot possibly have according to the whole approach of the rest of the prologue and the Gospel.[15]

Barth is concerned that pushing "that which has come into being" into the subject of the sentence in v. 4 introduces an abstraction that, as he has been showing, is foreign to the flow of John's thought. For John, there is no abstract being, no life or light in general apart from the Word; to think and speak of being, life, and light is to speak of the Word, namely, Jesus Christ. *All things* came into being *through* him. There is no other basis in human nature or the external world to know what it means to be, to live, and to explain the truth of God and creaturely being.

In keeping with this emphasis, Barth contends, second, that *ho gegonen* belongs with v. 3 because it punctuates the totality of the Word's creative act. Not one thing that has come into being—including the darkness that defines humanity as the object of God's light—has being except *through* Jesus Christ. "The *dia* . . . denotes the role of the means or, rather, of the mediator whose existence and function . . . explain the unheard-of fact that the dark, lower world is possible and actual alongside the pure and lofty God."[16]

The subordinate comes into being with the super-ordinate, the lesser with the greater. There is no other account to give of the world except this account. God wills to exist and be known as God in the event that this is so, in the place

15. Barth, *Witness to the Word*, 30.
16. Ibid., 31.

and moment that he is Lord not in the abstract but in the concrete refulgence of light among dark, which takes place in the mediator who brings light to the dark, Jesus Christ—indeed, as we have been saying (and as vv. 4-5 make plain), in the event that the light is distinguished and seen per se as *light-among-dark*.

The world is thus dependent from first to last on God, but specifically when and where "God" exists and is known in terms of his Word. When and where the Word happens, then and there is God, then and there is creation. "So great is God that it is only the Revealer who can originally bind him and the world together. So great is the riddle of the world that only the Revealer can secure its original relation to God. So great is the Revealer that in him we see not merely a later, ad hoc fellowship between God and the world, set up merely for the purpose of redemption, but a fellowship that is original."[17]

God is great and creation a riddle. The two, however, are brought into a determinative relation by the Revealer. In fact, in him, in Christ Jesus, the relation between God and creation is proper, basic, original. Creation is not merely a foil for an eventual work of God, but is willed by God "in the beginning" to serve as the theater of God's power and authority, his God-ness.

What Barth has done in this is to translate the mediatorial character of the Word out of metaphysics and into event ontology. The Word is the condition of all being, when "being" is understood as the coming-into-being of all things *as* the object of God's address, as the dark upon which light shines. There is no being at all outside of this happening, outside the life and action of the Word. In fact, God has his "being" in just this happening.

Barth acknowledges that John and other NT witnesses stand close to Philo and others in presenting the *logos* as the condition of all being (rather than, as we saw above, the principle of revelation). But he argues that in doing so it is their intent, unlike their Hellenistic predecessors and interlocutors, to describe and extol the *logos* per se and not use the *logos* to describe and extol a prior account of God and the world. "Jesus Christ was their first concern, God and the world their second concern. . . . The aim is to give Jesus Christ his place, and then to give God and the world their places."[18] The apostles only thought and spoke of "God" on the basis and under the power of Jesus Christ. They knew him only in these terms, in the dialectical event of coming to humankind without losing his eternal Self in doing so. Similarly, they only knew the world in the terms of this God, as the object of his eternal charity. To them, Christ is primary and

17. Ibid.
18. Ibid., 32.

everything else secondary; to them and to us, all that *might be* is given in what *is*, in the incarnate Word.

John's intent, in other words, is to *relativize* being in the light of the Word. There is no being or becoming (*egeneto*) except in the event of the Word:

> He does not say that they were created, or that God created them, but *egeneto*, "they came into being." The emergence of things is not seen from above but from below, in terms of themselves, as their own function. Yet this very quality of what they themselves do, their coming into being, is relativized. It is not their own. They have come into being not through themselves but through the Logos.[19]

All things are absolutely dependent on the Word for their individuated being, when that dependency is characterized by an active coming into being relative to another. Being is not static but dynamic. Everything that exists does so *for* something, for purpose, relation, realization. But coming to be as such happens only in and through the Word.

Only in and through the Word are beings seen for what they truly are. They cannot be perceived otherwise, except falsely as independent and therefore non-beings. "This is how things are with all that is. It is related to God. It is something and not nothing. But it is something only as it is related to the Word. Its existence is conceivable only in the light of the Word."[20] Creation exists in relation to God or not at all, which relation is established moment by moment in the Word of God. The Word makes creation to be. We might say, in the language employed in the last chapter, that only as the Word places entity within a reference frame of utter dependency on God does it come into being. Only there and then is it something and not nothing.

The Word reverses the order by which fallen humanity knows itself and God. It places us in a posture of obedience to God as our very condition of being. That is, it grounds our coming-into-being upon his ever-prior act of coming to be-with-us. It does this when and where it makes God *known* as God, when and where it *exegetes* the Father. Or more exactly, it does this when and where it shapes our every perceptual possibility after God, which is to say, when and where it restructures space-time (when and where it gives "when"

19. Ibid.
20. Ibid., 34.

and "where" a new orientation) to be the theater of God's loving union with the creature. As all possibility is shaped after God's reality, then and there is being as being–for–God.

EN AUTŌ ZŌĒ ĒN, KAI HĒ ZŌĒ ĒN TO PHŌS TŌN ANTHRŌPŌN;

In him was life, and the life was the light of men;

Having established that the Word is one with God in the beginning, and that therefore in the Word all things come into being, John begins "a new and third train of thought, which is concluded in v. 5. . . . The life that was in the Logos is the light of man, and it shines in the darkness, but the darkness does not cease to be darkness. This is the point. By life, provisionally and very generally, redemption is meant, and by light revelation."[21] It is not, of course, that this "new" direction is at odds with what John has thus far taught us; we note, on the contrary, a parallelism with what we have learned in the dialectic of light coming to the dark but as light that is perceived as such among the dark (which does not cease to be dark).

Nevertheless, Barth observes a newness to John's presentation in this sense: "*zōē* in John's Gospel is not the life that is already in us or the world by creation; it is the new and supernatural life which comes in redemption and has first to be imparted to us in some way."[22] The life that comes to be in the Word is the eternal life that humanity by nature fails to appropriate and therefore must be given. We recall in our discussion of sin and death in chapter 1 that Barth sees the human as by nature mortal. Death is not only the sign of our sin but also the reminder of our utter need for God. The life, then, that is given in the Word, when and where the Word reigns, is the true life intended for the creature specifically as God's child. It is salvation.

Barth recognizes that in understanding John this way he stands "against a whole flock of exegetes, many of whom have to be taken very seriously."[23]

21. Ibid., 36.
22. Ibid., 39.
23. Ibid., 36.

From Augustine to Luther to Calvin to Schleiermacher, interpreters of John 1:4 have found in "$z\bar{o}\bar{e}$ the general life of creation (with reference back to v. 3), and in $h\bar{e}$ $z\bar{o}\bar{e}$ the life that illumines humanity."[24] In other words, these exegetes have taken the anarthrous first instance of life in the verse to refer to a kind of general, created life that the Word bestows on humanity in a distinguishing manner (the particular life set off in the second use by the definite article), that is, as giving life to the human qua human in the form of spiritual sustenance, or consciousness, or transcendent self-awareness.[25] They make this move because they see vv. 4-5 as simply specifying what has come into being in v. 3, rather, again, than as taking them to move the narrative in a new direction.

Barth flies against the flock because, as he says, "I know of no passage in the whole of John's Gospel where it is possible to equate $z\bar{o}\bar{e}$ with being that brings forth other being, with the life of all things in the idea, with *continua inspiratio*, with the source of life, etc. Always in this Gospel the term $z\bar{o}\bar{e}$ (with or without the addition of *aiōnios*) has soteriological–eschatological significance."[26] Life in John is always eternal life even when the adjective "eternal" is not present. It is never an abstract living characterized in various formulations passed along through an intermediary being, but always the gift of God in the Word as the ultimate intention for his creature.

This way of thinking about life informs Barth's reading of light. "I have still to find in John a passage in which light is the light which is present by creation, which is given in and with the life of creation, which is there as the uncreated light of the created world, which does not rather come only with the life of redemption, which is not the light of revelation, which perhaps comes from the beginning but still comes."[27] The saving life that comes in Christ Jesus comes in and with revelation (Christ Jesus being the revelation of God in and among sinful humanity, that is, light among the dark). It was there in the beginning but comes again, present tense, to the darkness here and now.

As the self-revealing of God, light, like life in Christ, is "a separate action that goes beyond creation. In relation to what was made, to its life and to the knowledge that may be gained from it, *phōs* is a new and different light which is only arising."[28] The light that comes in the Word, revelation, is illumination of the life that God wills for the creature, not the frame of reference in which the creature passes its existence in moving from dark to dark, from the nothingness

24. Ibid., 37.
25. Ibid., 37-38.
26. Ibid., 39.
27. Ibid.
28. Ibid., 40.

that precedes its life to the nothingness that awaits it. This light is coming, dawning in Christ, or we might say, the Word itself is the dawning of the true life that God wills for the creature, of her full potentiality, of what she might be.

Thus, concerning the life we have in the light of Christ, in the redemption-revelation event, Barth summarizes:

> After the author has said in v. 3 that without exception everything made is mediate to God because it is made by the Word, and that nothing is *chōris autou*, now, making a new beginning, he goes on to say that in him was life, namely, the life which is indispensable to men but which in a fearful way they do not have, the true, authentic, eternal life which is immune to corruption and death, life such as God has in himself.[29]

As we have been observing, for Barth, creation has to be understood in the light of revelation. It has to be comprehended in view of the life that God intends for the creature and not the life that the creature has made for itself or a generic principle of life philosophically described. We can really know life and light only in general as preparation for the eternal life and light being brought to humanity and darkness in Christ Jesus. They otherwise have no significance. We only know who we are, what authentic humanity is and can be, in the light of the Word.

It is no surprise, then, that Barth thinks in terms of an *ongoing encounter* when it comes to the life given in Christ; of a living confrontation between this life and the mortal horizon of our lives; of the experience of humanity's great need—the deep urgency and profundity of our essential inadequacy made known in the light of this supply. "*This* life—in the Word which is spoken from eternity into time, and which may be heard in time with all the seriousness of eternity—is present as the life that is indispensable but is still missing, as the true life that overcomes death. *Is*, I say, although not excluding the *was*. The imperfect *ēn* includes a present here."[30] The imperfect verb form connotes a continuing effect—the dialectic of God's confrontation with humanity in sin is made real here and now in encounter with *this* life, with immortality among mortality, light among darkness.

29. Ibid.
30. Ibid., 41.

KAI TO PHŌS EN TĒ SKOTIA PHAINEI, KAI HĒ SKOTIA AUTO OU KATELABEN.

*The Light shines in the darkness, and the
darkness did not comprehend it.*

As noted, for Barth, "v. 5 stands in a special relation to v. 4."[31] Together, the verses introduce a new direction in the Gospel—the life and light of revelation that confronts the world in its darkness, within which confrontation the authentic being of the world is made manifest. With this verse, then, we are in a position to draw together Barth's insights concerning the opening unit of John's prologue for our present inquiry.

We have noticed how Barth stresses the present-tense character of the event of the Word. Revelation is not a merely past occurrence, a past confrontation, but an ongoing event, a present encounter with the life and light of God in Christ, or else it is not the revelation of God. God is God in confrontation with the dark, which is the same thing as saying that revelation is revelation in revealedness.

Therefore, in speaking of the light's *phainei* in v. 5, Barth makes an overarching observation regarding the formal effect of the Gospel (beyond just its material content): "the historical part of the first chapter, the story of Lazarus in ch. 11, and finally the resurrection in chs. 20–21 are all marked by a strikingly fluid use of the present tense which, in places where readers would expect past tenses, necessarily confronts them with the events narrated and hauls them out of their seats to action on the stage."[32] Barth recognizes that it is the Gospel's intention to involve the reader in the narrative. Or, John's testimony to the Word takes such a shape as to become one with the Word, to be the medium by which humanity today is identified, and in fact identifies itself, relative to God.

For Barth, the Word takes place again in these words. It is the condition of being for the hearer of these words as it was for their author. But it takes place for us as it took place for that author. The Word happens here and now as the line of demarcation between God and what is not God specifically in the act—that is, in this very revelation event!—that God crosses that line. This,

---

31. Ibid., 44.
32. Ibid., 44.

once more, is pneumatocentric thought and speech, an emerging theology of the Third Article shaped after the christo-logic of an-enhypostasia.

Our involvement in the event, then and now, can in no way be conceived of as a process of deification. Our involvement, the happening of eyes and ears to see ourselves addressed in these words, the event of faith, can only be characterized as a *confrontation*. "Revelation confronts non-revelation, concealment, indeed, a power that acts inimically against revelation. This is *skotia*."[33] The human recognizes itself in revelation not as a fit recipient of revelation but in a sphere of existence opposed to it, as a citizen of darkness. "Darkness is the atmosphere which contends against light and redemption. Men, all men, walk in this atmosphere (8:12; 12:35; 1 John 2:11). But as disciples of Jesus they must no longer walk in it; as believers they must not abide in it (12:35, 46). But according to 12:35 darkness can still overtake . . . once again those who walk in the light, like a mist that unexpectedly rises in the mountains."[34]

Human existence is described as the object of the light's shining, which persists in its resistance to the light even as it is illuminated by the light and made the recipient of God's gift of life. We exist in the real dialectic of being unfit for that gift but nonetheless being made by God to receive it. As we saw last chapter, precisely in the revelation event (as a *continuing* event), God is at once our need and promise. And he exists and is known as God in the establishment of just this need and supply.

It is within this framework that Barth explains the apparently contradictory shift from v. 3 to vv. 4-5. If *all things* come to be in the Word, how can a *new* thing, a new life, now be spoken of? And what of the darkness? How does one account for that? Would both not have been included in the *panta di' autou* of v. 3?

> If in fact *panta di' autou*, what need is there of the special life that comes, or of its revelation? Revelation has no basis or origin, or it is not revelation. Similarly, the darkness is simply there. It is an incident. It is not part of any program. Opposed to every program, it is simply an event. This incident on the one side and the Word of the revelation of life on the other are what the Evangelist finds to be the determinations of human existence, i.e., of his own existence. Hence he cannot "reflect" on them. Both of them, in different ways,

33. Ibid., 45.
34. Ibid.

are incomprehensible. Hence in different ways he can only take up an attitude to both as to facts of an existence that is determined by both.[35]

Barth continues to reject, as he did in his commentary on Romans, any account of sin and death as willed features of God's creative work. And of course, he rejects the alternative, Neoplatonic speculation of a rival, evil deity.[36] In contrast to both, "the darkness is simply there." It is in fact a nothingness that God passed over in creation, which nonetheless was actualized by creation in rebellion against God, and which now determines creation's existence on the one side.

On the other side, standing in contrast to the dark is the equally unexplainable revelation of God, but which is unexplainable for the very different reason that it derives from an entirely unforeseen and unmerited grace of God. Human being is constituted by both determinations. We have to say that all things come to be through the Word in the twofold sense that (1) they originate from the Word in the beginning, yet only as existences in the Word, existences before God, which are thus (2) made real as they are made known in the reiteration of the Word in each new time and place. They are "made real as they are made known" in that their life is taken up by God in revelation to be the theater of his glory—the place and moment of his rejection of the darkness unwilled by him but willed by the creature, and, as the reverse side of the rejection of sin and death, the place and moment of his gift of life.

The evangelist simply *finds* this existence in darkness, on the one hand, and in receipt of God's gift of life, on the other, to be his own existence in the event of the light. He does not place himself there by piety, existential resolve, ethics, or any other avenue of religious transcendence. He cannot reflect upon the twofold determination of his existence but can only confess it as he encounters it in God's Word.

"We simply have a conflict in which the Evangelist finds himself engaged and in which—perhaps this explains the urgent *phainei*—he wants to engage his readers."[37] Encounter with God is existential affirmation of our infinite and qualitative distance from him, which takes place in revelation as an ongoing event. It takes place as the Word takes place in words that are not fit for it. Once more, it is precisely in their unfitted-ness that they declare the Word as *God's*

35. Ibid., 46.

36. Ibid., 45: "Naturally darkness is not for John a second god as it is for Marcion. We are not in fact to restrict the *panta di' autou* (v. 3). At the same time we are not to excuse or explain the fact of darkness with the help of the *panta di' autou*. Incomprehensible in its origin, it confronts the light."

37. Ibid., 46.

Word and not the transcendent impulses of humanity. "John is trying to say that the light stands in conflict with an opponent that could not become its friend even if it wanted to do so. It is in a conflict that cannot end with a compromise. Darkness has never appropriated the light and never will. The light, when it shines, can expect nothing from the darkness except that it was and is and will be darkness."[38]

The event of revelation is the happening of a confrontation between the light and the dark, in which confrontation the light shows the dark for what it is, an existence that cannot comprehend the light but which is thus comprehended by the light. It is just this dialectical situation of the light being light-among-dark, of God being God-with-us, and of the dark being the object of the light, of humanity existentially perceiving its predicament and solution—together, the situation of God the Word—that determines all reality and possibility. In the Word, God is who he is and will be, and so are we.

We noted that human life is taken up by God in revelation to be the place and moment that he rejects sin and death, on the one hand, and therefore gives life, on the other. This is, plainly enough, not a general observation, but a specifically christological claim. The determination of creaturely reality in the event of faith is, for Barth, given both formal and material shape in Christ Jesus. It is in his existence that we see both God's rejection of sin and gift of life. His reality is the shape and substance of all reality. Who he is, is determinative of who God is as God and who we are as creatures before God; he is Lord over creation from first to last, from the life of death to the life of life, so to speak. Indeed, so utterly must we think and speak of existence in Christ that we can only have a sense for who and what God *might be*, and who and what we *might be*, in him. He establishes all reality *and* possibility, this in each moment that he stands before us.

We thus have to think of reality and possibility as a conjunctive event taking place in and with the event of revelation. It is as such the life and work of the Spirit. It is the Spirit who makes the christological confrontation to be real as it is made known here and now, or better, who has his life-act in ongoing realization of the Word today. It will help to flesh out the conjunctive event of reality and possibility in the Spirit if we consider the fuller treatment of it in Barth's Göttingen Dogmatics in this chapter, and in the *Church Dogmatics* in chapter 4. We will see in these treatments that Barth construes the dialectical event of faith as the "time" of the community (or church), which exists in a movement from sin and death to the new life of revelation. It does not leave

---

38. Ibid., 47.

the old time of darkness or enter yet into the new time of the light, but exists in revelation time, transition from dark to light according to the power and authority of the light. This transition is life in the Spirit. Because he thinks of this life not in a metaphysical sense but in terms of space-time, between the end of this chapter and chapter 4 we will fill in some details of Barth's conception of time itself by setting it in conversation with modern philosophy and science in chapter 3.

INCARNATION, FAITH, AND OBEDIENCE IN THE GÖTTINGEN DOGMATICS

The movement from divine reality to all possibility, not vice versa, is a recurrent feature of Barth's dogmatic work. It emerges already in his initial lecture cycle in dogmatics. Barth made three attempts at systematically laying out Christian teaching. The first stretched over four semesters: three terms at Göttingen (summer 1924, winter 1924–25, summer 1925), and one at Münster (winter 1925–26), where he offered a brief, supplemental series on redemption. These "Göttingen Dogmatics," eventually published in three volumes,[39] can be characterized as presenting a highly actualistic account of God and his relation to humanity. Barth's second attempt spanned three semesters at Münster (winter 1926–27, summer 1927, and winter 1927–28). He intended that the "Münster Dogmatics" (titled *Christian Dogmatics*) should comprise a multivolume work itself, but he abandoned the effort relatively early, construing his thought in this material to be too much beholden to existential philosophy.[40] He published only its extensive prolegomena.[41] One gets a sense of Barth's intellectual power

---

39. Barth, *Unterricht in der christlichen Religion*, vol. 1, *Prologomena 1924*; vol. 2, *Die Lehre von Gott/Die Lehre vom Menschen 1924/1925*; vol. 3, *Die Lehre von der Versöhnung/Die Lehre von der Erlösung 1925/1926*, Gesamtausgabe 17, 20, 38 (Zurich: Theologischer Verlag, 1985, 1990, 2003). The first eighteen sections—thirteen from volume 1 and five from volume 2—have been translated into English as *The Göttingen Dogmatics: Instruction in the Christian Religion*, ed. Hannelotte Reifen, trans. Geoffrey W. Bromiley (Grand Rapids: Eerdmans, 1990). The translation's stopping point (§18) is an unhappy one in that it breaks off partway through Barth's treatment of the doctrine of God (§§19 and 20 treating Creation and Providence, respectively).

40. See CD I.1, xiii; Barth summarizes the turn from *Christian* to *Church Dogmatics* by saying, "I have excluded to the very best of my ability anything that might appear to find for theology a foundation, support, or justification in philosophical existentialism." Barth credited his 1931 work on Anselm for providing the impetus to ground theology in the concrete history of Jesus Christ rather than a philosophical system; see Barth, *Fides quaerens intellectum: Anselms Beweis der Existenz Gottes im Zusammenhang seines theologischen Programms* (1931), Gesamtausgabe 13 (Zurich: Theologischer Verlag, 1981), 6.

and stamina just by considering the length of these unsatisfactory attempts: together, with commentary, they total 2,030 pages in the standard collected works. It is correct to say that Barth set aside or rewrote more systematic theology, *constructive and provocative* systematic theology, than many influential theologians ever produced!

Barth's third attempt took; his four-volume, thirteen-part *Church Dogmatics* was published over thirty-six years (1931–1967) in Bonn and Basel. It was incomplete at Barth's death. He never finished the last volume on the Christian life,[42] and he was not able to undertake the planned, fifth volume on redemption.[43]

Barth had no fear of deep revision and outright reconstruction. Comparing the Münster prolegomena to Göttingen, for instance, he likened the degree of alteration to that of the second edition of his commentary on Romans relative to the first edition: "here again no stone stands on another."[44] It is tempting, in view of such a protrayal, to conclude that by the *Church Dogmatics* Barth had all but discarded his earlier work, making its study of value only for the historical theologian interested in demonstrating the contrast between the early and late Barth by tracing out significant shifts and points of development. But differences between Barth's early and late thought are easily exaggerated. It is often the case that rewording, expansion, and structural amendment have little or no effect on the *essence* of the theme being explored, and indeed, that such revision is natural as one thinks through the given idea in greater detail and continues to set it relative to the wide array of Christian doctrines. At the least,

41. Barth, *Die christliche Dogmatik im Entwurf: Die Lehre vom Worte Gottes, Prolegomena zur christlichen Dogmatik 1927,* Gesamtausgabe 14 (Zurich: Theologischer Verlag, 1982).

42. Barth published only a small segment of what he intended in CD IV.4. For an indication of what Barth had planned, see the posthumously published, *The Christian Life: Church Dogmatics IV.4 Lecture Fragments,* trans. Geoffrey W. Bromiley (Grand Rapids: Eerdmans, 1981).

43. Writing about the unfinished portions of the *Dogmatics,* Barth acknowledged, "I have gradually begun to lose the physical energy and mental drive necessary to continue and to complete the work which I had started. . . . For this 'late Barth,' which I now am, it is indeed too late to do this in worthy fashion; he begs understanding and forgiveness" (CD IV.4, vii–viii). Besides the toll taken by age, Barth identified two developments that had made continued work particularly challenging. In 1962, Barth retired from full-time teaching: "there ended . . . an essential part of the impulse which lay behind my work thus far" (ibid., viii). In 1965, his longtime assistant, Charlotte von Kirschbaum, was diagnosed with brain disease, moved into a care facility, and thus put "out of action in relation to the *Church Dogmatics,* in whose rise and progress she had played so great a part" (ibid.; see also Busch, *Karl Barth,* 472 and passim).

44. Cited in Barth, *Die christliche Dogmatik im Entwurf,* 11.

areas of continuity ought to be as significant for the systematician as points of discontinuity are for the historian.

The movement from divine reality to possibility is a theme that Barth explored with notable consistency between the Göttingen and Bonn/Basel Dogmatics. Once again, this chapter examines Barth's treatment of it in the former. Chapter 4 does the same in the latter.

We noted in the last chapter that, for Barth, the task of theology is at one with the task of preaching, namely, the Word of God. This conviction forms the cornerstone of the Göttingen Dogmatics. "The problem of dogmatics is scientific reflection on the Word of God which is spoken by God in revelation, which is recorded in the holy scripture of the prophets and apostles, and which now both is and should be proclaimed and heard in Christian preaching."[45] Barth opens his lectures with this thesis. In light of the talks discussed in chapter 1 above, we notice right away that now Barth has included preaching as a form of the Word of God. It is not just that preaching is concerned with the Word, and that theology shares this object with preaching, but also that preaching in some sense is one with the Word and theology studies *it*.

Barth characterizes the subject matter of theological study as an event involving not only God's historical revelation in Christ Jesus in 1–30 c.e. but also the prophetic and apostolic testimony to that revelation and the proclamation of that testimony. The Word is not a fixed, historical datum that the theologian dissects. On the contrary, theology systematically reflects upon an object that continues to realize itself here and now.

The Word of God is ongoing. It consists not only of the life, ministry, death, and resurrection of Christ Jesus, but also of the scriptural witness to Christ and of the continuing witness of the church. It does not consist of each independently or we might say, "modalistically," but as a unity. In each form is the full and total Word, thus also in each form are the other forms. "God's Word abides forever. It neither is nor can be different whether it has its first, its second, or its third form, and always when it is one of the three it is also in some sense the other two as well."[46] The Word of God is a living reality; it is not a fixed or predetermined utterance but a threefold reiteration, with each iteration complete in itself and at once present in the others. They are thus "neither to be confused nor separated."[47]

Barth draws upon both Nicene and Chalcedonian logic to express that the Word of God is coordinate with the triune being of God, the God who can be

45. Barth, *Göttingen Dogmatics*, 3.
46. Ibid., 14.
47. Ibid.

a second and a third time without ceasing to be the one true God. It exists as three in one and one in three, and as such, as it can never be affixed to a single instance but encompasses in each single instance its other instances, the Word *happens.*

Barth recognizes that at the heart of the Christian confession from its earliest formulations is affirmation of God's livingness, that it is of the essence of the triune God (more exactly, of God as triune) to be God in moment-by-moment self-relating. The God who has his being in and as Word is a God who exists in eternal self-repetition, who *can* turn outside himself to be again himself because he *does* turn thus, because he has his being just in this turning. But it is in the Word *by the Spirit* that this is so. It is not in abstract trinitarianism that God has his being in eternal self-repetition, but in the concrete modality of the Word's *ongoing* realization. Here and now, in this event, in God again making possible who he is, we perceive God as God.

It is not that God's speech hovers above revelation, Scripture, and preaching, but that God reiterates who he is *in* revelation, Scripture, and preaching. He is the incarnate and at once inverberate deity. A community hears the voice of God in these works when it perceives them as a unity; to the extent that in preaching, for example, revelation and Scripture are present. That is, a community hears the voice of God in preaching to the extent that its words reflect and are informed by Jesus Christ and the prophetic and apostolic testimony to him. It hears God's voice in Scripture to the extent that the prophets and apostles bear witness to Christ and their testimony brings about further witness to him. It hears God's voice in Christ to the extent that he calls disciples past, present, and future, that he is the object of prophetic expectation, apostolic announcement, and ecclesial confession.

In its threefold form, the Word is not dead but living. God *speaks*, not just spoke. "God's Word is to be regarded as a living, actual, and present factor, the Word of God which now both is and should be proclaimed and heard. Now! Should be! Note in these expressions first of all the movement, the qualified temporal element, the turning from past to present denoted by them. The Word of God is God's speaking."[48] The Reformation principle *deus dixit* – God has spoken in such a way as to demonstrate and establish that he is the speaking God – is, for Barth, "the problem of dogmatics." Theology studies a contemporary event when its object is God's Word, nothing less than the event of God's eternal reiteration.

---

48. Ibid., 15.

But how does one study the living moment of God's self-repetition, the event of the Word by the Spirit, God inverberate? Obviously enough, such study can only be an exercise a posteriori. It must take place ever anew, as a happening and only a happening, which occurs with and is brought about by the prior presence of God. Theology emerges out of the Word by the power of the Word as reflection upon the Word, this, specifically in the Word's third form, for it is in this form that the Word meets us today. Preaching is "the starting point and goal of dogmatics."[49]

Christian preaching supplies the concrete locus of theological work in that it is the medium of God's *contemporary* presence. It is the event in which God again comes to be God with man. Barth here endorses the Reformation insight that the redemptive presence of God is not a substance to be ingested but God's living encounter with humanity, which as such engages human thought and speech. God is the *living* God in the occurrence of the Gospel's preaching in that this message is commanded and brought about in obedience, and commands and brings about further obedience. God is Lord when and where humanity is actually placed in dependent submission to him. This takes place in the act of witness to the Word:

> The Christian church begins by listening to the address of the prophets and apostles, which was not babbled, or mimed, or put to music, or danced, but spoken and written in statements and groups of statements. . . . It adopts this address, not mechanistically, not repetitively in simple copying or recitation . . . but primarily by its own responsible thinking and speaking, not passively but actively as it sends out the original witness as its own witness.[50]

The church is formed around the prophetic and apostolic statements and groups of statements proclaiming Christ Jesus, not passively but actively. The church itself is a living organism in that it comes to exist in continued obedience to the scriptural witness, in attentively listening to it and responsibly taking it in, running it through the mill of each new generation's thought and proclaiming it again as its own defining testimony. It is this activity that makes the church to be the community of Christian discipleship: continued

49. Ibid., 23.
50. Ibid., 24.

instantiation of "the Word of Christ" (Rom. 10:17) as an authoritative Word, when and where the message of Christ is proclaimed and people hear and obey that message.

"I emphasize, Christian *speaking*. This is where *dogmatizein* begins."[51] Theology takes place as reflection upon the Word of God in its present-tense form. Unless the presence of God is a present-ness, theology, human thought and speech of God, has no basis and norm. Unless the Lordship in which God is God takes place here and now, there is no knowledge and confession of God.

Inasmuch as theology is reflection upon the event of the Word of God today, Barth continues to describe the discipline in close continuity with preaching. "A dogmatics which along with its specific aim does not also function as Christian preaching is an extremely God-forsaken dogmatics."[52] Theology derives from and reflects upon the Word of God, which preaching also derives from and outwardly transmits, and therefore, like preaching, theology bears the quality of testimony. Its tone, content, and, unavoidably, its intention take the character of being a witness to God's Word. But as noted, preaching participates in the Word. It is one with revelation, whereas theology is not. Theology serves the Word (and does not presume to become it) by thematically investigating the extent to which Jesus Christ and the testimony of the prophets and apostles actually define reality in the church's preaching:

> As a critical authority dogma and dogmatics stand above Christian preaching, which may not escape their service (not their lordship) insofar as preaching is a human act that needs a norm. Yet they also stand under it, for they have their origin in it and must yield to it as the moon does to the sun insofar as preaching, proceeding from revelation and scripture, is itself God's Word.[53]

Theology originates in preaching, not the other way around, and therefore, like the moon relative to the sun, theology only reflects the light of the Word that occurs in the preaching of Christ according to the witness of the prophets and apostles. Its thought and speech never become the light that they reflect, and they are not meant to do so. They remain within the atmosphere of

51. Ibid., 25.
52. Ibid., 16.
53. Ibid., 18.

darkness even as the light illuminates them and, in doing so, may allow them to enhance the light's shining, to make it brighter and clearer by analyzing its happening in the darkness of human preaching.

In short, Barth is sketching already in Göttingen a Third Article theology. Theology springs from and takes as its subject matter the *contemporary* event of the Word as the determinative reality of God. It is an event that takes place in and with the ever-prior event of God being God in speaking to humanity with unmatched freedom and authority, as an echo of that speech. That is to say, human thought and speech (theology) come about in the event of divine thought and speech, *but as an event*, not as self-referential or self-sustaining insights but as constantly provoked and produced *reply*. Theology is called forth by God's thought and speech and rendered true insofar as it bodies forth the truth of that thought and speech itself. Theology does this inasmuch as it reflects the character of the thought and speech to which it is responding: insofar as it manifests the real dialectic of preaching, of God's Word in human words. Theology identifies and describes that dialectic and takes shape after it. It confesses the unveiling of God in the veil of humanity, but again, in the present tense. It only confesses this situation as it encounters it; only as theology recognizes and affirms its own incapacity does it declare God's capacity—thus reflecting the fact that revelation is in fact also *un-revelation*— and find its basis and norm.

Barth construes God's revelation in the terms of Reformation sacramentology: God is present *consubstantially*. "Naturally, in, with, and under Christian preaching, revelation and scripture are present, too, but not otherwise."[54] That is, we encounter God in the dialectic of coming to humanity without sacrificing his being to the media of human thought and speech. He remains Lord over those media by being their source and conception just as the Word was the source and conception of Jesus' flesh, and the enfleshed Word was the source and conception of the prophetic and apostolic words. The Word, God's all-determinative exegesis occurs today precisely as it did in 1–30 C.E.: *indirectly* identical with the medium of revelation.

"The best preaching is as such an equivalent to the kerygma that the Roman Catholic church offers every day in the form of the sacrament of the altar."[55] Whereas for Rome, the presence of God is mediated in the Eucharist, that presence is encountered in Reformation theology in the event of the sermon. God is there as he has always been—in media that cannot bear him. It

54. Ibid., 16.
55. Ibid., 31.

is precisely this incapacity of the minister's words that declares *God*. Here, the line is drawn between heaven and earth, deity and humanity, but crossed by the God who is so much God as to be God with humanity, to be present in words to which he is absent. So God shows up in the sermon as the *living* God, not the *outcome* of sacramental ritual but the *condition* of Christian thought and speech. And God shows up in the event of preaching as the living *God*; neither given over to the media of the event nor aloof from them, but having his being in command over the media, making them adequate to him. Thus, we must also state the dialectic in the reverse: God is indirectly *identical* with the human media of his presence, un-revelation is also *revelation*:

> From the very first Protestantism has involved a belief that the Logos takes human shape in spoken human words. . . . If some do not recognize the word that is spoken today as such, they are not following the Reformers but the Baptists, and they should ask themselves whether, with their rejection of God's Word in preaching, they are not secretly denying it in holy scripture and revelation as well.[56]

Barth found the livingness of the triune God at the heart of historic Christian confession to have been restored by the Magisterial Reformation's theology of divine presence. At the core of the Reformation concept of revelation is not simply a dialectic between God's visibility and invisibility. Logically more basic is the actualistic Lordship of God. The reason that God is hidden in his revelation is that he makes himself known by that which cannot make him known: he is unveiled in the veil of flesh and language. He has his being as Creator and Preserver of the minute constituents (flesh, ideas, and words) by which he is known *as Creator and Preserver*, that is, as the One who makes and rules over these media even in their occurrence and thus is as absent to them as he is present in them, or better, *as God* he remains absent precisely in his moment-by-moment presence.

In preaching, then, we are dealing with the possibility of God's revelation patterned after the reality of revelation, Christ Jesus. We are dealing with God's freedom to be with humanity as God, the concrete fact of his Lordship, the real dialectic of his veiling and unveiling on which all further knowledge and

56. Ibid., 33.

confession depend. *As such*, we are dealing with the basis and norm of human thought and speech of God. "We can seriously raise and treat the problem of the possibility of revelation only when we know its reality. Fundamentally we can construct it only a posteriori. All reflection on how God *can* reveal himself is in truth only a 'thinking after' of the fact that God *has* revealed himself."[57] All *reflection* upon how God can speak to humanity, all *theology*, can only be reiteration of the fact that God *has* spoken. It can only be a "thinking after" the prior thinking and speaking of God in human thought and speech. We encounter this prior thinking and speaking of God in preaching, but as reiteration of God's own thought and speech in Christ Jesus.

Theology can only examine preaching as the event of God's Word—it can only ask how far the Word of God speaks in these words—insofar as it is asking about the revelation of God in the flesh of Jesus. Theology can only query the possibility of God's revelation in this un-revelation insofar as this collective thought and speech direct the hearer to Christ. Or, theology only finds its basis and norm in the contemporary event of the preached Word when and where this event is neither more nor less than space-time reiteration of the reality of Christ Jesus, when and where it is the possibility of God being God-with-us here again as he was in 1–30 c.e.

Thus, Barth treats both the *objective* possibility of God's revelation and its *subjective* possibility. The objective possibility of God's revelation is the unique freedom and authority of God to place himself before us. This freedom and authority determine who he is: he is that which *can* come to humanity as Lord. "We must always understand revelation as God's revelation. In revelation God is always, not quantitatively (for what is gigantic or infinite does not make God God), but qualitatively different from us."[58] If *God* is to be revealed, if *God* is to stand before us, then it is by God's being uniquely free and powerful, not by the occurrence of some action or feat deemed to be sufficiently greater than ourselves, which we equate with the manifestation of "God."

The objective possibility of revelation is simply the establishment of God's impossibility, the non-capacity of revelation in human terms, and the overcoming of that impossibility by a freedom and power that are not known to humanity. It is the revelation of authentically *divine* freedom and power, which *is such* only in showing the human impossibility and negating it; the objective possibility of revelation *is* revelation in un-revelation:

57. Ibid., 151.
58. Ibid,. 134.

What if God be so much God that without ceasing to be God he
can also be, and is willing to be, not God as well. What if he were
to come down from his unsearchable height and become something
different. What if he, the immutable subject, were to make himself
object. What if he who is indivisibly one were to take the form of a
second. What if he who is unconditionally here were to be also there.
What if he who is unchangeably who *he* is were also to meet me as a
thou.[59]

God is *God* in making himself to stand before the creature, but as the
basis of the creature and not the other way around. He remains the immutable
subject that he is. But his immutability is not in a fixed "non-creatureliness," so
to speak, for then he would simply be the antithesis of my subjectivity, which
is merely a subtle way of making him after me (via negation). On the contrary,
He is the immutable God in becoming something different, eternally making
himself an object before me, in being known in the third-person voice precisely
by engaging me in the second-person, as a "he" who is at once a "you."

The objective possibility of God's revelation, then, is that revelation,
Immanuel. "I could not seriously raise the problem of the possibility of
revelation without knowing its reality, without starting with the fact that
God does reveal himself, without implicitly talking about Jesus Christ."[60] The
dialectical possibility and impossibility of God's revelation are given in the
dialectical reality of the Incarnation. God's becoming Man is not a merely
logical construct, which proves useful for understanding and explaining how
God relates to us today. No, God has his existence in the flesh of Christ—he
is with this flesh by anticipation from all eternity—and that determines *how*
he comes to be with us here and now. Unless and until we perceive that
God *is* God-with-us, that this is the nature of his being, we have no basis for
understanding and explaining that and how he *might be* with us. (A theology
that might take its center from the contemporaneous presence of God can only
do so when and where that presence amounts to reiteration of God's history in
Jesus of Nazareth.)

In the Incarnation and the biblical testimony to it is revelation of God
who can be God with us because he was God with them, who has and can
have his God-ness in indirect identity with the constituents of the here and

59. Ibid.
60. Ibid., 142.

now, this space-time, because he did so in that history. The possibility of God's revelation is given in the reality of God *being* God-with-Man, of Immanuel, of the Incarnation determining who God is and who he might continue to be. Therefore, the objective possibility assumes the subjective possibility, that in making himself fit for humanity God remakes humanity before him.

"How can God come to us without ceasing to be God? The doctrine of the incarnation has given us an answer. But how can we humans stand before God without ceasing to be human? This is clearly a second question apart, no less difficult and urgent than the first."[61] We must ask after the subjective possibility of revelation with no less earnestness than that with which we asked after the objective possibility. We cannot assume this corollary possibility. In fact, as we have seen in the light of the doctrine of the Incarnation, we must assume the opposite, that there is no such possibility. "We humans who stand before God, we now have to say, are precisely those who *cannot* stand before God (just as we saw earlier that precisely the God who reveals himself is the God who conceals himself). We have no quality, capacity, or possibility whereby to stand before God, we must now say. We would no longer be human if any such could be ascribed to us."[62]

Humanity is not overridden in the event of revelation. Rather, the distance between time and eternity is maintained in God's proximity to us. "The Yes itself means a No . . . in the very closeness of God our distance from him is disclosed."[63] As discussed in chapter 1, the contradiction that defines human being—our complete alienation from that upon which we are utterly dependent, the tragic attempt to realize our being by rejecting its only source, means, and goal—takes place moment by moment as we perceive existence according to the reference frame of self-interest. "We do not merely suffer from this contradiction. We constantly produce it by the free responsible act of our existence."[64] Thus, the possibility of receiving revelation as *revelation*, as that which is the *truth* of our intended being, must entail showing us who we are, creatures that cannot receive revelation because we have not done so. It must be such an act of God that overcomes the contradiction right when and where it affirms and makes it good, right when and where it renders us as the humanity immersed in self-contradiction:

61. Ibid., 174.
62. Ibid.
63. Ibid., 175.
64. Ibid., 174.

As God can step out of his deity, so we can step out of our humanity, although without surrendering but rather activating it. . . . In other words, there will have to be an activation of the humanity that is entangled, definitively entangled, in the contradiction. God will have to bear and fill and make good our human incapacity by the capacity, the sufficiency, the adequacy which can be present only in God himself for God himself.[65]

Just as God takes to himself what he is not without forfeiting what he is in coming to humanity—and in fact he comes to be again what he is in this act—so do we take in what we are not without losing ourselves, our un-readiness for revelation in receiving it—and in fact we come to be again who we *truly* are in this receiving. It must, however, be a *receiving* of revelation. It must not be a "having-received-and-now-possessing," for that would mean overriding the humanity entangled in its contradiction, obliterating the condition by which humankind actualizes its alienation from God and with it human being. If we really are to remain God's counterparts in the event of revelation, the creature relative to the Creator, then our need must remain in force. We must not become gods. Just the opposite, God as God must bear and fill and make good our need even as he supplies it. He must remain God and we must remain human even as he restores humanity to its source, means, and goal.

The human stands before God as one who by definition does not stand before God. She does so not only by God standing before her but also by the *activating power* of his Word, by his indwelling and enabling. *We*, who cannot hear and know and obey God, really do encounter him as God:

Those who do not stand before God do stand before God. They do so not only because God stands before them as an object but also because, for all their impotence, God is with them and indeed in them as the subject, so that God makes the connection, building the bridge that they cannot build. They stand before God because God's revelation is a here as well as a there, something subjective as well as something objective, because God not only reveals himself in the *Son* but reveals himself in the Son by the *Spirit*.[66]

65. Ibid., 175.
66. Ibid., 176.

The Spirit is the activating power of human being whereby it receives what it cannot. It is in the Spirit that we stand outside ourselves without losing ourselves, that we stand before God as fully human beings at once dead in our contradiction and alive in its overcoming. We will talk more about the fact that life in the Spirit is not a euphoric abandonment of creatureliness into some utopian synthesis with divinity. For now, the Spirit is the hereness and nownesss of revelation, without whom and without which there is no revelation. The Spirit is the condition by which the Son reveals God, by which the Word of God is received, without whom, then, there is no Word of God, yet about whom we cannot speak apart from the Word of God. The Spirit is the subjective possibility of revelation, whose life and identity as such are given in the objective reality of God with Man.

The Spirit is indirectly identified with the media of contemporary faith and obedience in just the way that the Word is indirectly identified with the flesh of Jesus:

> I have had in mind the miracle of the Holy Spirit who creates faith and obedience in us and thus places us before God. He "creates" them. That is to say, as he creates the world out of nothing, and as he makes a particle of human nature in the body of the virgin the dwelling of the Logos, so he makes a piece of broken humanity into human knowing and doing, with himself in his revelation as the object. As in creation and the incarnation, so here, too, we have a *miracle*, an event which has its only ontic and noetic basis in the freedom and majesty of God.[67]

The Spirit has his life and identity in the power by which he brings things into being out of non-being, by which no thing has being apart from him (he creates the world *ex nihilo*). By this selfsame power he makes the flesh of Jesus the medium of the Word and in a parallel fashion makes broken human thought and speech, human being and doing embroiled in its contradiction today, the medium of God's revelation. The parallelism that Barth identifies here is the main point. The life and identity of the Holy Spirit are coordinate with the

67. Ibid.

life and identity of the incarnate Word. They are structured and described by it. The Spirit is no less a miracle, no less the nonrepeatable event of God with humankind than the Word is. Indeed, the Spirit is the action and power of the Word precisely insofar as he reiterates the same dialectic that existed in the flesh of Christ and in the prophetic and apostolic testimony to that flesh. The Spirit is the possibility of the Word's happening here and now *as Immanuel*, as God being God-with-us.

We might say that the Spirit has no independent content, or that we think and speak in terms of the Spirit where and when we think and speak of God being God-with-humankind again in a manner after his being this God in Christ Jesus. We think and speak in terms of the Spirit where and when we witness to God in his ongoing self-repetition, in the act of assuming the constituents of human being without losing himself in the assumption. We think and speak in terms of the Spirit where and when we confess the Lordship of God over our thought and speech in their very happening just as the prophets and apostles did. We think and speak in terms of the Spirit where and when we testify with the prophets and apostles to God's Lordship over all creatureliness in the flesh of Christ even as he has his existence in that flesh.

We think and speak in terms of the Spirit, do pneumatocentric theology, where and when we perceive and reflect upon the reality of God being God in the act of turning outside himself to exist as the singular condition of all that is. We ground theological reflection on the Spirit where and when he becomes the condition of all life and true being, all life and new life. The Spirit is the center of theology where and when he structures our every where and when, that is, as he comes to be the possibility of encounter with God, the possibility of revelation, according to the reality of revelation.

The Spirit is the a priori condition of theology as he makes the human to see and hear what the human cannot see and hear, opening and restructuring her perceptual framework such that she stands before the God before whom she cannot stand. Pneumatocentric theology is a posteriori reverberation of the event of God's Inverberation, his being God in the ever-new verbal formulations of the church's proclamation, of being with and under these formulations such that he is indirectly identified with them. It is reflection upon this event that takes place only through this event.

The Spirit is the condition of theology as he makes humanity new in and by making the Word *known*, which is to say, in and by being the selfsame repetition of the Creator and Reconciler. The Spirit is the center of theology in and by being the Redeemer, God with *us*. We think and speak in terms of the Spirit insofar as he comes to be just that possibility, as he makes and sustains the conditions of our thinking and speaking of God by moment-by-moment placing us in utter dependence on God.

Pneumatocentric theology is a highly dynamic undertaking. It is a happening and only a happening. Its knowledge is as nonrepeatable as the God it knows, the God who is its a priori condition of possibility:

> The relation between God and us in which . . . revelation becomes manifest to us, has to be something that is a free and not a natural event on both sides. It must not set up anything constant or given, any natural necessity. It must not involve the immutability of a mathematical relation. It must be fully flexible. It must be a relation which, in order to remain true, must be renewed every moment both by God's work and word and in our own knowing and doing. . . . The relation has to be a conversation, a drama, a struggle, in which there are dangers and turning points, surprises and discoveries, repulses and advances, victories and defeats, standings and fallings. . . . Each moment must be unique and nonrepeatable, for our other partner is God and he demands that we hazard our whole existence. How could things be any different if this relation is really the subjective possibility of revelation, our opening up to the light in the darkness of our being, to the triumph over the contradiction, to the end of our alienation?[68]

God's reality does not determine his possibility and ours mechanistically. The relation in which he exists with us and we exist with him is characterized by freedom and flexibility, not necessity and mathematical immutability. Its constancy is simply the fidelity of God to be God with us, not a metaphysical constraint. Faith and obedience must be as alive as their giver and defender, or we could not meaningfully speak of light coming to darkness, of our illumination yet not obliteration.

This is a staggering understanding of the event of the Spirit and the life made possible in that event, of redemption. Barth concludes that life in the Spirit remains human life, life that remains itself even when and where it is made to stand outside of itself. Life in the Spirit is fully embodied existence, the continued happening of which engages sense, reason, language—the complete

68. Ibid., 180.

continuum of modalitites that constitutes space-time existence. It is *not* escape from these modalities but their exercise in living conversation, exchange, tête-à-tête with and by their Maker. And as such, as a fully embodied life, it entails newness, discovery, and victory alongside stale familiarity, frustration, and defeat. Life in the Spirit is darkness coming to the light that it cannot comprehend.

However much other religious or philosophical traditions think dualistically on this matter, the Christian concept of spirit cannot oppose material, corporeal existence with undefined immaterial, non-corporeality. The Spirit has his life and identity in the conversation taking place moment by moment between God and Man after the event of the God-Man, which is to say, the Spirit has his life and identity in the coming of God to be again today who he is in Jesus Christ in 1–30 c.e. and in the beginning. The Spirit is God a third time as he was a second and a first, the Spirit of Redemption and Creation understood according to Reconciliation, the Spirit of the Word, so that life in the Spirit is genuinely active, fully enfleshed, new life in Christ Jesus.

Redemption, then, is life defined by the obedience—concretely expressed in belief, confession, action—revealed and embodied in Christ. It is hopeful expectation of this life coming again, being realized here and now as the defining cadence and realm of the future—of what might come to pass and in what way. Redemption involves anticipation of the consummated lordship of Christ Jesus by the Spirit's activation of true human being, by making and illuminating the thinking, speaking, and doing in which God exists as God and the human comes to exist relative to him in living faith and obedience.

As noted, Barth was not able to complete his planned work on redemption in the *Church Dogmatics*, but he did treat it in the final lecture cycle that comprised the Göttingen Dogmatics. This makes the Göttingen material significant for understanding the direction that Barth might have taken in Basel had he retained the strength to do so.[69] For our purposes, Göttingen is especially important inasmuch as Barth handles redemption as the third locus of dogmatic study alongside and in unity with creation and reconciliation. Indeed, creation, reconciliation, and redemption are the *ad extra* operations proper to the triune Father, Son, and Spirit, respectively. Thus, it seems plausible that when Barth called for Third Article theology near the end of his life, he

---

69. Daniel Migliore draws the same conclusion in his introductory comments on the translated portion of the Göttingen Dogmatics. "Since Barth did not live to write the fifth volume of the *Church Dogmatics* that was to deal explicitly with this doctrine (redemption), the final section of his earliest dogmatics holds special interest and will be carefully examined by readers for clues as to how Barth might likely have unfolded his eschatology in his magnum opus" (*Göttingen Dogmatics*, LVII).

envisioned subsequent dogmatic work to begin again where he once left off, to think and speak in terms of the Spirit as the starting point and center of theology, but in a manner consistent with the way we think and speak of the Spirit at the end, eschatologically, which manner of thinking and speaking Barth outlined already in Göttingen. We therefore conclude this chapter with a few words about what Barth taught in his earlier work on redemption, and the shape and structure of a pneumatocentric theology deriving from this.

THE CONTEMPORANEITY OF JESUS CHRIST IN THE GÖTTINGEN DOGMATICS §36

Barth handled the doctrine of redemption in four sections: hope (§35), the presence of Christ (§36), the resurrection of the dead (§37), and the glory of God (§38). Because it is the "content" of hope, that to which the work of resurrection "corresponds," and the "immediate knowledge" of God in his glory, I will focus here on §36, "The Presence of Jesus Christ." The case can be made (I am not making it here) that this section forms the logical core of Barth's treatment of redemption.[70]

Barth opens this material with the following thesis:

Redemption is like creation and like reconciliation, but apart from them as a new, third, and final thing, real and active through and in the Word of God to humankind. The Redeemer is therefore no other than the eternal Son of God, through whom all things are created, no other than the one become flesh, through whom God has reconciled the world with himself, Jesus Christ. His arrival, direct knowability and presence in glory, in which he is resurrected as true God and true Man—this is the promise, this the content of hope. Its hour comes as the final hour of all humanity, of all nature and of all history. It is near in the lightness and darkness of the ultimate possibility and reality of nature and history. It is already there, wherever and whenever grace finds faith and obedience in the true church.[71]

---

70. As a start to such a line of argument, it is worth noting that Barth calls the *parousia* of Christ, by which he means his full presence in a manner consistent with yet distinct from the Incarnation, the "chief and central concept" of eschatology (*Unterricht in der christlichen Religion* 3:438)

71. Ibid., 431.

Four issues present themselves for comment. The first is a matter of vocabulary and translation. When Barth speaks of the "presence" of Christ in this citation and throughout this section, he overwhelmingly prefers the term *Gegenwart*. This is so even when his train of thought would lend itself to other options—when, for example, speaking of the "arrival" (*Ankunft*) of Christ, *Erreichbarkeit* might seem more natural, or "appearance" (*Erscheinung*) would connote *Vorkommen*.

Among the possibilities (including the straightforward *Präsenz*, which is used occasionally), *Gegenwart* has the most directly *temporal* semantic range. Barth is manifestly not thinking of redemption as some kind of suprasensible, nonembodied, extraspatial, extratemporal, extrasensory "presence." He is thinking of a concrete living in the here and now. "I have translated, "*presence*," (*Gegenwart*) of Jesus Christ in the title of our paragraphs. Insofar as it is *hoped* for, it is of course his coming, his advent, his arrival (*Ankunft*), future (*Zukunft*), but one hopes for it longing for the goal and result of this coming, his *present* (*Gegenwart*) to be made with it."[72] The redemption of the human is not self-transcendence, being lifted outside of one's corporeally situated frame of reference, moved beyond the dimensionality of space or pitched forward to a nondescript, extratemporal immanence, but holistic expectation of a *time* of Christ, of a *now* in which he reigns. The human lives toward this lordship, anticipating a present defined by Christ by tangibly *thinking, speaking, and acting* after Christ, for him, by his example and power, under his authority here and now.

Barth rejects any sort of disembodiment or escape from creatureliness in his construal of redemption. "The problem of the immortality of the individual soul, the other side of death *except* for the resurrection also of the flesh has *absolutely* nothing to do with the novissima, the eschata in the *biblical* sense. . . . The hope of the *reconciled* human relates directly to the resurrection of the bodily-ensouled (*leiblich-seelischen*) totality."[73] The human does not look forward to the dissolution of the flesh and a weather balloon flight of the soul into the ether, but to fully corporeal living. In the eschaton the creature exists *as a creature* before its Lord, obeying him in the actuated power, sense, reason, speech of a body–soul unity.

That brings us to the second matter. The hope that Barth has in mind is, as indicated, the hope of *reconciled* existence. Although as we will discuss, Barth does distinguish redemption as a "new, third, final thing" in God's life

72. Ibid., 438.
73. Ibid., 433.

and work, he at once intimately relates it to reconciliation. In fact, he locates the former within the latter. "Creation, reconciliation, redemption, these are the three points on which dogmatics has to orient itself: *reconciliation* as the essence (*Inbegriff*) of divine dealing with humankind, as it comes to be known through God's Word, *creation* as its condition in reference to God and humankind, *redemption* as its consequence, its goal, its culmination."[74] Redemption is the zenith, the climax of Christ's *reconciling* work, not vice versa. "Redemption" just means deliverance, emancipation from the power of sin and death. It means release, or more exactly, re-lease, being restored to another charter, course, and bond of agreement, to a new covenant (Luke 22:20; 1 Cor. 11:25). Barth is simply recognizing that the content of redemption is Christ's work of reconciliation. The two cannot be divorced. Indeed, the former is known only in terms of the latter. *"Knowledge of redemption results from knowledge of reconciliation, only from it.* And therefore its object is primarily the Reconciler, who is also the Redeemer, Jesus Christ."[75]

Knowledge of redemption is of the same substance as knowledge of reconciliation. Thus, as Christ is the Reconciler, so is he the Redeemer. If we are to speak of the *Spirit* of Redemption, then we must understand his content, so to speak, his identity and operation to be none other than that of the Word made flesh. As we do not think and speak of God's redemptive agency in isolated differentiation, neither do we of the agent. "We must thus establish above all that the *waiting*, which . . . we have recognized as characteristic of the reconciled human, the human in the status gratiae, is not a waiting on an undefined, formless, neuter something, the *content* of hope, the *other side* of the eschatological boundary not some things, happenings, and developments, but *he, Jesus Christ.*"[76]

Existence in the state of grace, expectant existence, has a definite substance to it, a distinct form, a nameable object, a "he," Jesus Christ. The human lives eschatologically when she lives, though not yet in a state of glory, in the *name* of the glorified one, he who is on the other side of the boundary of mortality; not in a vague wish to cross this line for formless immortality but waiting on *his* coming again, *his* being-present, *his* eternal reign.

While Barth is clearly operating within a trinitarian rubric (creation, reconciliation, redemption), he does not interpret each act individually, or evenly treat each modality in terms of the others. Rather, he centers creation

---

74. Ibid., 432.

75. Ibid., 434–35 (italics in original).

76. Ibid., 437.

and redemption on reconciliation as that act which has a "primary, central meaning."[77] Reconciliation, once again, is the "essence" of God's dealing with humanity, creation its "condition," and redemption its "consequence," not the other way around. Therefore, we must think of Christ as the "for," "in," and "through" which of creation and redemption because he is the Reconciler, the cause and means of all true life and being. Life in the Spirit, then, is *this* life, life in Christ Jesus. The Spirit's identity and work are in making this life reality, not another, not his own as if such a thing could be separated from life in Christ. Redemption is the ongoing work of bringing all existence under the eschatological rule of Christ, hence there is no Redeemer beyond the one who mediates the defining content and power of the Reconciler.

In the light of this, two options emerge concerning how best to carry forward Barth's eventual call for pneumatocentric theology. One option would take him to be encouraging an outright rejection of this line of thought, to construct something fundamentally alternative to his early concentration on Christ and reconciliation. In this case, theology would somehow make the Spirit and redemption of "primary, central meaning," and in this, understand creation and reconciliation in terms of redemption. Just as Barth had once read all other doctrines for, in, and through the lens of Christ's reconciling activity, now he would be commending others to do the same kind of thing for, in, and through the Spirit's redeeming work.

But obviously enough, this would entail having access to a second content besides the Word, which would now become the basis for understanding the Word. It would mean knowing what it is for God to redeem logically *before* knowing what it is to reconcile, which is to say, knowing eschatological substance *before* we know the substance of deliverance from the power of sin and death, in fact understanding God's deliverance *in terms of* his un-revealed yet presumed eschatological unity with the creature. It would mean knowing the definition, form, and substance of the Spirit in the same way that Christ is known, in order then to speak of Christ in these terms. It would mean understanding revelation as revelation of the Spirit, whose existence structures and informs the existence of the Word. It is for this reason that I can*not* see Barth intending this option.

To what could the theologian turn for the content of the Spirit that would not ultimately amount to the kind of speculation Barth deplored? How can the Spirit be the objective possibility of revelation as Christ is? And if he is not, if he remains the subjective possibility of revelation but now in a determinative

---

77. Ibid., 436.

reversal of direction, such that the subjective moment of revcaledness defines and delimits the objective moment of revelation, how can the Spirit be distinguished from the human? We recall that it was exactly this subjectivization of revelation that Barth strove so hard to overcome vis-à-vis his liberal predecessors. It is not insignificant in this respect that in Göttingen he cited the right relationship between reconciliation and redemption as being of decisive import for correcting Schleiermacher. "As Revelation and Reconciliation sit opposite Creation as a new thing breaking in from above, come from Heaven, from God out as a new beginning, thoroughly corresponding with the becoming of the beginning of Creation, so also Redemption sits opposite Revelation and Reconciliation. This is what *Schleiermacher* above all did not grasp."[78]

Somewhat paradoxically on the surface, reconciliation must remain the center, that to which redemption corresponds as the for, in, and through which of God's *ad extra* activity, even in a pneumatocentric theology. Unless we are to recommit the error of Schleiermacher—or positively, if we are rightly to construe a means of resolution between Barth and Schleiermacher—then we must see redemption as the consequence, the outcome of reconciliation, sitting opposite from yet thoroughly corresponding with it, the content of which is given in the revelation of the reconciler, not vice versa. Any reversal of this order makes the fateful mistake of locating Christ on this side of the eschatological boundary, of making the human into the condition of knowledge of the divine, of construing reconciliation with God as the transcendence or supra-eminence of the human.

The second, preferable option for understanding Barth's call for Third Article theology is therefore to understand the content of the Spirit's work in the terms of Christ's work and in this to perceive the Spirit as Spirit of the Word. Then we might be in a position to demonstrate how in the creation space-time comes to be shaped after God's self-election to be-present with what he is not, and how in reconciliation space-time is reshaped after God's election of what he is not to be-present with him; again, more on these possibilities in the coming chapters.

Such an approach would not suggest that, for Barth, redemption is merely "an evolutionary result arising from Revelation and Reconciliation."[79] Redemption sits opposite reconciliation and revelation as a new thing no less than reconciliation and revelation are new relative to creation. But the "sitting opposite" would have to entail formal and material continuity. The newness

78. Ibid., 446.
79. Ibid.

of redemption, of Christ's presence in and by the Spirit, would have to be of precisely the same quality and in fact form as it was in the Incarnation. That would represent a step beyond what Barth laid out in Göttingen, even as it learns from this his initial attempt at eschatology. The nature of this step is our third matter for discussion.

As the thesis above indicates, at Göttingen Barth presses the distinction between the presence or present-ness of the incarnate Word and the character of his full, consummated presence to such an extent that, in the light of subsequent doctrinal development, it will have to be revised. "The Redeemer is no other than Reconciler and Revealer, but his coming, the manner (*Art*) in which he is perceptible, the way in which he is there, is something totally other."[80] Barth employs the same language that he used in his commentaries on Romans vis-à-vis God's otherness from creation to express the differentiation between Christ's *parousia* and Incarnation. He does so to highlight the very same eschatological boundary, the infinite and qualitative gulf between eternity and time. Meeting Christ in his return is to enjoy his *eternal* presence, to perceive him in the fullness of his deity, which at this stage Barth still thinks of as being veiled by God's en-fleshing. That is, he still thinks that absent the flesh there is an entirely other quality to God's glory, wherein humiliation is overcome and canceled out.

In time, in the Incarnation we do not perceive Christ in his glory, but only in his humility. "We know Christ this side of the parousia in the status exinanitionis [state of humility]. . . . The status exaltationis [state of exaltation] remains for us in indissoluble correlation to the status exinanitionis."[81] We cannot see the exalted Christ this side of glory, but only believe in him, only know him indirectly, in and through his humiliation. By contrast, "it must be seen and said that we do not have to do in the parousia with a repetition or continuance of *these* circumstances, that Christian *hope* and its ensuing *eschatology* is doubtless judged to be about a wholly other coming, being known, being present of Jesus Christ."[82] Christ's second coming is as different from his first as heaven from earth, eternity from time. Barth understands Christ's return as a coming in exaltation and *not* humiliation, indeed, in *contrast to* his (first) coming in humility. He has not yet attained the insight that Christ's exaltation *just is* his coming in humility, which is to say, that servanthood is not

---

80. Ibid., 440.
81. Ibid., 441.
82. Ibid., 442.

something God takes on in Christ for a season and then sets aside in glory; but rather, God has his eternal lordship in the eternal submission of the Son.

By way of his discoveries concerning the doctrine of election, which again we will address in chapter 5, Barth will realize that the humility assumed in the Incarnation is proper to God's eternal being. Inasmuch as God's lordship extends first over himself, inasmuch as he is so much God that he can be God in and through servanthood, God has his being in the moment-by-moment act of his self-election to be God-for-us. In other words, we have seen that while in his early work Barth is on his way to concluding that there is no God beyond Immanuel, that God has his divinity in coming to humanity, he is only *on his way*. We recognize that in his treatment of redemption at Göttingen, Barth has not fully thought through what it means to understand God in terms of his being-with-us as the incarnate Word. He is still able to differentiate between Christ's states of humiliation and exaltation rather than relate them in a real dialectic, something eternal and therefore not merely descriptive of a stage of God's being.

We can appreciate the character of the revision that would have to take place in an eventual doctrine of redemption by contrasting Barth's remarks on the *parousia* in Göttingen to his later treatment of the subject in CD IV.3.1 (1959). Here, Barth stresses that Christ's "glory" is the *glory of the Mediator*, which as such entails *both* humiliation and exaltation:

> In the glory of the Mediator as such there is included the fact that He is in process of glorifying Himself among and in and through us, that we are ordained and liberated to take a receptive and active part in His glory. . . . His humiliation as the Son of God took place *propter nos homines et propter nostram salutem*. . . . And his exaltation as the Son of Man took place in order that he might draw us all to himself (Jn. 12:32). . . . With those who in the wider or narrower sense, virtually or actually, are his own, He thus forms a unity and totality. . . . There is a strict and indissoluble distinction of position and functions. . . . But in this order and distinction there is a totality. He can as little be separated from them as they from Him.[83]

83. CD IV.3.1, 278–79.

Christ's self-glorification involves humankind. His humiliation is "for us men and for our salvation," as the Second Article of Nicaea has it, and his exaltation is similarly for the purpose of drawing humankind into his saving life—both eternally. Now there can be no question of setting aside the former in view of the latter, since both together are means of understanding the reality of Christ's existence as a totality that involves *human* being from beginning to end. Humanity is proper to him as the object of humiliation, the actualized negation of its sin being the condition of his (and our) exaltation. That does not mean that Christ is dissolved into humankind. As Barth noted, "there is a strict and indissoluble distinction of position and functions." Nevertheless, the Word cannot be separated from humankind. His *eternal* identity is in and with the creature that he creates and redeems.

Thus, in the Redeemer we simply have the coming again of the one who came before, the Reconciler who exists in unity with the Creator in the beginning. Redemption is the third iteration of this God's eternal presence. As such, it is the consummation of God's being God as Lord, God's coming to be who he is without contender. It is the event in which God ultimately brings all of creaturely existence, all space-time under his unimpeachable authority. This brings us to our fourth and final set of observations concerning the thesis cited above and the significance of Barth's treatment of redemption in Göttingen for pneumatocentric theology.

The coming again of the one who came before—this perspective, this anticipatory waiting—determines existence here and now as "existence-being-redeemed." It is the reality according to which all creaturely possibility is framed in that it is the reign of God standing as the non-negotiable future toward which all being is heading and therefore around which all of existence is oriented. This reality is given in the revelation of Christ as Reconciler. "The revelation of this *midpoint* of time reveals at once its past beginning and its future end. It reveals *God* as the *Lord* of time, we can say with a word."[84] Standing between creation and redemption as God's revelation and his reconciliation with creation, Christ reveals both the whence and wherefore of creation. He gives time its essential direction by situating it as God's—as deriving from God, on the one side, and coming to God, on the other.

What creation might be is given in what it was and will be, which past and future are structured by the present knowledge of Jesus Christ. Creation will be God's as it was and in fact is, the theater of his reign, and therefore whatever it can be, whatever prospect or *hope* it has is defined by *this* eternity,

---

84. Barth, *Unterricht in der christlichen Religion* 3:451.

God's existence not outside of time but at once bounding time and impelling it forward to become his kingdom. When and where Christ's presence is consummate, which is to say, when and where he is eternally *present* such that all before and after really are his, really point to and derive from him, then and there is *parousia* and the culmination of redemption.

In other words, for Barth, Christ's coming is already here and not yet here. According to the thesis cited above, "it is near in the lightness and darkness of the ultimate possibility and reality of nature and history. It is already there, wherever and whenever grace finds faith and obedience in the true church." Nature and history are not givens but are open, susceptible to newness; they are possibilities as much as they are realities. Indeed, their reality is the theater of God's being and doing, and this is also what they might be. They come to be what they are as they move along a trajectory toward redemption, toward the consummated Lordship of God in Christ. That Lordship is already being realized in the life of faith, in the obedience of those who live after Christ, in his power, and under his authority. The life of the Spirit is taking place in the true life of the (true) church.

Barth is able to think of the day of redemption in these terms, as both future and present—or, more exactly, as the future that defines the present—because these are the terms that describe and determine the days of reconciliation and creation. "The day of Jesus Christ . . . breaks in as radiant dawn (*Morgenglanz*) of eternity, as beginning and end of all history, but as a real day *in* the midst of history. . . . The day of the Parousia breaks in as the day of epiphany has broken in and, we hasten to add, as the day of creation has broken in as the eternal day of the divine dealing with the world."[85] The eschatological presence of God comes as eternity to time, each (eternality and temporality) without losing its essential character. Just as was the case in revelation and creation, God does not forfeit his deity in coming to time, he does not give up the unique characteristic of eternality, and neither does he obliterate the creature, who does not lose her historicity before her eternal Lord. This is as true in the eschaton as it was in the beginning and is now. God comes to time, but as a day in time, historically. As such he stands not only as the basis of time but also as its goal, not only as its reality but also as its condition of possibility, not only its origin but also its means and end.

In short, Barth understands time to have an inherently subjective quality, or a preferable way of expressing it would be that true time simply takes place with the subjective possibility of revelation. It comes to be-after the

85. Ibid., 450.

objective possibility of the incarnate Word. That is, inasmuch as the Spirit is the subjective possibility of revelation, authentic time takes place in and with his work of making Christ reality here and now, of bringing about *his* present. True time is an event coordinated with the life of faith and obedience. It is the means by which the specific cadences, the sequences of thoughts and behaviors that define the reign of Christ and the life of faith take place, and more, it is just those cadences and sequences. It is existence both rimmed and determined by the eternal God's coming to temporal humanity. It is the in which and as which of life in the Spirit. We will explore this further in the next two chapters.

CONCLUSION

What is real? God, and only in him, creation; God is more basic to "reality" than is creation, than is space-time in part or whole. But what "God?" In what way is "God" the determination of reality? God is the determination of reality in and as *Word*. That is to say, God is the determination of reality in the initiative, decision, and act that characterize his being "in the beginning." God determines reality insofar as he is *God* in concrete Lordship first over all that he is, in the freedom not to be defined and delimited by given concepts of eternity and God-ness and, second, over all that he is not. God is the determination of reality in the primal event in which he determines his being as the basis and norm of all being.

But this primal event, the Word of God, takes place here and now; indeed it must take place here and now if it is to be the determination of all reality. *En archē* refers not strictly to a time long ago but also to the readiness of God, the power and authority in and by which God commands and rules all things. Given in the reality of God, then, is the potential or possibility of God to be-again, his ability and right to have his being in command and rule of all things, to be the Lord here and now, and in this, for "here and now" to be called forth by God as the theater in which he lives and acts. Given in the Word of God is the possibility not only of God but also of the full reality of existence which depends on God, and its every possibility.

In fact, it is only in the here and now, in the reality and possibility of space-time as it is called forth by God to be the theater of his Lordship, that God exists and is known *at all*. It is only in the concrete happening of his Word contemporarily that God stands as Lord before what he is not, for apart from this happening there is no reality and possibility, only the artificiality of a self-sustaining creation, only a creation inclining to un-creation, only a creation in the convulsions of sin, only a factory of idols. Only as God continues to be *God* with us and for us *today*, in consummate refusal of every force of non-being, idolatry, and death, is he known and confessed as God *in the beginning* (in both senses of that phrase).

That means, as Barth helped us to see, that the locus of encounter with God in space-time is the happening of the Word in its third form. It is in the event of Christian proclamation that God exercises his prerogative as God to determine all things by assuming what he is not and having his life in this act of assumption. It is in the event that thought and speech in the form of witness to Christ, taking place in conformity to the thought and speech of the prophets and apostles, is generated and brought into conformity with Christ himself that God is God and creature is creature, which is to say, that the relation in which Creator and creation exist *as such* is properly established.

This event is the life and work of the Holy Spirit. He is the subjective possibility of God's determinative revelation in that he is the means of God's objective address. He is the generative source of contemporary witness to Christ and the giver of faith by which it is perceived. He is not the objectivity of God per se, but he is the condition and incidence of Christ's objectivity. Thus, he is objectified as the divine agent not in himself, but only in the happening of Christ as the determination of all reality and possibility.

The Spirit is the power and authority by which space-time comes to exist authentically, not according to the rebellion of sin but as the theater of the Word. He is the Redeemer of all human reality and possibility insofar as he is the event of God causing all reality and possibility to be conformed to the image of Christ Jesus. It is the aim of the next two chapters to flesh this out.

3

The Spirit of Truth and Time

God's Word is God's Spirit, who blows where He will. God's Word happens when God is spoken of, ubi et quando visum est Deo.
-Karl Barth[1]

Chapters 1 and 2 argued that thought and speech of God necessarily begin with recognition of a chasm between God and humanity, of a basic human incapacity for God, which is given in the pronouncement of John 1:18 that "no one has seen God." This chasm exists not because humanity was created without the equipment to know its Creator in his full glory. Rather, it exists because of humanity's free exercise of that equipment to substitute God's genuine majesty for a hollow alternative by thinking and speaking of him from a center in itself. It exchanges his imperceptibility for perceptible beauty, morality, and religious consciousness, thus placing itself in the position of God. It fails to perceive the factual priority of God and instead places itself as the eternal a priori. From this position, it then determines what things also might be; it construes all possibility in terms of this artificial reality.

In his exegesis of John 1:18, Barth showed that if God is actually to be known *as God*, then he must make himself unknown in moment-by-moment rejection of human "reality." He must posit his reality anew in confrontation with ours, becoming hidden or absent to our perceptual framework, to our sequences of possibility, precisely in his presence as Lord, which is to say, in

---

1. Barth, "The Authority and Significance of the Bible: Twelve Theses," in *God Here and Now*, trans. Paul M. van Buren (1964; London: Routledge, 2009), 66. The Latin is a citation of Article V of the Augsburg Confession, which concerns the ministry (or office—*Amt*) of the church. The English translation of the Latin is "when and where it pleases God," which reflects the German (the Confession was produced in both Latin and German), *wo, und wenn er will*. However, given the context of Barth's citation, he probably intends to indicate that God makes his invisibility "visible"—from *visum*—whenever and wherever the event of the biblical witness to Jesus Christ "happens," that is, whenever and wherever the Spirit and Word coincide in the event of corporate hearing (the faith of the church).

his presence as the true a priori, the true reality within which all possibility is given. He must mercifully turn our upside-down searches into dead ends. And in so doing, by rendering ineffectual every native human attempt to transcend mortality, he must make himself the bridge across the chasm.

Barth explained this paradoxical situation in his early lectures on "The Need and Promise of Christian Proclamation" and "The Word of God as the Task of Theology." In these pieces, he demonstrated that God makes himself known as unknown specifically *in Christ Jesus*.[2] In the incarnate Word, God crosses the boundary between deity and humanity but without erasing the boundary in doing so. God is revealed, but in the flesh, above all in Christ's cry of dereliction, "My God, my God, why have you forsaken me?" God is the answer to human searching not as its outcome but as its singular condition of possibility, that is, as its refusal and reconstitution. He is answer precisely by making our mortal question his own, rejecting it, on the one hand, and rightly asking it, on the other.

We observed that Barth's logic in these pieces is necessarily pneumatological. The dialectic of God being known as God in the veil of human flesh is an ongoing *event*. It is characteristic of Christian proclamation and theology today as ever simply to be reiteration of the incarnate Word. Because the event of the Word is for Barth the only true thought and speech of God, then we disciples at second hand must encounter the same Word if we too are to know and proclaim God. In that case, the Spirit must be the contemporaneity of the Word. He is God inverberate, taking up humanity's question and asking it as his own *in the words of proclamation here and now*.

We summarized Barth's insights by concluding that, by the Spirit of the Word, God confronts humankind objectively, which objectivity remakes our subjectivity. God's Inverberation creates and informs the capacity to perceive him as Lord, that is, as the source and not the outcome of human inquiry. That verberation in concrete language—the sensate pulsing and ingestion of sound formations materially and formally particular to the Word—is the nature of God's spatial-temporal presence today.

We noted that the dialectical-pneumatological nature of God's reality and possibility, which involves humankind, continues in the Göttingen Dogmatics.

2. As Bruce McCormack noted (*Karl Barth's Critically Realistic Dialectical Theology: Its Genesis and Development 1909–1936* [Oxford: Oxford University Press, 1997] 327 and passim), having discovered the christological dialectic of *an-enhypostasia*, Barth transferred God's eschatological otherness to the self-determination of the divine Word. God's otherness now is in the freedom to come to humanity in Christ, which is to say, in assuming this flesh but *in* the hypostasis of the eternal *Logos* and so *as God*. He remains imperceptible in the perceptibility of Jesus of Nazareth.

We saw that the starting point of all that God can be, and all that humanity can be, is determined by all that God *is* in his moment-by-moment act of bridging the chasm between us. God's reality in Christ Jesus is the shape and content of God's possibility, that is, who God might be in himself. And human destiny is given in its existence as creature before this God.

God's eternal essence, his aseity, his self-grounded freedom—all of this is defined according to his spatial temporal being, selfhood, and (paradoxical) sovereign obedience. We do not know what we are saying if we extrapolate from human liberty the ideal of limitless autonomy and ascribe it to God. God is God precisely in his freedom to remain Lord even in the kenotic act of becoming man.

Exegetically, Barth showed us from John 1:1-5 that by virtue of being God in the beginning, the Word is the basis for all thought and speech of God here and now. God has his God-ness, so to speak, in the eternal freedom, initiative, and decision to be-with-us. And by virtue of God being God-for-man, human beings can be-for-God. Everything that we might be as creatures defined and delimited by space-time is given in who God is as Lord of space-time.

In the same way that the Spirit instantiates God's subject-determining objectivity, he is possibility-determining reality. It is as Spirit that God has his being in the moment-by-moment action of human thought and speech; he remains Lord in that thought and speech in that he is their constant source. Yet it is *human* thought and speech and as such the instantiation of what the human might be: man for God, the new man, the man of faith.

The first two chapters have thus identified the Spirit with space-time existence. They have avoided speaking of the Spirit by way of abstraction to nonsensate modalities, and, on the contrary, have thought and spoken of the Spirit in terms of God's concrete engagement with the world of sense, which determines the shape and content of the world of sense, that is, which makes space-time to be what it is. But can this account of space-time itself, as at once the object and condition of the Spirit's reality, be correlated with contemporary understandings of space-time? Indeed, this chapter shows that Barth's pneumatocentric dialectic is not merely clannish speculation but something that fits well with the essentially relative and subjective character of space-time.

Chapter 3 supplements Barth's thought with insights garnered from other fields, which serve to reinforce his basic claims. It sets the character of spatial-temporal "truth" in conversation with Barth's theological exegesis of John 1:6-9. This conversation then frames contributions made to our understanding of the world's truth, its fundamental structure and potential, by two influential figures, Jacques Ellul and Albert Einstein.

Within the broader context of this work being prologue to a theology of the Third Article, this chapter draws a series of conclusions, which, taken together, sketch a doctrine of creation after the contemporaneity of God. Space-time exists in the dialectic of coming to be out of nothing. When and where God is inverberate, the veil of fallen space-time is peeled back, but not in a fixed or static way. God's Inverberation is an active movement, a dynamic revelation of his Lordship over even the rebellious impulses of creaturely existence. Thus, our corresponding movement toward newness is a movement that is not completed. Space-time's unveiling involves showing its veil in fresh and poignant ways.

What Is "Truth?"

Thematically addressing the character of *truth* is necessary as we consider the event of revelation as subject-determining objectivity and possibility-determining reality.[3] That is, inasmuch as God refuses disengaged examination from our perch of false independence but institutes participation in his motion toward us, we are compelled to consider what it is that makes our thought and speech not only of him but also of ourselves and our worldly existence

---

3. The following discussion is comprehensive neither in judgment nor in reference. Both are impossible. Pilate's question is for every field. So, for example, Karl Jaspers's magisterial *Von der Wahrheit* (Munich: R. Piper, 1947) takes more than eleven hundred pages to construct an exclusively existential and psychological answer. My page count is more modest. Besides classical sources, Enlightenment thinkers, and the texts singled out for detailed investigation, the following have influenced my thinking on truth, subject–object encounter, and scientific knowing: Jürgen Habermas, *Knowledge and Human Interests*, trans. Jeremy J. Shapiro (Boston: Beacon, 1968); Michael Polanyi, *Knowing and Being: Essays*, ed. Marjorie Grene (Chicago: University of Chicago Press, 1969); Klaus Rosenthal, *Die Überwindung des Subjekt-Objekt-Denkens als philosophisches und theologisches Problem,* Forschungen zur systematischen und ökumenischen Theologie 24 (Göttingen: Vandenhoeck & Ruprecht, 1970); Hans-Georg Gadamer, *Truth and Method*, trans. Joel Weinsheimer and Donald G. Marshall (London and New York: Continuum, 2004)—a revision of the 1975 edition; and Charles Taylor, *Sources of the Self: The Making of the Modern Identity* (Cambridge, Mass.: Harvard University Press, 1989). A recent text in the Radical Orthodoxy movement also deserves mention. In *Truth in the Making: Creative Knowledge in Theology and Philosophy*, Radical Orthodoxy Series (New York and London: Routledge, 2004), Robert Miner makes the case that systematic awareness of the constitutive character of knowing predates Kant and can in fact be traced to the seventeenth-century Italian philosopher Giambattista Vico. Though Miner seems unaware of it, George Steiner draws a parallel conclusion in *After Babel: Aspects of Language and Translation* (New York: Oxford University Press, 1975).

functional and accurate. If in fact theological truth occurs at the ontic-epistemic nexus of object and subject (God's becoming Man and the Spirit's continued reiteration of this circumstance in contemporary thought and speech), a purely objective theory—for example, unqualified correspondence—will not do. Likewise, a purely subjective theory of truth—for example, unqualified coherence—is insufficient. What our subject matter obligates is a dialectical account of the True, at once adequate to the object–subject constitution of that which we perceive, and which we, as perceivers, are.

But asking after truth from within its constitution is not an easy undertaking. There is inherent open-endedness in such inquiry. We therefore cannot avoid some turns of impressionistic rhetoric aimed to engender a sense of resonance, rather than strict deduction. To be as clear as possible: we will ultimately see that truth is a *living quality*. It is neither transcendent *standard* nor immanent *resonance* alone. It is these things always operating together. Therefore truth is principally the *translation* of existence in the event of object–subject interface.

On Truth 1: General Considerations

In a default manner of thinking and speaking, "objective" connotes that which is received by sensation, especially ocular and tactile. Conversely, "subjective" suggests imperceptible state (of mind, emotion, activity) or agent/agency (unfortunately for many, "spirit").[4] The one indicates that which is external and at a measurable distance, to which we correspondingly stand as object; the second, that which is internal. But without severe qualification, such facile, default dichotomy is nothing short of disastrous for both science and faith. Imperceptible processes of the natural world as well as states of being and spirits should not be considered, by definition, nonobjective. Likewise, neither perceptible nature nor worshiped idol should be considered, by definition, nonsubjective. There is division between "subjects" and "objects" of the world and of faith, *and yet not*.

The best means I know of demonstrating the fluidity among entities, or an actualistic and relational kind of ontology, is by referencing the coordinated

4. There is no accepted, standard definition of *objectivity* and *subjectivity* that obtains for all science and theoretical discourse. What I am articulating is, I think, unobjectionable, which is to say, a generally granted and helpful understanding of these modalities, epistemologically and ontologically. At the very least, the designations are inextricably bound up with sensory perception, the role of which in *knowing* and *being* is central to my inquiries here.

act of speech and hearing. Spoken words are the creation and harnessing of sound; creation in the sense that no established stock of words statically exists in any language, and so the capacity to bring into existence a new formulation of sound is *everready* (for instance). Words are at the same time simply a harnessing, in that the human does not generate sound *ex nihilo* but selectively appropriates or exercises the extant modality.

Successively, a sound formation is ingested, made internal to us through the organs of auditory reception (the ear canal, but not only—the force of words can literally be *felt*) and conducted into the human organism. It is "processed" in the brain, yes, but more: the expression and reception of specific word formations involves the entire person as a unity, inasmuch as words provoke, sustain, annihilate, and otherwise give us manners of physical existence. Language expression and reception take corporeal form in the muscling of speech, inwardly in thought and emotions like stress, to state a self-evident example, which are manifested in bodily functions—altered rate and intensity of blood flow, rapidity of synaptic firings, accelerated breathing and varying volumes of air in/exhalation—so that words are quite physically produced, received, and reproduced. By this organic process, words are "birthed" into *action*, thrust into public for partaking.

In and through the cooperative, physical/psychic operation of language we arrive at a preliminary understanding of *truth*. *Truth is the event of resonance between an object, its communication, and reception, which reciprocally constitutes the object, its producer, and receiver.* The reality of any thing is its constitution *in* communication and reception. That is not to say that a thing lacks reality apart from communication and reception, but rather that its reality per se comes to be as it is given and partaken. Properly speaking, there is no thing in and for itself, but all things *are* insofar as they *come to be for* something. What a thing *is*—its being or truth—is determined, on the one hand, by its elemental properties, not statically but by their potency, what they can be in this light rather than that, and, on the other, by their reception in a corresponding light.

We have, in other words, two subjects in conversation, who stand relative to each other as objects. The reality of each is the nexus of her objectivity and subjectivity, of her speaking in this way and her reception in this way. She comes to be who she is in this event.[5] Moreover, objectivity and subjectivity

---

5. A limit case, of course, is the person who is deaf and/or mute. Does such a person never encounter truth? I acknowledge that the challenge of sensory deficiency presents a corresponding challenge to *being*; that is, to transformative, shaping encounter with meaning and to transforming and shaping meaning (which reciprocal reception and projection is truth). As I see it, however, with the rich challenge of sensory deficiency comes enriched opportunity, indeed enriched capacity for truth and being. That is

concern the words that define her being in this moment. A word stands as object before us in one sense, and yet takes us into its constitution in another. The objectivity of word is not in doubt; sensibly perceived, it is definitely *there*. And yet its where is irreducibly a function of its being *here*. *I* render its being, too. We cannot wall off creations and exercises of the tongue. They coalesce with us in their very occasion. Their being is perpetually in the process of expression and constitution, which action concomitantly shapes our being.[6]

Special attention should be paid to a particularly significant feature of the interrelationship between subject and object in language: word's unity and diversity. A peculiar creation and harnessing of sound is consistent on one level—a word *is* this given wave pattern. But a word is not statically that pattern because the formation can determinatively vary in pitch and frequency. Without changing the word's makeup in one sense, variation in pitch does change the truth character of a word. A word that is spoken *in the physiognomies of anger* frames subject–object existence differently than the same word spoken *in love*; this, insofar as the same word variously spoken bears and shapes distinctive psychic/physical states. And determinative reverberation carries forward by the word's restatement in other moods, that is, in the ongoing interchange of speaking and responding. Truth (and being), then, has to do with *both* the consistency and the inconsistency inherent in any word formation. *Truth is both unconditional and relative in its occurring.*

Now, it is tempting to see this dialectical construal of truth as unique to language. But I am convinced that the same definition and description of truth just given apply to all realms and modalities of human engagement. The truth

because the sense-challenged person is typically more intuitively aware of relationship in the constitution of being. It is precisely a sense deficiency that heightens sens-itivity to the fluid character of all being and all truth. One modality works harder to compensate for the lack of another; the deaf individual, for example, takes in the same shaping action of word, now via the organs of sight, but in doing so more readily apprehends the action of shaping inherent in dialogue because of increased awareness of the actions and reactions of the dialoguing agents (whether "reading" words on the page or lips and faces of interlocutors).

6. See Charles Taylor, "The Importance of Herder" and "Heidegger, Language, and Ecology," in his *Philosophical Arguments* (Cambridge, Mass.: Harvard University Press, 1995), 79–99 and 100–126, respectively. Herder's importance, argues Taylor, is that he articulates an understanding of language as being more or less a matrix into which humankind is thrown (hence a pre-Heideggerian phenomenology of language), as opposed to a collection of terms that humanity has built over time. The former allows for the shaping effect of language even in its employment, or its "constitutive" task even in its "expression." In this we recognize a kindred thought structure to the dialectic discussed in the last two chapters: language measures that by which it is constituted, as it cooperatively constitutes its subject matter in and through its performance.

of natural science (fields given largely to ocular and tactile investigation—sound waves, too, are read or measured by conventions of sight) is not essentially different from the truth of language-oriented, human science. A fully orbed occurrence of truth involves the entire range of sensory perception.

We must continue to explore the determinative and dialectical nature of truth in its pluriform occurrence in order to fill out our understanding of the inverberate truth of God as the condition of all possibility. By his Spirit, the unconditional God continually places himself in a relative state, existing as he is known and spoken by us without giving his being over to our knowledge and speech. In this way, the living Truth retains his objectivity even as he places himself in a state of subject–subject mutuality.

That is, God's contemporaneous en-wording (Inverberation) repeats the same dynamic of his historical en-fleshing (Incarnation). Person-to-person proclamation of the Word exhibits the same motion of the Word's becoming flesh/the light's shining in the darkness: precedent objectivity of God's action and coordinate subjectivity of human agency. Revealedness is not described just by the latter but by the whole; it takes the same quality as revelation. That is because, as Spirit, God has his being in the *interchange* (and not in the speaker or receiver), which is to say, his being is in the *coming* of his revelation again and again to the living thought and speech making up this act of proclamation. Barth's theological exegesis of John 1:6-9 makes this clearer.

ON TRUTH 2: BARTH'S EXEGESIS OF JOHN 1:6-9

EGENETO ANTHRŌPOS, APESTALMENOS PARA THEOU, ONOMA AUTŌ IŌANNĒS;

> *There came a man sent from God, whose name was John;*

As we saw with v. 2 in the last chapter, John's prologue contains material that is best described as interruptive. Verses 6-9 form a disruptive textual unit in that they abruptly suspend exposition of the Word in order to introduce "one sent from God named John." But here, too, Barth recognizes that the disruption itself is instructive and even intentional:

If [these verses] disturb us—and in some way that reaction is certainly justified—then we have to ascertain the significance of the disruption which the author himself effects either with his own or with alien materials. Or rather, we have to ascertain the sense in which these statements are obviously intended to alert his readers and suddenly to steer their thoughts in a new direction.[7]

Just as with v. 2, the reader of John's prologue must attend to the formal structure of the text as well as its content. The interruptive force of vv. 6-9 turns thought in a new direction, namely, to a dialectical relationship between the Word and the one who bears witness to him.

John is not the Word. "What we see in v. 6, in the light of what precedes, is the contrast between the Logos and all that has come into being. He to whom v. 6 refers is to be seen on this side of the contrast. The *anthrōpos* confirms this."[8] John is not in the beginning with and as God. He is man, *anthrōpos*, the recipient of God's revelation and not that revelation itself. He belongs "to one of the points in the history which according to v. 5 undoubtedly must lie in the sphere of *skotia*."[9] John is of the darkness, not light. The light is addressed to him.

Yet in receiving the light, John is brought into conformity with it. He is made a participant in the light's shining. "If the *egeneto* and the *anthrōpos* definitely distinguish [John] from the Logos, the predicate *apestalmenos para theou* brings him close, and even in a sense puts him in the same sphere and gives him the same function."[10] On the one hand, John is created, a man who comes into being with a definite beginning and end. Again, he is not the Word. But, on the other hand, John is identified with the Word. He is brought close, summoned into the sphere of *to phōs*, because he is sent by God, for God.

John's being is bound up with his calling, its whence and wherefore, so far as the Gospel of John is concerned. It cares about nothing else in naming this one except to establish that he is *from God* (*para theou*). First-century Jewish custom expects that John is identified by family vocation and geographic heritage, but as with the prophets of old, these indicators recede in significance

7. Barth, *Witness to the Word: A Commentary on John 1. Lectures at Münster in 1925 and at Bonn in 1933*, ed. Walther Fürst, trans. Geoffrey W. Bromiley (Grand Rapids: Eerdmans, 1986), 48.

8. Ibid., 49.

9. Ibid., 48.

10. Ibid., 49.

relative to another. John is distinguished as the object of God's activity. "Within the world that has come into being, within the human world that has fallen under darkness, not as an exception to the determinations that are posed for all and every creature, there is among the determinations this qualification: sending by God, separation for a task or mission, and in this sense prophecy."[11]

Among darkness, light shines and distinguishes its recipients. Among the wicked kings and deceiving prophets, a true prophet speaks. Among religious and irreligious alike who speak of God according to false ideology and misshapen introspection, there is one sent from God (*apestalmenos*), an "apostle." There is one in whose thoughts and words God still stands objectively before mankind, a corner of darkness become enlightened. Yet once more, God stands thusly in coming to the dark, *in* the vocation that he gives moment by moment. In John's freedom to bear witness to God, which is to say, in the receipt and discharge of an inclination toward the light that he neither is nor prevails over, we encounter the living Lord. In the contemporaneousness of his revelation as in its beginning, God does not stand opposed to the dark as if allergy or autonomy demands it, but as Lord, the one who *can be* who *he is*. He exists in the possibility that attends his reality, in fresh means of declaring his Lordship, which is to say, in the Spirit of Christ Jesus.

HOUTOS ĒLTHEN EIS MARTYRIAN HINA MARTYRĒSĒ PERI TOU PHŌTOS,
HINA PANTES PISTEUSŌSIN DI' AUTOU.
OUK ĒN EKEINOS TO PHŌS, ALL' HINA MARTYRĒSĒ PERI TOU PHŌTOS.

> *He came as a witness, to testify about the Light, so that all might believe through him.*
> *He was not the Light, but he came to testify about the Light.*

In vv. 7-8 and continuing until v. 15, we encounter something of a structural *inclusio*. Sandwiched between the "this one"/"that one" construct of vv. 2 and 18, which we discussed in the last chapter, John presents us with another *houtos/ekeinos/houtos*. In these inner verses, the intent is to further associate and

---

11. Ibid.

dissociate John the Witness and Jesus Christ, to show both John's proximity to Jesus and the extreme distance between them. That is, the structure reinforces the basic relationship between the being of the messenger and the content of his message.

"This one" testifies to the light. His very being, as just noted, is defined by this act of testimony, by the receipt and execution of his calling to be Christ's witness. John is known only in intimate relationship with Jesus. He has no identity except in view of Jesus. In turn, he is identified as one designated by God to bring God's self-exegesis close, to bring Christ Jesus into the sphere of our living and being and doing. In and through John's witness we perceive God here and now. We see and hear the God who has his existence in the media of space-time, in flesh and language. In other words, the proximity of John to Christ translates the proximity of God himself to us:

> *Elthen* is here undoubtedly the same solemn *erchesthai* with which Elijah came according to the Synoptics, the same as that with which the kingdom of God has come near, the same as that with which the Son of Man will come at the end of days, the same as that which serves both in the Synoptics and in the Gospel to denote the first epiphany of the Lord.[12]

Barth tightly associates the "coming" of John not only with the coming of a prophet (Elijah) but also with the in-breaking of the kingdom and the coming of the Lord himself. In the proclamation of his message to the world of darkness is the appearing of God. God involves the proclamation of his witnesses in his revelation, which is to say, in the event of his Word. "If the appearance of the Baptist as a total phenomenon . . . is described by this solemn *erchesthai*, this embraces its coordination with the office of the Revealer himself."[13]

Expositors have long observed that such is the character of *faith* in the Gospel of John: when and where proclamation of Christ becomes the defining action of the witness, that is, when and where he receives obedience in that he becomes consumed by his task and cheerfully has no identity outside of it, then and there occurs a unity of messenger and message. According to Rudolf Bultmann, the Gospel of John "achieves a unity of Proclaimer and Proclaimed. . . . [It] radically develops the thought that God's word and act are a unity. In the word we meet God's act, and in God's act is His word. . . . ἀκούειν

---

12. Ibid., 51.
13. Ibid.

[to hear] can be equivalent in meaning to πιστεύειν [to believe]."[14] Really to hear proclamation of God's action relative to what he is not is to encounter that action itself, to experience the contemporaneous reality of God-with-man, for the revelation of God's dealings with humanity is the content of those dealings. This is primarily the case with the Word of God, Jesus Christ. Being the self-exegesis of God, Christ reveals God as God-with-us, in the act, that is, of turning from all eternity toward us. The Word *is* the God he reveals.

But unity of Proclaimer and Proclaimed occurs, secondarily, between the witness to the Word and the Word himself. The action of God extends through Christ Jesus into testimony about Christ Jesus. God makes himself to be with us, too. His act involves us. To hear the Word is to have faith in the Word. To receive the Word is to be made an obedient respondent. When and where in our proper turn we proclaim the Word of God, Jesus Christ, we are only acting in accordance with the verberate quality of the Word. Indeed, apart from that experience we can*not* proclaim the Word. We can only think and speak as ones drawn into God's movement, as participants in his light. In this respect, we do not at one point hear and another believe. No, to hear just is to believe; one cannot hear except as a child of the Word. The witness to the Word lives and moves and has being in the Word himself. He becomes a child of God, reborn of the Son's obedience to the Father.

Dialectically, however, the witness is not the message. John is not God's self-exegesis. "That one" is not the light. "One may believe, i.e., come to faith, through John," Barth notes, "but the Revealer himself is the object of faith."[15] The messenger does not proclaim himself, but Christ Jesus. As such, the messenger can never replace the content of his message with his own charisma, personality, and so on:

> Witness is truly and in the best sense speaking about a subject, describing it exactly and fully, pointing to it, confirming and repeating it, and all in such a way that the subject remains itself and can speak for itself, that it is not in any way absorbed in human speech or shouted down and overpowered by it. Only where we have supreme concern both to be as close to the subject as possible,

14. Rudolf Bultmann, "πιστεύω κτλ. (D IV.2)," *Theological Dictionary of the New Testament,* ed. G. Kittel and G. Friedrich, trans. G. W. Bromiley, 10 vols. (Grand Rapids: Eerdmans, 1964–76), 6:222–23; with particular reference to John's idiomatic use of *pisteuō* with the dative (for example, v. 12 below; 2:22; 5:47; 8:40, 45). But the application is manifestly broader.

15. Barth, *Witness to the Word,* 51.

and yet to keep at a distance so that it may speak for itself, do we have *martyria*.[16]

Barth observes that the very character of witness is compromised if its subject is absorbed into the medium. The medium must rather remain paradoxically far from the message. The content of John's message is light, but John participates in the light of Christ without ceasing to be dark. In this way, the dialectical character of John's witness reflects the dialectical reality of the one about whom he witnesses. God is revealed in his witness to the extent that God remains its objective source and goal (and is not conflated into the witness or its words).

John "came as a witness in order to witness" (*ēlthen eis martyrian hina martyrēsē*). As noted, we must not rush to conclude that the Gospel's pleonasms are *unnecessary* redundancies. As with *houtos* of v. 2, the repetitious specification here of *eis martyrian* is significant. A "witness" is one whose biorhythmic orientation has been refashioned to know and speak what it cannot, a moment of dark that has encountered God's self-exegesis and, in a secondary fashion, exegetes after him:

> What v. 8a affirms in definition of the term "witness" is the servant-relationship, the subordination, the dependence which applies to the one thus named over against revelation. But what vv. 6-7 affirm on behalf of v. 8b is that being a witness (even if *only* a witness) means a positive share [in revelation] even if this share be only indirect and on a lower level.[17]

Of himself, John is removed at a great distance from the one about whom he thinks and speaks. He is a dependent servant. "A man can receive only what is given him from heaven. . . . The one who comes from above is above all; the one who is from the earth belongs to the earth, and speaks as one from the earth. The one who comes from heaven is above all" (John 3:27, 31). Yet by the calling of God he becomes a participant in the self-giving activity of God.

---

16. Ibid., 52.

17. Ibid., 56; brackets in original reflecting a revision Barth made to the text.

He receives what is given him from heaven and speaks a message that, although earthen, is charged with God's own life and action.

God is inverberate. The inverberate deity brings about our seeing and hearing, making us to have existence in the light of his revelation *as perceivers*. Thus, as we proclaim the Word as John did, the material constituents of space-time are placed within a new reference frame. In our message, the world is set into a new order—an alternative sequence and cadence, a "time" of *response*. Both for us and in us, it is set after-Word. It becomes a realm of then- and than-predicates corresponding to the living Lordship of its Maker. God's presence in the words of his witnesses simply is his reign over creation now as ever; in the moment-by-moment meeting of these human words and their reception, there is the Living God.

One area we have neglected but are now in a position to discuss is the traditional teaching that the flesh of Jesus was without sin. The New Testament is reasonably straightforward about Christ's sinlessness (2 Cor. 5:21; Heb. 4:15). Doctrinally, the church has contended that the flesh assumed by the Word was not tainted by sin as ours is. Pope Leo I made this position definitive in his "Tome" of 449, when he argued that even though it was sinless, Christ's human nature was fully *human* because it was of a pre-fallen, Adamic quality. Sin does not make us human. God does. Just as Adam was still a human before sin, so could Jesus be a bona fide *sinless man* (and not just God appearing as a man).

But I have explicitly stated that the thought and speech of human witness today brought about and assumed by the Spirit of Christ remain sinful even as the Spirit produces and commandeers them. They do not enjoy the same, pre-fallen, Edenic quality as Christ's flesh. How, then, can the Inverberation of God here and now be construed in terms of a correspondence to the Incarnation when the former suggests that God is revealed in something sinful, whereas the latter does not?

In view of John 1:8 we are, in the first place, given salutary occasion to remember that *Inverberation is not to be understood as a second Incarnation*. We are not contending with two Words of God, first Christ-the-Word and now Witness-the-Word. No, Inverberation refers to the continuing reality of the singular Word made flesh. In that sense alone is it a correspondence to the Incarnation; it is lived reiteration of the history of God's being-with-us *in Jesus of Nazareth*, not another history alongside it. It is imputation of Christ's life, ministry, death, and resurrection to our time, not the creation of a third history between God and humanity—first the time of creation, then the time of reconciliation, now the time of redemption. No, the time of redemption just is the time of reconciliation, which itself is simply restoration of creation to its Creator.

In the second place, however, there *is* a genuine correspondence to the Incarnation in the an/enhypostasis of God's Inverberation. John really does testify about *the light* and not just his own sense of illumination; it is really *God* who is present *in* the church's witness. In the same way that the flesh of Jesus did not preexist but was brought into being by the Spirit at a particular point in history as the medium of *God's* revelation, so, too, do the church's thoughts and words, as the collective vessel of God's presence, derive moment by moment from the Spirit's creative power. Indeed, it is the same action of the Spirit to bring life into being out of non-being that operates in both cases, for he overcame the concupiscence of Mary from annunciation to conception no less than he overcame John's insurgency and overcomes our own. It is only heresy that has tried to retroject the sinlessness of Christ back on to his mother in her natural state. Of herself, Mary is no less dark than we are. In keeping with this fact, she is not the origin of Incarnation's *carne*, but the Spirit is. We are not the origin of Inverberation's *verba*, but the Spirit is. He is the God of light bearing upon darkness and chaos there and then, here and now.

Our obedience, like Mary's, is merely the Spirit-enabled corollary to his initiative, decision, and act. It is our response, "Behold, the bondslave of the Lord. May it be done to me according to your word" (Luke 1:38). As we obey with her, our thoughts and words become the medium of God's revelation, but only the medium.

There is an infinite, qualitative chasm between the media of the Word and the reality of the Word even as the Word has his reality in the concrete media of Jesus' flesh and the witness to his life, ministry, death, and resurrection. Both flesh of the revealer and language of revealedness remain what they are in God's conceiving and assuming them. If they are in fact to become vessels of *revelation*, then they must be brought into unity with God's self-expression without entailing the forfeiture of deity or the annihilation of creatureliness.

There is, of course, still a difference between the flesh of Jesus and our language. The product of the Spirit's work in the Incarnation is not directly identical to the outcome of the freedom of his life within us. Even in being born of God, we remain children of sin until redemption's miracle fully encompasses our space-time. The history of the sinless man Jesus *is* redemption's miracle. Therefore, the thoughts and words of witnesses to Christ—of prophets, apostles, and pastors—are a *secondary* form of the Word. They must become the Word in a way that is not true of Jesus of Nazareth.

ĒN TO PHŌS TO ALĒTHINON, HO PHŌTIZEI PANTA ANTHRŌPON,
ERCHOMENON EIS TON KOSMON.

There was the true Light which, coming
into the world, enlightens all men.

Human witness *participates* in the life of God, self-determined by his history in Christ Jesus. The witness is not Christ Jesus. That one is not the Word. He is not the true light but a reflection thereof. The witness becomes the Word by the Word being who he is, the self-translation of God into the media of space and time.

The Word is the true light in the sense that it is the revelation and achievement of authentic life. "Over against the witness *peri tou phōtos* there stood and stands the *phōs alēthinon*, the original, uncreated, primary light, the direct and immediate revelation of life that bears witness to itself."[18] For Barth, the light of Christ is differentiated from that of his witnesses in that it is generative, which quality is self-authenticating. God is known as God in the event that true life is seen among humankind. God is known as God, then, in the event that witnesses derive from the self-authenticating, generative happening of the Word. "Not just an activity but an effect of light is meant here. It illumines men, it fills them with light, it sets them in the light."[19] The Word creates participants in its light, agents of reflection or, again, reverberation, and it is in this happening that God has his truth, or that God is *God.*

God exists and is known in *coming* to the world. His existence here and now is self-consistent with his existence there and then. The Word is not static, but God in the beginning, God in the initiative, decision, and act of coming to humankind. "This light was (the same time-embracing *en* as in v. 4 and v. 8) *coming* into the world. . . . The *being* of this light in the world is its *coming.* But its coming in full reality!"[20] The light here in v. 9 is described according to the same temporalizing verb "to be" that we saw in v. 4: it *was,* that is, it takes on life (*zōē*) and history (the future reconciliation that confronts our past and breaks into our present). It comes to space-time as space-time's truth,

18. Ibid., 61.
19. Ibid.
20. Ibid., 62 (italics in original).

its illumination, and indeed has its being in this action of embracing space-time. But this action in full reality! The coming of God's Word to space-time, his Inverberation is determined in content and form by who he is and not by speculative consideration of who he might be. Once more, Barth asserts the *reality* of God's revelation as the condition of God's *possibility*; even as Spirit, who God *is* among man determines who he *might be* among man, not vice versa. He is Spirit of the Word.

God sets himself relative to what he is not here and now as always. Just as he had his being in moment-by-moment self-identification with Jesus of Nazareth, so does he now identify with the proclamation of Jesus. And the former reality governs our understanding of the dynamics of the latter. God's dialectical engagement with space-time applies here and now no less than it did there and then. It is not the flesh that is divine but God's *coming* to the flesh that reveals the shape and substance of his divinity. Human language is not divinized, but God's *coming* as Spirit to our thought and speech reveals the shape and substance of his divinity; this, insofar as his contemporaneity is of the same nature as his historical temporalizing in Jesus.

It implies no dishonor to God to confess this since we would have nothing else to think and speak of God if he were not this way. Anything else—any more "honorable" depiction of God by which he exists autonomously from human thought and speech—could only initiate within the non-being of an independent creation. It could only amount to the projection of a No-God.

God comes to the world as its *true* light in the sense that he is its disclosure (*alētheia*). He uncovers what it is and might be. The Greek modifier is a composite term, made of an "alpha-privative" (the letter "a" functioning like the prefixes "un-" or "dis-" do in English) attached a word meaning "close" or "cover" (*lētheia*). God's coming is the un-covering of himself as God-with-us, and therefore the corresponding dis-closure of our genuine existence, revealing its many layers of sin and self-derivation and at once making free use of the thoughts and speech of sinful man to bear God's charitable self-determination forward.

The true light *shines*. Refulgence always entails a corresponding event of translation as darkness is turned away from itself toward newness. This is so in the proclamation of the Word today as it was in the enfleshing of the Word two thousand years ago. Thus, God's self-translation is not "out there," but in and with us here. The light's shining takes place in earthen vessels for the simultaneous enlightening or re-creation of those vessels. Our world, really this space-time, becomes the raw material of the Creator's initiative, decision, and act. Pulsing outward from particular speech-acts made after God's speech-act in Christ Jesus, creation comes to be remade in the midst of its fallen rebellion.

But is this really so? Can it be? Is creation's possibility really susceptible to reformation after God's reality, specifically his *inverberate* reality? Is space-time susceptible to the Spirit of the Word as we have been describing him? The remainder of this chapter is dedicated to demonstrating that the answer to these questions is yes. Exactly to the degree that the truth of creation exhibits the same dialectical quality as the medium of revelation described exegetically, we can meaningfully correlate the dialectical-pneumatological insights we have been culling from Barth with those of other thinkers.

To accomplish this, we must follow some challenging guides across lofty peaks. Now we are neither laypeople nor scholars but equally displaced learners. We first engage the language-based conclusions of Jacques Ellul, in conversation with the physical insights of Albert Einstein.

On Truth 3: Jacques Ellul

Although I have been using the terms somewhat interchangeably, Ellul introduces a qualified but helpful distinction between *truth* and *reality*. By this he intends that "there are two orders of knowledge . . . . There are references to the concrete, experienced reality around us, and others that come from the spoken universe."[21] Ellul bemoans the fact that pursuit of the first order of knowledge, of "what is seen, counted, and quantified, and is located in space,"[22] has become so dominant in contemporary culture that truth has been almost uniformly confused with its measure. That is, we confuse "truth" of an entity with quantifications corresponding to ocular observation.

Ellul takes part in a tradition of criticism dating at least to Søren Kierkegaard, which challenges the primacy of ocular stimulus and response in the constitution of The True, as if being was nothing more than the result of a thing's optical capture and corresponding description.[23] The essence or truth of an entity is more than can be encapsulated in sight and sign, Ellul contends. In fact, the experience and references that genuinely constitute existence are creations of the "spoken universe," of word.

"I am certain that from the beginning, human beings have felt a pressing need to frame for themselves something different from the verifiable universe,

---

21. Ellul, *The Humiliation of the Word*, trans. Joyce Main Hicks (Grand Rapids: Eerdmans, 1985), 22.

22. Ibid., 10.

23. On Ellul's appreciation for Kierkegaard, see Ellul, *Humiliation of the Word,* 37 and passim.

and we have formed it through language. This universe is what we call truth."[24] Despite comfortable predilection for empirical demonstration, it is more elemental for humankind to frame an existence at variance to what we perceive optically. Language "forms," it creates, it speaks forth the "surreal, meta-real, or metaphysical," the sphere of the unverifiable and free.[25] The world of language is not one of mere symbol. (It is also this.) That kind of referencing presumes that symbol and object are stable enough to maintain connection, which obtains in the *practicality* of banal, quotidian discourse. But such stability is a façade of visual depiction. *Truth,* of word, is open-ended, uncertain. "The Word contains fuzziness, a halo that is richer and less precise than information."[26] Empirical demonstration conveys data, information, a precise and fixed content and frame of reference. Language contains "blessed uncertainty," a capacity for possibilities beyond those afforded by sight and touch.[27]

Truth is *agreement,* carved out of discourse, which is neither stable nor predictable but a function of word's appetite for otherness latent in semantic range. That is, concordant potency relies on the gradations of similarity and dissimilarity making up the background of every conversation; what the topic is like, sort of like, sort of unlike, and totally unlike with regard to each descriptive word's ability. Without these degrees, meaning is never achieved. Connotative timbre is an occurrence given in the capacity of word for diverse interpretation; without the continuum of near and far—many of which spectrums are concurrently operative in any conversation, as many in fact as there are words in play—there is no meaning.[28] And because of this, truth is not invariable and final. In the terms of Barth's exegetical observations, truth is always *coming* to expression:

> All language is more or less a riddle to be figured out; it is like interpreting a text that has many possible meanings. In my effort at understanding and interpretation, I establish definitions, and finally, a meaning. The thick haze of discourse produces meaning. . . . But we must be careful: this happy result is achieved only to the

24. Ibid., 22.
25. Ibid.
26. Ibid., 17.
27. Ibid., 18.
28. This is not the same thing as saying truth is infinitely in flux, that it is irreducibly contextual. Words contain a directive orientation; they do not just receive meaning in discourse but also determine it.

degree that—exactly to the degree that—we have experienced all the "interference" of meaning: the rich connotations, the polyphony, and the overtones produced. In the midst of all this, and because of it, a common understanding springs forth and is formulated. It is not exactly what I said (fortunately!). Rather, it is more than that. Nor is it exactly what a tape recorder could have taken down. Instead, it is a symphony of echoes that have reverberated in me. Our agreement commits us to a renewed relationship that will be more profound and genuine. We will be continually reinventing this relationship, just as our speaking must continually recommence.[29]

In the course of conversation, of creating and harnessing sound, a "symphony of echoes" builds to crescendo out of the polyphony of possibility, and this building is meaning or truth, which although definite is never final. The moment of reverberating resonance between the world another creates by putting to word and that of which I partake is peculiar to living discourse (as opposed to that frozen in image or tape recording); it occurs in the act of honing old definitions and obtaining new ones, of encountering and sifting manifold con*not*ations and in*ton*ations. Thus truth is established in continual relationship: in the relationship internal to language in its livingness, which is necessarily reinstated as we grow in language and engage again and again in statement and response.

Ellul makes a compelling argument for a concept of being that is determined not by sight but by hearing. Optical perception prejudices one toward fixedness and to defining essence according to the material. In this world, being and beings are affixed to a signifying characteristic, readily identified. Oral and auditory operation, by contrast, opens to what is Other, what is by nature not able to be captured but submits continually to reframing. This includes, for instance, "the establishment of a scale of values," "everything related to the debate over Love and Justice," and "anything concerned with the ultimate destination of a human being."[30] It is not too strong to say that the ocular is concerned with things of finite now, whereas the auditory deals with things of infinite tomorrow. (Yet as I will show, both, together, constitute *true being*.)

The shaping dynamism of word over against the sterile signifying of image obtains for Ellul even in language's written form. Image refines reality into a momentary depiction that is made to stand for (signify) some whole. This is

29. Ellul, *Humiliation of the Word*, 19–20.
30. Ibid., 28.

not how word operates. Ellul acknowledges that written words shade toward image as they leave the realm of hearing and encroach upon sight, but he rejects the easy conclusion that scripted words are therefore merely elaborate signs.[31] The issue is that written word is an isolated form of spoken word, and so even though it is "weaker," it has not lost its "aim, meaning, or intention."[32] Written word suffers the frozenness of symbol only when it is no longer read aloud and spoken. Then it becomes an instant of distillation. But word's genuine intent is speech, wherein it does not reduce and condense but differentiates and endows (we notice contrastive trajectories—the one toward reduction, the second toward propagation):

> The Genesis passage that establishes creation on the basis of separation contains the germ of the most modern ideas about language; it tells us that difference both establishes the word and proceeds from it. The word bestows being on each reality, attributing truth to it. . . . Individual being comes from the word, because it is distinguished from the whole and given meaning by the word.[33]

Word does not stand for the whole; it individuates being from the whole and relates one to it. In speech (proclamation *and* response), words shape and are shaped in an open, ongoing process of hewing. The oral and auditory operation brings forth meaning in ever-continuing nuance, conditioned in statement and reception by the speaker's and hearer's personal suggestions. At the same time, by these processes the speaker and hearer are shaped—words' intonations and gradations of meaning sculpt thoughts, behaviors, and desires, altering our physique here and now—so that being is a function of the word's coordinate activities of receiving shape and bestowing it.

I have drawn attention to the intersection of physicality and mentality in Ellul's treatment of language because truth resides there, at the conjunction. It is holistic coincidence of subject and object occurring in the process of inquiry, as the seeker asks and answers after the material of her discipline. The human does not just receive truth but also participates in its constitution.

The relevance for our understanding of Inverberation is obvious. The Word takes place as the coming of truth in person-to-person proclamation,

31. Ibid., 42–47, 160–61.
32. Ibid., 44–45.
33. Ibid., 53.

which activity is mutually conditioning exactly to the degree that the Word retains its primal objectivity. God identifies himself with the structures of linguistic interchange in that he has his being in the event of resonance (obedience of faith) taking place in the proclamation of Jesus, that is, in the shared thoughts and words unique to Jesus. Yet he remains *God* in this event to the extent that these thoughts and words point away from themselves by confessing their inherent inadequacy for this event. They speak of one who makes them adequate in the same way that he bridges the chasm between eternity and time in Christ Jesus. In this, they perpetually reconstitute the understanding, conventions, and expectations of their speakers and hearers.

Once again, linguistic interchange is the most obvious modality in which the creative happening of divine truth takes place. But the constitutive and co-determinative character of truth obtains in the domain of nature generally. To perceive this via physics, we turn to Einstein.

On Truth 4: Albert Einstein

Einstein made his "special" theory of relativity public in 1905 and, by extension of its formative principles, offered a general theory of the same in 1916. Both appeared in a single publication in the latter year. That book, translated into English in 1920, was reissued through fifteen editions until 1952, when Einstein added a fifth and final appendix on space as *extension* (with regard to space, Einstein offers a sophisticated elaboration on Descartes).[34] For the next several pages I must entreat the reader lacking background in physics to persevere. For our understanding of *truth*, the yield is worth it. Inasmuch as I, too, am not a theoretical physicist but a theologian in the tradition of Augustine thoughtfully "plundering the Egyptians," I have endeavored to interact with Einstein's theories in terms of their formative logic.[35] It is not the refined mathematical equations that are of especial importance but their philosophical implications and underpinning.[36] Indeed, Einstein remains a figure of great

34. Einstein, *Relativity: The Special and General Theory*, trans. Robert W. Lawson (New York: Three Rivers, 1995).

35. I am indebted to Lene Jaqua, Ph. D. in theoretical nuclear structure and associate professor of science at Colorado Christian University, for reviewing this material. Her several comments improved my understanding of Einstein's theories and, I hope, clarified my expression of their significance here.

36. So, for example, Paul Arthur Schilpp, ed., *Albert Einstein: Philosopher – Scientist*, Library of Living Philosophers 7 (London: Cambridge University Press, 1949). In this volume I found the following essays particularly insightful: Victor F. Lenzen, "Einstein's Theory of Knowledge," 355–84; Kurt Gödel, "A Remark about the Relationship between Relativity Theory and Idealist Philosophy," 555–63; Gaston

value in such inquiry as ours because of his ability to maintain contact between issues of being and mathematical expression.[37] And for this reason the theoretical physicist, also, may find the following enriching.[38]

Bachelard, "The Philosophical Dialectic of the Concepts of Relativity," 563–80; and Aloys Wenzl, "Einstein's Theory of Relativity Viewed from the Standpoint of Critical Realism, and Its Significance for Philosophy," 581–606.

37. See Thomas F. Torrance, *Space, Time and Incarnation* (London: Oxford University Press, 1969). Torrance likewise contends that we must understand God's presence in space-time according to modern as opposed to classical paradigms. This is necessary, he contends, because it is only in modern physics that we attain space-time constructs adequate to the Incarnation. These constructs surfaced in an incipient fashion during the patristic era but became obscured by Greek thought. Specifically, Torrance contrasts the concept of space inherent in the Nicene affirmations of God's transcendence, on the one hand, and incarnational presence, on the other, with what he terms a "receptacle" or "container" notion of space and presence deriving from Hellenistic philosophy (pp. 1–22). In the former, God stands relative to space as its Creator and in the Incarnation engages it as the place of meeting and interface with the creature. Space does not exist except as the junction of being, the realm in and through which being stands relative to being; it is implicated by that relationship as its occasion. According to the latter, by contrast, particularly at the hands of Aristotle (in which space is the quantitative containment of substance), space is simply "that which receives and contains material bodies." In this concept, the Incarnation could only "be thought of as an intrusion into the creation," as God merely enters a preexisting container for a period but has no real relation to it or its contents (p. 24). Unfortunately, the patristic understanding of space in contrast to that of the Greeks obtained only in the East. In the West, medieval thought took over the Aristotelian, receptacle model, engendering a series of unfortunate consequences for theology. My only concern with Torrance is that construing the entire Western tradition of physics before Einstein on the question of space as being given to a deficient, *container* concept lacks requisite nuance. While it is true that Newton himself seems to have thought along these lines, and because of this tended toward an Arian disjunction between the material world and the absolute being of the Infinite, not all Newtonians followed suit. Torrance one-sidedly contends that, because of their adherence to Newtonian thought, Protestant scholastics of the eighteenth century labored under dualistic structures that inevitably cashed out in Enlightenment deism. But Jonathan Edwards, utterly stamped by Newton, was at best a "quasi-receptacle-ist," if you will, and certainly *not* a dualist. Edwards's thought consistently inclined toward *monism* because he came to understand space not as the static container of material entities but as the dynamic *extension* of God's creative potency; it is not just *in* which but also *as* which entity exists (as it is known and loved). A commendable treatment of Edwards along these lines is Sang Hyun Lee, *The Philosophical Theology of Jonathan Edwards* (Princeton: Princeton University Press, 1980). Moreover, one of Torrance's underlying convictions is that Reformed theology in general managed to avoid the problems of the container model of space, yet as I just showed this engenders logical difficulties when we observe that Reformed theologians also take up Newton! Torrance treats Reformed theologians as if they were somehow immune to Newton even as they followed him.

38. A potential project in historical philosophy that has occasionally grabbed my interest traces the conceptual lineage leading from Kant to Barth, Heidegger, and Einstein (through, in particular, the Hegelian tradition of phenomenology, on one side, and nineteenth-century field theory, on the other, especially Ernst Mach).

Related projects for the like-minded are Iain Paul, *Science, Theology and Einstein,* Theology and Scientific

I focus on the first of Einstein's theories, that which deals with uniform or rectilinear motion.[39] In brief, the distinction between the special and general theories of relativity has to do with the kind of movement under examination, and in this the particular coordinate systems specific to both the movement and the observer. The special theory treats the Galilean axiom that bodies sufficiently removed from each other either remain at rest or travel in a straight line. Such bodies and movement can be conceptually mapped along a four-dimensional grid: x, y, z (the three dimensions of observed space), and t (the dimension of time, which permeates the spatial coordinates). Einstein expanded his conclusions concerning uniform motion into a general theory governing non-uniform motion, which paradoxically qualified or limited the applicability of the first theory.[40] But in both theories the fundamental issue remains: the elemental properties of space and time are relative in character to a frame of reference.

For Einstein, all explanations of observed phenomena, whether in science or everyday life, take place from the standpoint of *experience*. Relativity theory

Culture 3 (New York: Oxford University Press, 1982); idem, *Science and Theology in Einstein's Perspective*, Theology and Science at the Frontiers of Knowledge 3 (Edinburgh: Scottish Academic Press, 1986); and idem, *Knowledge of God: Calvin, Einstein, and Polanyi* (Edinburgh: Scottish Academic Press, 1987). A kindred work to the project I described above has been written by Roy D. Morrison II, *Science, Theology and the Transcendental Horizon: Einstein, Kant, and Tillich*, American Academy of Religion Studies in Religion 67 (Atlanta: Scholars Press, 1994).

Einstein was ethnically Jewish but famously rejected classical monotheism in favor of a basically pantheistic "cosmic religion." The most comprehensive account of Einstein's faith remains Max Jammer, *Einstein and Religion: Physics and Theology* (Princeton: Princeton University Press, 1999). Although Einstein conceived of God impersonally, he frequently spoke of "God." Jammer cites the well-known German author-playwright Friedrich Dürrenmatt, who quipped that "Einstein used to speak so often of God that I tend to believe he has been a disguised theologian (p.7)"; see Dürrenmatt, *Albert Einstein: Ein Vortrag* (Zurich: Diogenes, 1979), 12.

39. That is, movement along a straight line and of a constant velocity. For a brief description of the relationship between the special and general theory of relativity, see Einstein, *Relativity*, 83–87. While some have taken the second to undo the first, Einstein rather emphasizes the distinct types of motion each adjudicates and thus understands the general to qualify the applicability of the special, and the special to "live on" in the general as a "limiting case."

40. On the general theory of relativity, see Einstein, *Relativity*, 67–116. As we will see, one of two givens in the special theory of relativity is the constancy of light's speed. This measure remains constant because the special theory deals only with light's motion along a rectilinear vector (which limits the theory's applicability largely to the ways we experience light on earth). Conversely, in the general theory light's speed is variable, because Einstein accounts for its curvilinear motion, which involves constantly changing vectors and thus accelerating frames of reference. In this theory, Einstein accounts for light's motion in the universe around massive objects and thus at once extends and delimits his findings in the special theory of relativity.

begins here: "every description of the scene of an event or of the position of an object in space is based on the specification of the point on a . . . body of reference with which that event or object coincides."[41] Observation of the world is conditioned by the projection of a matrix, a system of coordinates to which being and motion are referred. Language itself gives expression to the situated-ness of existence; *up*, *left*, *west*—such words indicate the "body of reference" according to which entities coincide with measurement (even prereflective description of the scene of an event is a kind of reading or measurement). Our active mind, in other words, intuitively and ceaselessly correlates that which we observe with us. But that means there is no such thing as a single, given x, y, z, t axis "out there," according to which all description of reality takes place, with which all measurement must agree to be *true*. For, where are the zero-points? Our designations of place and motion are in fact dependent on or relative to our own positioning.[42]

Accounts of existence are determined by coordinate systems from which observation takes place and toward which it is directed. There exists a "perspective" of and from the event, and one(s) at point(s) outside the event. Consider, for instance, a train moving along a straight section of track.[43] If a passenger throws a stone from the train, what is the character of the stone's motion? It depends on the points of reference. From the thrower on the train the stone seems to fall in a straight, downward line, so that the only dimension necessary to plot its trajectory is the y. But from the embankment looking across at the train, the stone moves parabolically, across both the x and y dimensions. Likewise, if one was suspended above the train, a parabolic motion would be observed along the x and z lines. What is the stone's true motion? All three, but not all three in a unified schematic.

---

41. Ibid., 6; see also p. 67: "*from the point of view of the idea it conveys to us*, every motion must be considered as a relative motion" (italics mine). There is no Archimedean point from which motion is rendered absolutely, but all description of motion involves our position relative to the moving, as we, also in motion, perceive it.

42. Longitudinal and latitudinal references, for example, do not alter this. Such coordinates represent only collective suspension of local coordinate systems, which still operate, in order to facilitate agreement in measurement for communal and pragmatic reasons (for example, uniformity in global navigation). We simply disregard our own frame of reference temporarily in favor of a singular, arbitrarily constructed system outside the earth. But the privileging of one reference body does not undo the fundamental fabric of human knowing: *our designations are still relative to a reference body*, which means the truth of an entity is not fixed even though the reference body of its rendition is universally accepted.

43. The moving railway carriage is Einstein's chosen illustration for his special theory of relativity. What I am conveying vis-à-vis a stone thrown from a train car can be found in *Relativity*, 10–11.

Even when we synthesize our observations by accounting for *t*, we could only construct a unified, complete model of the stone's motion if we lived in a vacuum. One might be tempted, in other words, to suggest that each of our three observers utilizes a stopwatch to plot the stone's position at various stages of its fall according to her respective axes. The three trajectories could then be combined to render the motion *x*, *y*, *z*, *t*. This procedure can be usefully employed in *practice* but does not obtain in *truth*. One of the most enduring and significant components of Einstein's thought is the manner in which he demonstrated the relativity of time, in his special theory by showing the relativity of simultaneity.

The accuracy of the composite model of the stone's trajectory is contingent upon the simultaneity of the observers' temporal markings. If one of our observers was farther removed from the throw than the other two, then her markings at points along the stone's fall would be delayed by the additional time it takes for the light of the event to reach her. Again, the practical difference in this scenario would be so negligible as to suggest total simultaneity of action and observation. Yet already we are beginning to appreciate the salient issue: *in truth*, time is a variable function of velocity and distance, or motion in space.[44] "Simultaneity" is thus a term of relative meaning. We need to consider this in greater detail. In doing so, I relate Einstein's thinking in the order that he unfolds it.

The *principle* of relativity—a maxim of classical mechanics—is the departure point for Einstein's special *theory* of relativity. The principle states that "if, relative to K, K′ is a uniformly moving coordinate system devoid of rotation, then natural phenomena run their course with respect to K′ according to exactly the same general laws as with respect to K."[45] Imagine we stand on the train embankment with our back to the passing train and, looking across a field, observe a car driving along a straight road. Likewise, a passenger on the moving train looks across the same field and observes the same car. According to the principle of relativity we assume that the laws governing and conveying the

44. This is not overcome by the clever, contemporary scientist employing technology beyond that of Einstein's day: say, three digital cameras instead of human observers, triggered by a transmitter placed within the stone. That experiment removes human perception but only transfers properties of observation from light to the medium of a digital signal, which still has a measurable velocity. Distance is thus still a determinative factor. Moreover, the addition of a transmitter represents an implicit, philosophical choice: to privilege the coordinate system of the stone itself, as if to stand at its zero points is to enjoy the only objective reference frame, all others being subjective.

45. Einstein, *Relativity*, 16.

motion of the car from my stationary perspective (K) are exactly the same as those vis-à-vis the moving train (K').

In particular, we suppose that the light reaching me from the car travels at the same speed and in the same, linear fashion as it does to the train passenger. It does not, in other words, come to me straight and at a fixed speed and to the passenger, by virtue of her traveling, in a curvilinear manner, which would cause her to render the motion of the car (plot its trajectory along her K' system of coordinates) in a way that could not be reconciled with my representation.

But is it legitimate to assume the regularity of light's motion in principle? Let us do an "about face" for a moment and turn to the train. If at the same instant our passenger turns away from observing the car and takes a step in the direction the train is moving, how shall we calculate the total speed and distance she travels relative to the embankment? It would seem that we merely need to add the speed of her gait relative to the train, to that of the train itself relative to the embankment: if the train is moving at a rate of 100 meters per second by my reckoning and she steps at a rate of 1 m/s (as communicated to me by a second passenger sharing the train's motion, observing the first), then from my point on the embankment she steps at a rate of 101 m/s, or covers 101 meters in that second of my observation. To any child who has watched a train from a station platform, this appears quite obvious and intuitive.

However, we are thrust into acute intellectual difficulties if the movement we consider is that not of a person but of light. Let's say the motion we are dealing with is the color of a chair from which the first passenger stands up, brown, traveling to a second passenger in the front of the train. From my perch on the embankment I intuitively calculate that the total velocity of the motion (c, the speed of light in a vacuum = 299,792,458 m/s) = v (train's velocity) + vb (velocity of the color brown relative to the train). The immediate problem is that light's magnitude is thereby rendered inconstant. In other words, $vb = c - v$, so that light (from the chair as the second passenger observes it) is slower than light; according to the arbitrary values given above, the former would be required to move at 299,792,358 m/s.

Either, therefore, the principle of relativity is undone or light as a constant value *in vacuo* is overthrown. That is, either the laws governing an event are not the same in principle, or the light governing observation behaves inconsistently. Einstein reconciles this difficulty by showing that it is not the laws of nature or light's speed that is inconsistent, but the m (distance–interval) and s (time–interval) as measurable magnitudes.

The addition and subtraction of speeds just conducted obtains only insofar as the respective, basic units of measure are standard and nonfluctuating, that is, only insofar as "meter" and "second" indicate absolute magnitudes unaffected by motion. But Einstein demonstrates that these values are entirely relative to motion. We cannot calculate the speed of the passenger relative to the embankment by simply adding her walking velocity relative to the train to that of the train (relative to the embankment), nor can we arrive at the velocity of light relative to the train by subtracting the train's speed from c, because the magnitude of meter and second depends on one's particular body of reference. To put it simply, we have added and subtracted apples and oranges; *a second on the moving train is not the same as a second on the embankment.*

Einstein contends that time is not a static datum, a given modality in and through which beings pass existence. It is rather the necessary corollary of spatial events.[46] Time is both the *as which* as well as the *within which* of an event; the passenger's walking with the train structures the time units that measure her walking. Time is, dialectically, the measure of the experience it is constituted by: though we may suppose we have time in given units used to quantify any event, in point of fact time is an event-determined quality. The test case that suggests this is the experimental verification of simultaneity.

The simplest definition of "simultaneous" is *multiple events occurring at the same time*. But if we ask, What constitutes the time's sameness?, we answer, "an equivalent and uniform distance-relationship to the event." Time is simply characterization of an event made with observation of that event's defining motion in space.[47] Take our train again. As I stand on the embankment I notice two flashes of lightning, X to the left (corresponding to the rearward point of the train) and Y to the right (front of the train), which appear to strike at once together. But of course, this could only be the case if I stand still, exactly at the midpoint between the strikes, so that the distance along which the events'

---

46. Einstein stands in line with Kant in the general sense that all being is spatially and temporally rendered. But Einstein moves beyond Kant in that space and time are not independent, prethematic, a priori modes of thought through which entity is mediated. On this, Kant is clearly in line with Newtonian physics. For Einstein, space-time is rather the physical conjunction at which being occurs. Because this conjunctive state is relative to the coordinate system of its observer—that is, the spatial-temporal point of being is constituted by both the event and its observation – Einstein's relativity is continuous with a Kantian dialectic. On the relationship between Einstein and Kant, see Bachelard, "Philosophical Dialectic of the Concepts of Relativity."

47. Reading the hands of clocks at two different events does not apply, because doing so assumes that we already know what time is and can measure it with devices. Along these lines, the movement of clocks is itself a matter of distance—for instance, how far a gear must turn to mark a passing time unit, and how quickly the turning moves if the clock itself is placed in motion. Part of Einstein's effort is to show that this movement is in fact variable (see Einstein, *Relativity*, 40–42).

medium (light) comes to me is equivalent, and the velocity of the medium is equal for each event/strike.[48]

Obviously, things change as soon as we involve motion. Let the strikes occur exactly at the point our moving train passenger is in spatial proximity with me on the embankment. Because she is heading toward the flash on the right at the train's velocity, its media will reach her before the strike on the left since she is closing the distance to Y and extending it to X, so that we do not have simultaneity but a "this-then-that." Moreover, if we were to construct a value for the "instant" of the strikes, we would arrive at different results relative to the embankment and moving train.

To illustrate with a wildly unrealistic example, let us round the speed of light up to 300 million meters per second. And to make the numbers a little easier to work with, let us imagine a train that is exactly 600 million meters long, so that she is exactly 300 million meters from each strike when it occurs. Now let the train move at 150 million meters per second. The light from the right will reach the train passenger in two-thirds of a second, but the light from the left will take 2 seconds, from the external perspectives of the strikes themselves, that is. The train passenger will not experience the event as taking 2 seconds (the "time" of the first strike is included in that of the second strike, since the second strike is not waiting for the first to reach the train passenger before it sets off), because she does not "feel" her movement toward and from the respective flashes and has no conception of them until they actually reach her. To her, it takes 1 and one-third second for both flashes to occur (the difference of time from the first to second flash, which is to say, after the first flash it takes 1 and one-third second for the second flash to occur).

Now consider the person on the embankment. Each lightning strike will take one second to reach her since she stands at the midpoint between them, but it will not be the same kind of "second." She will perceive the strikes as instantaneous and simultaneous. She will no more consider them happening in the past and taking time to arrive than she would consider the light from distant stars setting off and finally reaching her. She only knows them as strikes (and stars) because their light *has* reached her. But in truth, "time" is made of both her perception of the strikes and of the factual distance covered by their light (for although not realistic in our example, Einstein presupposes that she sees the front and back of the train – her sight places her beyond her specific geographic point even as that sight is constructed by the light coming to her

48. Of course, as soon as we involve "velocity" we circularly assume time, since velocity is merely distance-interval per time-interval along a vector. But we can proceed so long as we do not correspondingly assume a meaning of "time-interval."

from the environment about her, including the lightning strikes). It is the duration required for the event to be this event. So as with the train passenger, we have the experience of the event—its "as which"—and the measurement of the event—its "in which"—and both distinctly, yet together, are time. Most significantly, this "time" is not the same for the train passenger and for the person on the embankment. Both the as which and in which of the X-Y lightning event is longer for the former relative to the latter. Another way of saying this would be that the motion of the train passenger slows time relative to the stationary perspective of the embankment.

Paradoxically, to the person on the embankment, the "second" on the train is longer or slower than the "second" on the embankment (we recall that to the observer on the embankment the train passenger also passes her simultaneously with the lightning strikes and so from her perspective the passenger is part of the same lightning event – it is to her just an elongated event for the passenger). Yet both kinds of "second" are true time.[49] Einstein thus concludes that "the time required by a particular occurrence with respect to the carriage must not be considered equal to the duration of the same occurrence as judged from the embankment (as reference-body)."[50] The constitution of the moment at hand, the "second" as and in which each flash of light occurs in perception, has a different value for the passenger than for the observer. "Every reference-body . . . has its own particular time; unless we are told the reference-body to which the statement of time refers, there is no meaning in a statement of time of an event."[51]

Once more, the decisive issue is that instance and distance, time and space, are not absolute and independent constituents, but our *mutually-conditioned realm of existence relative to a frame of reference*.[52] Appropriately qualified, we are led by this to some important considerations with regard to objectivity, subjectivity, and truth.[53]

---

49. And to the person on the train, the "second" on the embankment is faster than her own. What makes one second, "one second" is simply its being the duration needed for light to travel 299,792,458 meters. But this "need" is relative to the velocity at which one is already traveling and the location of light's source, the passenger's rectilinear motion relative to stationary observation of lightning strikes at the back and front of the train.

50. Einstein, *Relativity*, 31.

51. Ibid.

52. "One meter" is merely that distance-interval obligated by $1/3 \times 10^8$ seconds of light. But if observation of that light is in motion, such as on the train, the "meter" it obligates is not exactly coterminous with the same on the embankment. That distance is reciprocally conditioned by time is demonstrated in Einstein, *Relativity*, 32–33.

In the first place, an object is not a thing statically existing "in" space-time. Things only have being at the intersection of reference frames, that is, at the nexus of constitutive qualities and their perception, which conjunction also shapes space-time. Einstein does not allow that things of the physical world are entirely determined by observation, hence that space-time is purely an idealist construct. No, he is manifestly a critical *realist* (so am I, and, as noted, so was Barth), meaning that entities and events per se[54] are governed and communicated by basic constituents, which are not simply internal to the observer. However, those properties are translated in perception according to a particular coordinate system. Hence, we can—in fact must—say that a being is *both* its singular and plural makeup, both its elemental properties and observation; all entities and events are *co-determined*. That is because space-time itself is determined by the physical relationships both governing and brought about by entities and events (that is, the transmission of light from point to point and the motion affecting its reception). Space-time is not only the "in which" but also the "as which" of all things.

Existence is not stasis but moment-by-moment occurrence. Specifically, the existence of any thing occurs as a dialectic between that thing's unique

53. The primary qualification is that with the special theory of relativity we are, as mentioned, dealing with space as a four-dimensional realm, and with a particular kind of motion *in* that space (rectilinear). Both represent a limited perspective. Ultimately, Einstein prefers a concept of space that derives from his general theory of relativity: as coincident with *field*. In the special theory, all matter and accompanying laws and fields are conceived as existing "in" the spatial coordinate system; that is, we can imagine space as that x,y,z,t emptiness left when everything and every governing property are removed. But in the general theory, fields are not "brought about," if you will, by matter, but physical reality *is* a field, the quality of which represents a generalization of the gravitational field (cf. *Relativity*, 155–78). In this, "space-time does not claim an existence on its own, but only as a structural quality of the field" (p. 176). Hence, space and time do not endure when all being is removed; rather, when the field is removed, *nothing* exists. Nevertheless, space-time as a mutually conditioned realm of being (as opposed to prethematic, independent, and absolute constructs), as well as the relative character of entity as it is observed spatially and temporally—these fundamental elements obtain in both theories. And that is sufficient for my purposes, my intention at this point not being to render a general judgment on the Newtonian versus Einsteinian concepts of space.

54. For Einstein, an "object" is *independent* in those characteristics not relativized by the perceiving subject's spatial and temporal situatedness (see Lenzen, "Einstein's Theory of Knowledge," 367 and passim). However, nothing exists outside its space-time structure. Hence, we see the dialectical character of Einstein's thought, much akin to Kant: entity is both independent and dependent, co-constituted by characteristics outside of perception (though rationally presumed) and by the mode and act of perception. When the subject is taken account of in the determination of the object, we are left with the dialectical affirmation that an object *is*, and an object is *as* its space-time rendition.

elemental properties and the plurality of points of reference both available to the thing and manifested external to it.

Second, then, the nature of *meaning* or *truth* is dialectical itself. If the time-interval of an occurrence is co-determined by any occurrence's fundamental properties and their relative observation, such that, as we saw, greater and lesser duration values correlate to the same event, then *sequence* is variable. That greater and lesser duration-intervals likewise correspond to later and earlier chronological designations is significant inasmuch as the co-sequence or *con*sequence intuitively associated with observation—myriad entities and events being coordinately observed by the senses every moment—is in strong measure determined by *sequence* in observing (measurement and expression). Evaluation or internal measurement correlates to the same in the external realm, sometimes directly, sometimes inversely. A basic example of this is the if-then construct. In it, reason and time are reciprocally bound; the logic is, "given this, that follows." But if "this" is not given because its *-er* is not as expected—say, the lynchpin event comes lat*er* and not earli*er* relative to spatial motion—then the evaluative judgment is altered.[55] It is this sort of recognition that led Martin Heidegger to conclude that all being is time.[56]

Therefore, we must conclude that truth is the dialectical constitution of entities and events in experience, agreement between or co-constitution by underlying properties and their perception. Truth is thus *coming into being as such,* that is, reciprocal determination by distinctive properties and of their (equally distinctive) reception. Here we stand on a knife's edge. Truth *is* the coming. It cannot be simply the before or after, the giving or receiving, for it is always both, not synthesized but cooperative. It must therefore be the condition in-between, so to speak, that quality by which entity and event are constituting and constituted. Truth is the circumstance of space-time beings in and through which there is *this* space-time, which incidence takes place in the

55. Another way of perceiving this is to recognize that than-statements—with an *a*—are quantitative yet related to qualitative then-statements of temporal judgment.

56. See Heidegger, *Being and Time*, trans. John Macquarrie and Edward Robinson (New York: Harper & Row, 1962). In the example of the lightning strikes, we noted that the person on the embankment only knows the strikes as strikes when their light *has* reached her. That is a past-tense statement, so that her present (the instant of the strikes) at once encompasses the past (the one second that it took for the light to reach her). And her future is already subject to the events taking place in this present, which have yet to reach her. Her being, then, is entirely situated relative to these temporal references; she only has being-as or being-there, being in the concrete modalities of perpetual reception of entities and events and projection into further entities and events.

manifold interrelationships of creation. Thus, we can never fix truth itself, but only formulate its becoming in an ongoing dialectic between reference frames.

On Truth 5: Concerning Truth and Speech

If truth is simply coming-to-be-thus, then thought and speech are given formal determination by their very attempt to ascertain and articulate the truth of any thing—as they *go after* (in following, manifest) the object of inquiry. They have an a posteriori character. Inasmuch as truth cannot be affixed to a given frame of reference but occurs, so the expression of truth is as dynamic as the occurrence of this or that object. It must always recur in, with, and after the more basic occurrence of the thing or event being described. Yet we have seen that the happening of truth is co-determined by its ascertainment; that even its elemental constituents of extension and duration are relative to motion and perception. Thus, even in their essentially post facto quality, thought and speech also participate in the constitution of truth. They are also structural in character. Now we can, *mutatis mutandis,*[57] reconnect with Ellul.

---

57. The unsympathetic reader may here object that I am crossing a line; namely, that by associating Einstein's conclusions vis-à-vis space-time, which are drawn in the realm of physics, with philosophical and theological products of the written realm I am committing a categorical error. Truth of these varied media cannot be harmoniously brought into dialogue, only confused. In response to this hypothetical but likely objection, I should remind that my choice to engage Einstein was premeditated, exactly because of the fluid way his thought traverses between physics and philosophy (and theology). Einstein is explicit that modern science has simply "taken over from pre-scientific thought the concepts space, time, and material object . . . and has modified them and rendered them more precise" (*Relativity*, 162). The contact point, as I see it, is *language*. Once more, Einstein's theory begins by making a statement about experiential observation—"every *description* of the scene of an event. . . ." For Einstein, physical and mathematic equations are a form of description; they are a highly formalized, highly representational form of linguistic commerce. It is for that reason that Einstein can move back and forth between equations and contemporary, vernacular discourse. I can only ask the reader to try out this fluidity. All sciences, human and natural, must reckon with the translative and dialectical nature of Truth. Part of the hesitancy, of course, is the assumption that physical science operates in a sterile manner, without value judgments, and by definition philosophy and theology are fields of value adjudication. Thus, the "language" of mathematical formulae is fundamentally different from the value-laden vernaculars of cultural speech. But this is a false assumption from the outset. Einstein reminds us that the very process of knowing does not begin in a vacuum but as an operation of judgment. The best we can do is ceaselessly try to identify the prejudices of our imagination, as Jonathan Edwards put it, and seek to hold these at bay as we draw paradoxically intuitable yet barely communicable conclusions. Yet because science is at bottom nothing more than the attempt to make *concepts* ever more precise and articulate, concepts outside of which we can never operate as we attempt new theories to explain part and whole, natural and

Ellul observes that word and time are correlative exactly because of the distance-interval implicated in the basic unit of wording, the sentence. Speech "engulfs us in temporality, because of the unfolding of discourse. . . . I must always wait in order to grasp the exact meaning of a sentence that has just begun. I am suspended between two points in time."[58] The remoteness between points in the sentence unit "engulfs" the subject in time in that the sentence places her at a distance-interval relative to beginning and ending. She now stands in the words, as it were, related to their starting and ending points (her proximity being a matter of her background knowledge, prejudices, and semantic consciousness and facility). And meaning or truth is that object–subject condition *where-when* the developmental agency of separated words and the agent developing in them converge:

> When I hear a sentence, I am in the present with it. I have grabbed hold of and memorized its beginning, which is now past, and it plunges me into the past with it. I am also listening carefully for the end of the sentence; I am waiting for the direct object which will clarify the meaning of the whole sentence. I am straining toward this future implied by speech.[59]

Truth happens in the event that my thought and speech are at once catalyzed by the sentence—they provoke and stretch my reference frame—and as they orient the sentence to me, they place its content within my reference frame. Unfortunately, Ellul contrasts this temporal construal of truth with that of the spatial realm, which is to say, he opposes the event-character of linguistic objects with the givenness of objects perceived optically. He acknowledges that truth, ultimately, happens at the intersection of language and image, of word and sight, but relegates their "reconciliation" to the end of time. "There is in the order of truth a deep, total, and essential rupture between word and sight in the present age."[60] In light of what we just observed in Einstein and will now discuss further in Barth, we must correct Ellul at this point.[61] We must

---

human sciences should not interact merely on the occasion of inevitable collision, but intentionally, as varied but related attempts at truth.

58. Ellul, *Humiliation of the Word*, 14.

59. Ibid., 15.

60. Ibid., 253.

allow that truth is multiply constituted both in linguistics and in the externally perceived, physical realm (in the realms of all sciences).[62]

61. Ellul should have recognized the reciprocal constitution of space-time *in and through language* (in that words do not merely describe but also constitute space-time relationships), exactly as I have related his thought here. Instead, he contrasts the sequentiality of word with instantaneousness of spatial image (see *Humiliation of the Word,* 14 and passim, esp. 221–27). He does this primarily to make a case against the propensity, pandemic in modern cultures, to reduce truth to the pragmatic output of technology or "technique." Truth becomes *that which works,* meaning *that which is tangibly at hand and able to be manipulated in knowledge and act.* I sympathize with Ellul's effort. However, Ellul so thoroughly differentiates between truth and reality, word and sight, time and space, respectively, that his occasional qualifications are without force, and such distinctions must be severely qualified. The sensate constitution of being is such a linked matrix that the same argument made against privileging one—sight/image—must be made against preferring others—hearing/word. (God did, after all, create the visual, too!) Unfortunately, I find the same shortcoming in Stephen H. Webb's otherwise creative attempt to introduce a "theology of sound"; see Webb, *The Divine Voice: Christian Proclamation and the Theology of Sound* (Grand Rapids: Brazos, 2004). Webb and I are close, certainly operating on parallel tracks, in that he too would return to Barth to critique theology abstracted from proclamation, argue for a robust account of the Spirit's work and life-changing presence in these disciplines, and construct what he calls a biblical/ecclesial "acoustemology" of worship and preaching (p. 27 and passim). However, like Ellul, Webb believes these efforts are enjoined with a concomitant priority of the oral over the ocular, hence with the common critique of modernity that alleges, by its propagation of technology and media, that contemporary Western culture has inverted the appropriate order of sensation to our peril. He thus separates the senses and locates their reconciliation in the eschaton. "Christian eschatology entails the proposition that heavenly grace will saturate our whole body, making synesthesia—the mingling and mixing of the senses in a unity that transcends their differences—a reality. Nevertheless, I want to do more than recommend sound as a neglected topic worth retrieving for theologians. . . . We need to explore the extent to which all aspects of Christian faith are soundful" (pp. 30–31). I argue that restorative, heavenly grace unites the senses today by the operation of Word and Spirit in proclamation primarily and theology secondarily, that sight is not to be disparaged in our attempts to hear again, and that by abstracting a future unity of grace and being from what is possible (by God) today we risk a kind of pantheism—the sublimation of all entity into God via some projected, great and final leveling of sense perception.

62. Basic, biological operations relate our being to time, such as hunger and walking. These are also sequential-dimensional, yet occur irrespective of language and light. Contrary to popular reception, Einstein does not make light alone responsible for time. He acknowledges a "subjective" and "psychological" origin of temporality as well (see *Relativity,* 159–61). Again, it is Einstein's range that makes him so appealing to me, more so than Ellul. Einstein recognizes the role of recollection or memory in the constitution of sequence, something that operates irrespective of light and sound (for example, in someone blind and deaf from birth). Any single comprehension brought somehow into repetition, produces intelligible sequence.

On Truth 6: Where-When Is Truth

Barth makes an instructive reference to Einstein in a sermon that he gave on Psalm 104:2 (April 1921). Commenting on the first part of the verse, which says, "He wraps himself in light as with a garment," Barth writes:

> If the discoveries, which a young scholar named Einstein has made in recent years prove to be even somewhat true, then one must think of light as a reality (*Tatsache*) that is actually not grasped any longer as a [given] reality (*Tatsache*), but rather as realization (*Erkenntnis*), as spirit, as truth, which appears somehow to form a gateway to another world beyond the space and time in which we live and think.[63]

The light that we perceive is not merely a component of the existence that God brings into being but a fundamental constituent of said existence. It is the realization of being; it is "spirit" or "truth." It is not something within space and time but the means of space-time, an essential reality in which and after which space-time itself comes to be. It is thus the gateway to the reality, the truth, the coming of God as the basis of all reality, truth, being.

Genuine reality just is the happening, the "where-when" or determinative present-ness of Christ Jesus. As he defines existence, so there is existence—its full range of possibilities comes to be in and with his reality. His truth determines all truth; his history conditions all history; his temporality gives defining shape and substance to all being in time.

Barth gives detailed consideration to the nature of time in his discussion of "The Creature" in CD III.2.[64] Again, he does not consider time in the abstract and then apply his conclusions to God and humankind, but rather assesses what time is and what gives it significance by thinking of it as a modality proper to Christ. He begins his treatment with a subsection on "Jesus, Lord of Time."[65]

Barth opens this subsection with two noteworthy preliminary observations concerning God, on the one hand, and humankind, on the other. In the first place, "even the eternal God does not live without time. He is supremely temporal."[66] We do not think rightly of "God" if, viewing him in terms of Christ, we abstract to some atemporal stasis as the condition of his being. The

---

63. Barth, "April: Psalm 104:2(a): Licht ist dein Kleid, das du anhast!" in *Predigten 1921*, Gesamtausgabe 44 (Zurich: Theologischer Verlag, 2007), 104–5.

64. CD III.2 §47, "Man in His Time," 437–640.

65. Ibid., 437–510.

66. Ibid., 437.

God who is God in and as the Word made flesh is *God of time*, who in taking flesh to himself also takes up its history and so has eternity in a distinct past, present, and future.[67]

In the second place, "man lives as he has time and is in his time."[68] True humanity is that revealed in the *historic* Jesus of Nazareth. Atemporality therefore has no place here, either. The creature is not a creature by transcending time—not, say, as a timeless soul whose destiny is to return to its timeless source—but by living according to the sense common to time, chronologically.

Moreover, echoing the thought structures that we saw in Ellul and Einstein, Barth thinks of human existence as both being-in and being-as time. The temporality according to which human being is realized is at once the inescapable framework of one's existence —her "in-which"—and something she makes to be—her "as-which." "We speak of 'created time,'" Barth writes, "but it would be more accurate to say 'co-created.' For time is not a something, a creature with other creatures, but a form of all the reality distinct from God, *posited with it*, and therefore a real form of its being and nature."[69] Time comes to be with reality as the form of reality. It is the field of all being and doing, on the one hand, the duration and (with space) extension according to which there is identifiable being and doing, and, on the other hand, it is proscribed as a modality only with its beings and doings. Just as it gives meaningful shape to entities and events, it is reciprocally given shape by entities and events.[70]

Once more, Barth makes these preliminary observations by focusing on the inherently temporal nature of the existence of Christ Jesus. He is at once in time, and by his living he gives defining structure to time; he is Lord of time.

What makes Jesus known to be Lord of time is his unique "second history," that is, the forty days of his *resurrected* life. "This [Easter history] is a key position for our whole understanding of the man Jesus in His time. It shows us as nothing else can, according to the New Testament, that even as a man in His time Jesus is Lord of all time."[71] From the perspective of Christ's resurrection

---

67. God does not experience past, present, and future in succession, Barth observes, but simultaneously, as his eternity is (dialectically) not collapsed into time (see CD III.2, 437-38). God has his eternal life in *perfection*, which is to say that he knows and lives the *fulfillment* of the past in the present and the present in the future; he is not ignorant and inexperienced of the present and the future as if they are, to him, strictly "not yet."

68. CD III.2, 438.

69. Ibid; italics added.

70. Ibid.: "Time is the form of the created world by which the world is ordained to be the field for the acts of God and for the corresponding reactions of His creatures, or, in more general terms, for creaturely life."

from the dead, he is known as a human in time, susceptible to origin, sequence, and end like all humans, and as ruler over time, he who makes his own end. By conquering death, time's end and humanity's existential frame of reference, Jesus demonstrates a power greater than time, a capacity not only for time but also for its restructuring. He establishes a new existential reference frame.

Easter time becomes the interpretive lens through which Christ's total time is understood, specifically as the center of all time. It defines the comprehensive "history," the total arc of Jesus' existence as an existence that gives history meaning—as life conquering death and non-being.

The time frame of the Gospel is structured after the event of Easter as the time frame of all creation. It represents *God*'s history with humanity, his giving life and light in the midst of darkness and chaos. It is this history that gives time, as a modality, purpose, meaning, and substance:

> It is wrong to suppose that the New Testament authors started with a particular conception of time as an ascending line with a series of aeons, then inserted into this geometrical figure the event of Christ as the centre of this line. Surely it was a particular memory of a particular time filled with a particular history, it was the constraint under which this laid their thinking, which formed and initiated their particular conception of time. What shaped and determined their conception of time was the fact that the God who was the Father of Jesus Christ stood before them as the *basileus tōn aōinōn* (1 Tim. 1:17).[72]

The New Testament authors did not start with a given conception of time, into which they inserted the history of Jesus, but the other way around. They conceived of time in view of the history of Jesus; inasmuch as they saw the Father in him, they saw the Lord of creation, of all times. The forty days of Jesus' resurrection placed a constraint on the apostle's thought and speech, forming their comprehension of all past and future around this present life, construing them as coming to be for it (and therefore from it), and moving out from it (and therefore for it).

71. CD III.2, 441.
72. Ibid., 443.

Contrary to ancient conceptions of *chronos*, then, as a given progression of ages culminating in an *aiōn teleos*, the New Testament understanding of time thinks outward from "the king of the ages." In Christ, time is neither more nor less than the field and form of God's covenantal dealings with creaturely existence. It comes to be and has significance as such. Christ's time becomes for the biblical authors the seat of all being, again, that for which God created the world and the foretaste of that—the victory over death—to which he will bring the world.

Our time is of course also Christ's time as our thought and speech are placed under the same constraint, as we take on the thought structures of the prophets and apostles. The church's time is a continuation of the New Testament time. In the church, we think and speak from the focal point of Christ's Easter victory, at once perceiving time past as preparation for this messianic moment and looking forward to the consummated messianic rule. As the Spirit of God gathers us *here and now*, in this time, around the thought and speech of the Messiah, he reveals a new time even as we continue to live in our time. We will talk more about this next chapter. Meantime, we notice that our time comes to be the time of redemption as we live and move by the Spirit in the proclamation, in the thoughts, words, and behavioral patterns of the resurrected Christ testified to by the prophets and apostles.

For Barth, this living and moving is no mere recollection of an idea or series of ideas. Christ really does have a defining history, a past, present, and future that give shape and tangible substance to our past, present, and future.[73] He is Lord of time to the extent that his biorhythms become our own through the dynamic event of knowing him here and know, which is again to say, through his reality becoming the determinative reality of here-now, through the reestablishment of reality and reforming of possibility after the Work and Person of his Spirit:

> Where the Spirit is, there is more than a mere tradition or recollection of Jesus. Of course there is tradition and recollection as well. But the message of His past is proclaimed, heard and believed in order that it should no longer be past but present. Life is lived in

73. Rather than mere recollection, we might better think of the event of Christ's time as *recapitulation*. Adrian Langdon has drawn just this conclusion from his own work on Barth's understanding of time. He interprets Barth in terms of this classically Irenaean construct, according to which Langdon thinks of God as the "eternal contemporary." See Langdon, *God the Eternal Contemporary: Trinity, Eternity, and Time in Karl Barth* (Eugene, Ore.: Wipf & Stock, 2012), 123–58.

contemplation of the kingdom already come, in which everything necessary has been done for the full deliverance and preservation of man, for the fulfillment of the divine covenant. Nor does this rest merely on a retrospective vision, nor on an interpretation and assessment of this past history hazarded at some point and in some way by the men concerned, but on the fact that this history, this time, is not merely past but present, overlapping objectively as it were the present time of the apostles and their communities, pushing beyond its own frontiers to those of this other time and beyond.[74]

The Spirit just is the present, the contemporaneity of Christ Jesus. He is not only the means of rightly remembering the person Jesus, but also, in and through contemplation of the decisive reign of Christ over all things, including death and non-being, he is the reality of Christ here and now. The Spirit is the form of the kingdom experienced today, the rule of God over hearts and minds in the same manner that Christ ruled over the hearts and minds of the apostles. Just as for them his rule was not merely their interpretation and assessment of time past but the defining condition of their present by his second history, so also does Christ's present-ness extend in the Spirit to us, as the determination of our time.

In this, the Spirit is not an abstract modality outside of time, a timeless principle, being, or way of being either for God or for the human, but the mode of true being in each here and now, as each here-now. Life *in* the Spirit is life *as* a disciple of Christ Jesus. It is holistic reiteration of the verberations, the thoughts, words, actions of the apostolic community, the realization of our being in the dynamic motion of their living, as an extension of that living:

> His past life, death and resurrection can and must and actually do have at all times the significance and force of an event which has taken place in time but is decisive for their [the apostles'] present existence. Hence they can and must and actually do understand their present existence as a life of direct discipleship; as their "being in Christ"; as a being done to death with him at Golgotha, renewed in the garden of Joseph of Arimathea, and on the Mount of Olives (or wherever the ascension took place) entering into the concealment

74. CD III.2, 467.

of the heavenly world, or rather into the concealment of God. Thus its continuation and formation here and now can only be a faithful imitation of their "citizenship in heaven" as it is already actualized proleptically in the man Jesus.[75]

In the event of Easter, the disciples see the assumption of a particular future, they see a life after death that is before them as accomplished, as now, as the present. They are confronted with the defeat of reality as they know it, even as they continue to live in this reality; they see the end of death even as they continue to stand on this side of death. And they proclaim what they behold. They declare the future *in* the now, *as* the origin, meaning, and goal of the now. Those who hear this proclamation, who find themselves in the citizenship of this kingdom, whose lives are taken up into the prolepsis of Easter and move at its cadence, stand among the dark as light to dark, as participants and bearers of a new reference frame relative to the old, which, again, still operates for them, too, therefore as utterly dependent on, yet redemptively contemporary with, the Lord Jesus Christ.

By the Spirit who raised him from the dead, Jesus is present. His is the time of our present as he reigns over the full range of our mortality, as he places us beyond death even though we die. "The day of His death was revealed on Easter Day to be the day of their life. And they now stand in the grey twilight before the dawn."[76]

Again, the Spirit is the present-ness of Christ Jesus not by mere recollection, but as determinative reality, as a life that becomes life for all humankind, as a light that gives light to the world. The Spirit of the Word defines reality according to the Easter history of the Word, bringing the full continuum of new possibilities into the scope of fallen human perception, actualizing that perception to apprehend a way of being that of itself, of its autonomous exercise, it cannot.

"Objectively and in fact He [Christ] Himself is the acting Subject who lifts the barrier of yesterday and moves into to-day, making Himself present, and entering in as the Lord. This is the inner connexion between Easter and Pentecost."[77] By his Spirit, Christ remains the acting Subject, the Word by which time came to be, the Reconciler of time to its Creator, the Redeemer

75. Ibid.
76. Ibid., 469.
77. Ibid., 470.

to which time at once comes and gives expression. He is Lord by being the prime actor and not the secondary object of action; by making history with the creature and not merely being the object of creaturely recollection.

Therefore, the Person and Work of the Spirit are together not merely the product of Christian recollection or tradition. Spirit is not the sum total culmination of Christian history, not the Synthesis of time in any sort of political triumph, social movement, or utopia. The Spirit, no less than Jesus, is the operative agent making time to be what it is, the object of God's intentions and the means by which he carries out those intentions. The Spirit is the contemporaneous Lordship of Christ, his presence in the church's determinative thought and speech by which time comes to be, here again, now again, *God's*. Being thus, he defines here-now according to the reference frame of life opposite death, of light opposite dark. "The community lives under the lordship of Jesus in the form of the Spirit."[78]

The Spirit is Spirit of time and true being to the degree that he is Spirit of the Word. To the degree that his being and doing in fact actualize ours, engage us in the full range of creaturely modalities, make our lives not only in time but also in reciprocal determination of time to submit in tangible ways to the lordship of Jesus—to the degree that his being and doing involve all of this, he is the Creator Spirit. He is not the Creator Spirit in any other way, in any timeless, extension-less, duration-less way of being, for we know of no such Creator. We know only of the Creator who exists as Lord of time, who has his eternal being in a determinative history, who makes time, and makes it to be *his*.

Time is the condition of being, not just the vessel, in that being is simply living according to the constituents that define existence. I have been speaking of this conjunctive reality in terms of perception, cognition, articulation, emotion, and kinesis. The Spirit of the Word actualizes these constituents, forming and framing them after the Easter reality of Jesus. He makes us to perceive reality to entail new possibilities, to think, speak, will, and move toward a new horizon of being, to live in a manner defined not by mortality but by resurrection, to be for *hope*.

In this regard, the Spirit gives time to the creature as he gives life to the creature.[79] "To be man is to live in time. Humanity is in time. This is involved

78. Ibid., 509.

79. "Given Time" is the second of five subsections comprising "Man in His Time" (see CD III.2, 511–53), each more narrowly assessing the character of time as constitutive of human being. As noted, Barth frames his account of time by analyzing the temporality of Jesus' life in the light of his resurrected history. He then differentiates Jesus' unique time from that of humankind generally and relates the two. Humanity is not lord of time but is constantly subject to the movement from darkness to darkness, from

in the fact that the being of man is his life, and that his life is reception and action, rule and service. If this life of his is real, so too is his time as the stage on which he lives out his being."[80] Creaturely being is not an abstract, static substance in which we participate humanly (anymore than the resurrected life of Jesus was an abstracted soul), but present-tense, embodied life. It is taking in and giving out, commanding and obeying in thought, word, and deed. These are inherently temporal modalities; the human does not receive, act, rule, and serve atemporally, but only in and through duration and sequence.

Apart from duration and sequence, the concept of "hope" is senseless. Hope entails an *after*, a tomorrow that is brighter than today and thus changes the configuration of today—the meaning of its events and the orientation of its creatures. In turn, duration and sequence are vacuous without hope, charity, ethics. The succession of creaturely moments comes to be with a *definite* end; it depends as a succession on an outcome. Life without tomorrow is no life at all, just movement from the vanishing nothing of yesterday to the groundless nothing of today to the ethereal ulterior of what may or may not come. "We might almost say that he is himself his time in the sequence of his life-acts. He is himself his time fulfilling itself in the sequence of his life-acts. So close is the relation between the real being of man and the real time in which he is."[81]

This is what I mean when I say that life in the Spirit is life as a disciple of Christ Jesus. To be truly human is to be temporally oriented in hope, to think,

the fleeting past to the unknown future. Nevertheless, in view of Christ the temporality proper to human being is validated as the form of God's activity in and with us. God gives us time as the means and manner of our living before him. He refuses our darkness *in time*. He comes to our darkness as light, as the Redeemer of our being in time, making us to stand face to face with him and at once move from darkness to light. The third subsection is "Allotted Time" (553–72). Here, Barth defines human being in terms of the unique past, present, and future that distinguish us as individuals before God. Whatever the makeup and extent of our lifetimes, the good news is that these are allotted to us by God as, again, the history needed for us to fulfill the lives given to us. The proper response to our histories is not dissatisfied longing for infinite time but gratitude and joy for the history allotted to us. Any dissatisfaction ought to be directed to the removal of those things that inhibit the fulfillment of our living before God. Our lifetimes, then, are bounded by a "Beginning Time" (572–87) and an "Ending Time" (587–640), the fourth and fifth subsections, respectively. We are conscious of the fact that on each side of our allotted time stands an abyss of non-being. We are not infinite souls but embodied creatures, always the unity of soul and body. That means that eternal life is graciously bestowed by God, not merely the return to a preexistent timelessness. And it means that our lives move toward a definite end; death is both the sign of God's judgment of sin and the boundary of our allotted time. It is the evil result of rebellion, and, in our return to non-being, it is our return to the life of God himself who called us out of non-being and gives us life. It is the tomb that will be opened for us too.

80. CD III.2, 521.

81. Ibid.

speak, and act according to the life-promoting dynamics of resurrection history. There is no other spirituality so far as the Christian faith is concerned, as there is no other Spirit besides the Lord of time, once more, no timeless deity into which we are drawn as fundamentally timeless entities, but only the God whose reality is to give and sustain life in the midst of death and non-being.

Reality (truth, being) is an event. It is the happening of God as God, God being who he is, the Lord who gives life and time, and therefore the corresponding happening of creaturely existence. Creaturely reality, in other words, is a secondary happening utterly dependent on the ever-prior, moment-by-moment instantiation of divine reality. We come to be as we are given the duration and extension required actually to live—to perceive, cognize, converse, will, and move—before God, which takes place only by God's prior self-giving for us:

> Time can and must be seen in the most intimate connexion with ourselves and our being and action. . . . What we have here is obviously an exact parallel to the other anthropological fact that man is as he has spirit, i.e., as he is established, constituted, and maintained by God as the soul of his body. Indeed, it may even be said that the fact that we are in time and have it is simply another aspect of the same fact. What emerges in both is that man is not God, but a needy creature of God. He does not have his existence and nature autonomously, but as they are given by God. . . . To say "man" or "time" is first and basically, even if unwillingly and unwittingly, to say "God." For God is for man as He has time for him. It is God who gives him his time.[82]

Humans are not autonomous entities, but partakers of the Spirit. We have being to the extent that we are given spirit, which is the same as saying that we have being to the extent that we are given time. We do not possess reality, truth, being, spirit, or time, but dis-cover our selves as real beings only as God continues to establish his reality here-now. We are only insofar as he is. Only as God is present, as he is present-tense and not timeless, are we present. We may be unwilling to say it, or unable, but the fact remains that apart from him we come from nothing, head toward nothing, and therefore existentially are nothing. Only as God comes to be with us and to set us before him do we have a future that gives meaning and orientation to our yesterday and today.

82. Ibid., 525.

Barth does not conceive of the absolute dependence of all being on God in a pantheistic way, but again, dialectically. Both God and creation have their respective beings in the act of God's turning to what he is not, or in the exercise of God's lordship over all, including himself, but as such, the beings of God and creation are dependent on God's elective self-determination. God wills to be thus, to bring a secondary reality into the existence of his primary reality, and thus remains the free Lord even in this determinative act. His being is being-for-us not by static necessity but by dynamic, moment-by-moment choice.

In short, the God who elects from all eternity to bring existence into being outside himself and relate to it self-consistently elects the same today or there is no creaturely reality. The Creator is the Reconciler is the Redeemer, not modalistically, but three in one. What he does today and therefore who he is today is the same as what he did and who he was in 1–30 c.e., and what he did and who he is in eternity. As Spirit of the Word "he is the same yesterday, today, and forever" (Heb. 13:8):

> Primarily . . . it is not we who are now but God who is now: God who created us and is in process of rescuing and preserving us; God who is not dismayed at our sin, and does not cease to be for us, nor reverse our determination to be for Him and in mutual fellowship; God in all the defiance of our unfaithfulness by His own faithfulness. He is now primarily; and we secondarily.[83]

CONCLUSION

God today is the selfsame Lord of history. He is this in speaking again as he has always spoken, now in the proclamation of his church. Just as he took flesh and mortality to himself, but as the omnipotent Word, so also does he assume language and human wisdom, but as the omniscient Spirit. He comes again as light to dark, as life to death. As he generated the flesh he assumed in history, so does he generate the language of his contemporaneity and vindicate it in the redemption of all things.

The Spirit continues to act as and be the giver of life among death and non-being in the moment-by-moment proclamation of Christ's victory over the grave in that he makes this proclamation to occur and be heard. The victory took place by the Spirit (Rom. 8:11). Its declaration takes place by the Spirit (1

83. Ibid., 529.

Cor. 12:3). Its hearing takes place by the Spirit (John 16:8-15; 1 Cor. 2:6-16). The Spirit is the condition of our living in Christ's life; as he was the condition of Christ's resurrection history, so is he the condition of that history becoming our own. He has his identity in this act of bringing life to death, reality to non-being, possibility to impotency, of redeeming what has been made according to the reconciliation accomplished in and by Christ.

To be as exact as possible, the event of God being God today is the proclamation of the Gospel. God has his being as Spirit in the lowliness of his church's witness to Christ, in the frailty of its all-too-human contingency, but also in the power of its message to transform humanity, to make it alive, real, and true. This coming of God to humanity is neither more nor less than reiteration of his being, of his turning to time as the eternal Lord, of his being Immanuel. The being of humanity simply happens in and with this ongoing event of God's being.

It is certainly the case that this truth, this life and time of the church takes place in the midst of falsehood, death, and darkness. The light shines among the dark. He comes to his own, but his own do not receive him. A life comes to a humanity that is unwitting of it and that is unwilling to acknowledge it. But that does not alter the message in which we encounter very God and our true selves. Being no less contingent upon the gospel for its being than the world is, the church may never proclaim Christ's Lordship triumphalistically. But it also may never be cowed away by the world from its proclamation to the world. With full humility and with full confidence in the power of its message, the church must say again by the Spirit what it has heard by the Spirit, that Jesus Christ is Lord to the glory of God the Father.

Whether that message is heard again, whether falsehood is brought to truth, and whether non-being realizes being in obedience before God are not things that the church makes to happen.[84] The messenger is not to be confused with the message. Truth and being are a matter of convergence between the

---

84. And it is not a principal concern of the church to prognosticate about the fate of those who remain unwitting of and unwilling to acknowledge their being before God. The church cannot of course ignore the word of judgment spoken by Christ, and it cannot neglect the fact that there truly is no reality, no truth or being apart from the event of God's being for us, which fact suggests that if we are not to face ultimate destruction then we must obediently respond to Immanuel. But not knowing and not desiring God do not negate the fact that he is Creator and Lord, that our being is in his hands from before the point of any knowing and willing, that we remain in his hands after our faculties of cognition and volition break down, that even being allotted the time not to know and not to love God is elective grace, that it is precisely in Immanuel that we comprehend the full range of grace's triumph and see that God will not finally be overrun by our secondary election to death and non-being. Thus, even for the unwitting and unwilling world, the Christian lives in hope and evangelizes not out of despair and threat

Spirit of proclamation and the Spirit of hearing, of words brought forth in this light and received in a corresponding light. That is as much the case for the world in this moment as it is for the church in this moment.

This is where Ellul and Einstein are helpful interlocutors. They enable us to comprehend the event ontology of truth, reality, being, and time in the proclaimed Word. Truth, reality, being, and time—all various ways of thinking and speaking of the same thing, hence we use the singular verb form—*is* a dialectic, a coming-to-be-again. It is the ongoing convergence of object and subject (in this order), which has a determinative effect on the object and its subject. The Spirit is the presence of God again, not differently than his presence to creation in Christ and in his eternal self-election. He is God not alone, but God-with-us, self-consistently the one who places his being in the event of proclamation and response. In its turn, space-time comes to be as the field of this God's life-acts. It has its truth only here, in the moment of the Spirit making it to be the realm of his reign, which is to say, in the moment of its coming-to-be for him. This coordinated happening, which again takes place in the ongoing event of Christian witness as a decidedly temporal modality, is redemption, the life and work of the Spirit.

(too much nineteenth-century American evangelism was mislead about this, a tragic legacy that continued into too much twentieth-century American evangelism) but out of joy and expectation.

4

———————

The Spirit of Being and Becoming

The Holy Spirit is the presence and Lordship of Jesus Christ Himself in the visible form of this [biblical] witness.
–Karl Barth[1]

Human reality is an event contingent upon the event of God *being* God, or more precisely, reality comes to be with the continued execution of God's decision to exist as Creator, Reconciler, and Redeemer; to give life where there is none, to make his life with that life as its Lord, and to bring that life into unity with him. Time itself, then, is an event. It is the theater in which God lives as he has purposed and continues to purpose. It is the modality in which he summons creatures to existence before him, according to which modality these creatures live and move and have being. Their being is a series of life-acts taking place within the temporality given in God's life-act, which co-determine that temporality.

Living in disharmony with God is therefore rebellion not only against God but also against life and time. To make oneself primary and God secondary, that is, to make oneself real and God possible is to place oneself outside of time. It is to negate one's own being by thinking, speaking, willing, and acting according to an artificial event sequence, engendering false consequences. It is to bring about and participate in a movement from nothing to nothing.

If humanity would truly be, which is to say, if it would encounter truth and take part in it, then it would discover itself within the movement of God's history. God confronts us *here and now* as he confronted the apostles and the patriarchs. He speaks here and now as Lord just as he did there and then. He establishes his own reality and draws us into it; he makes his covenant with humankind and so makes us *to be* his contemporaries.

---

1. "The Authority and Significance of the Bible: Twelve Theses," in *God Here and Now*, trans. Paul M. van Buren (1964; London: Routledge, 2009), 58.

He does this in spite of human infidelity. In spite of our open rebellion against God and time, in spite of our predilection for non-being, God self-consistently comes to us, has his being with us, and gives us life. In spite of the fact that we do not know him and are unwilling to love him, he knows us and loves us as his own.

In his contemporaneity, then, God acts as he has always acted and continues to have his being in this act. As Spirit, God has his life in the field and form of temporal relationship, of being our Lord precisely in the ongoing happening of human thought, speech, willing, and acting. Concretely, as Spirit, God has his life in the church's witness to Christ Jesus after the words of the prophets and apostles; he is inverberate as he was incarnate.

This chapter further develops these basic themes by focusing on two critical components of them. First, it gives more detailed consideration to the dialectical character of *time*. It explains how time is at once the *subject* of God's revelation and the *object*, that is, how it is at once the condition by which God speaks redemptively and, as the condition of our being, the object of redemption. In this, it also addresses how we live in rebellion against time, on the one hand, and come to time (being) as God's redeemed, on the other.

Second, the chapter elaborates on the event of the Spirit as the truth of church proclamation. It takes up Barth's insights from Göttingen concerning the three iterations of the Word, which were discussed in chapter 2, by locating and expounding on their reappearance in CD I.2. It shows that our possibility, our coming-to-be, is an act of hearing that corresponds to the act of God's speaking in proclamation of Scripture.

BARTH'S EXEGESIS OF JOHN 1:10-13

EN TŌ KOSMŌ ĒN, KAI HO KOSMOS DI' AUTOU EGENETO,
KAI HO KOSMOS AUTON OUK EGNŌ.

> He was in the world, and the world was
> made through Him,
> and the world did not know Him.

We noted in dealing with v. 1 that the existence of the Word, which reflexively defines the existence of God, is characterized by its being *en archē* ("in the beginning"). In and as his Word, God is understood according to that initiative, decision, and act by which God brings being out of nothing. Verse 10 echoes this reality. Barth notes that it constitutes something of a complement to v. 1. "With the necessary caution one might say that [v.1] refers to the transcendence of the Logos, [v. 10] to its immanence in the world."[2] Verse 10 restates the nature of the Word relative to creation, now emphasizing that creation is not merely the object of the Word but also the subject. The Word is alive insofar as he exists in actual, meaningful, determinative relation to what he has made, as his being is defined by engagement with the world, in responsive relation to it, that is, command, receipt, interest, discipline, and empathy. The Word was in the world.

"It is important to note, however, that the *en tō kosmō ēn* of this verse understands the immanence as an event in contrast to permanent immanence."[3] Barth observes that if we are not to lose the transcendence of v. 1 in the immanence of v. 10, then we must not construe the Word's being in the world as a given condition. The Word was in the world *as Lord*; he remains self-determining agent even in the determination of his existence among the here and now. *En tō kosmō ēn*—he *was* in the world, and he *came* to his own (v. 11). He is not of the world or a possession of its citizens. The Word is not some constant variable of creaturely being and doing, but a self-governing, living modality. That the Word's engagement and response might take place as they have taken place—that he is and will be in the world as he was—is a function of God's volitional self-determination to be this way, of his pledge or self-giving, not a calcified inference from the logic of necessity.

"It is act or action," Barth continues; it is not "a continuous relation."[4] We cannot, having perceived a glimpse of God's being-with-us in the revelation of his Word, allow ourselves to freeze it. We cannot abstract an ontology of "relation" from encounter with the Word and affix "God" to it. That would obviously enough amount to nothing but the great contradiction of human being once more rearing its head: to thinking, acting, and speaking as if, having perceived God and our dependence on him, we now have him to perceive again according to given constructs of mutuality. It would be to slip as usual into the darkness of self-priority that defines us.

But again, just as the past-tense coming of God prevents us from freezing his relation to time as a given quality of his being and instead makes us to confess that it is an act of his will to be with us, so also does it make us to expect

2. Barth, *Witness to the Word: A Commentary on John 1. Lectures at Münster in 1925 and at Bonn in 1933*, ed. Walther Fürst, trans. Geoffrey W. Bromiley (Grand Rapids: Eerdmans, 1986), 63.

3. Ibid.

4. Ibid.

his coming anew. *En tō kosmō ēn*—he was *in* the world. In having his being in this relation, God has shown us his determination to be with us and thus fostered our anticipation and in fact need of his continuing to be such a God, to be again in the world and come again to his own. The Word participates in the world that he made as its origin, means, and hope; he is immanent to that which he is at once transcendent. He assumes the time over which he is Lord and, in fact, has his Lordship in just this assumption, just this act. The Word is immune neither to history nor to a-history but exists as Lord of history. This also must be acknowledged if we are not to slip into the dark reversal of divine and human being. It must be said that God exists in the power of his coming to us, in his *authority and ability* to be neither dependent on nor independent of us, to be God today as he has always been, subject only to his will even as he exercises that will in determinative relation to us, indeed *as* he exercises his will here-now.

God today is once more the God who exists as life before death and non-being, light among the darkness. As Spirit of the Word, he continues to have his being in the *event* of coming to all that he is not.

EIS TA IDIA ĒLTHEN, KAI HOI IDIOI AUTON OU PARELABON.

He came to His own, and those who were his own did not receive Him.

Verses 10b-11 make a parallel claim: although the world came to be in and through the initiative, decision, and act of God, in and through the Word, it did not recognize God in his coming. Though the Word came to that which belongs to him, his possession by right of creation, his own did not receive him. "He belongs to [the world and its inhabitants] by right. They ought to receive him willingly and joyfully as one who is at home with them. For they themselves belong originally to him. They ought to see that they stand in an original relationship to him. But they do not. The absurd thing stated in v. 10c takes place and becomes an event."[5]

God has his being in bringing life and being out of nothing, and creation thus has its being in a contingent relation to this action of God. But the absurdity of creation is that it neither knows nor receives God's vivifying work.

5. Ibid., 67.

It thrusts itself into ontological contradiction, refusing its own being as it refuses its source of being.

This is not a strictly past occurrence, which now plagues the world. The fall of creation is not just a tragic misjudgment made by two people in a primal moment of shortsightedness that cast a catastrophic shadow over history. History itself is made up of the sequences of creaturely self-contradiction. Humanity's refusal of its Lord is an ongoing *event* in its contemporary refusal of the Word. Here and now, the primal reality is reiterated. God comes to his own, his place and people, the world and its inhabitants, and is rejected by them.[6] But he remains self-consistently God in the world's self-deluding, self-compromising act of rebellion. The Spirit of the Word refuses our refusal.

Thus more fully comprehended, history per se is the field of God's activity as Lord over all being. Time is *both* the outcome of God's external turn and the stage on which he exercises that turn in refusal of human rebellion, in constructive opposition to the empty hostility of chaos, in remaking what he has made by rejecting its unmaking. From humanity's perspective, then, time is the condition, the means by which it exists *both* in rebellion and in redemption. It is the means, manner, and substance of the life-acts that comprise both our descent into non-existence and our being raised into authentic being and doing.

6. Barth considers but does not agree with the interpretation of v. 11 that understands *ta idia* as a reference to the people of Israel. He acknowledges that "decision is not easy" and that such a reading enjoys the support of figures like Augustine, Calvin, Cocceius, Zahn, and Harnack, but concludes with Holtzmann, Heitmüller, and Bauer that this reading "would be strangely isolated and unmotivated and unfruitful" in the context of the prologue; see ibid.

HOSOI DE ELABON AUTON, EDŌKEN AUTOIS EXOUSIAN TEKNA THEOU GENESTHAI, TOIS PISTEUOUSIN EIS TO ONOMA AUTOU, HOI OUK EX HAIMATŌN OUDE EK THELĒMATOS SARKOS OUDE EK THELĒMATOS ANDROS ALL' EK THEOU EGENNĒTHĒSAN.

> *But as many as received Him, to them He gave the right, to become children of God, even to those who believe in His name, who were born, not of blood nor of the will of the flesh nor of the will of man, but of God.*

We are not merely to say of the human world that the darkness did not comprehend the light, that the world did not know the Logos, that his own did not receive him. There has also to be said the further and positive thing which comes into the world like a miracle, the inconceivable reality which finally and definitively confounds it, namely, that he gives to some the possibility of becoming the children of God.[7]

Barth considers vv. 12-13 to form "a first climax in the prologue"[8] in that they convey God's triumph over the darkness, the breakthrough of the Word. God will be God. He finally and definitively reigns over all that would not be ruled. He makes a nativity out of sullied ground; he perseveres in desertion and brings about ontological persistence, psychological, biological, genetic steadfastness amid self-abandonment; in the deep, before a hardened propensity to nothingness, he brings forth offspring.[9]

We encounter the universe as inhospitable, in fact in the vastly greater part of its expansiveness we find it to be hostile to biochemical life. Why

---

7. Barth, *Witness to the Word*, 69.

8. Ibid.

9. Although Barth could not have endorsed Einstein's pantheism, one can imagine Einstein, with the necessary qualifications, endorsing Barth's theism. Einstein was comfortable using God-language and thinking of the universe in genetic terms because he was struck by the universe's persistent comprehensibility, by its not-to-be-lazily-assumed accessibility to human thought and speech. That the universe exists in an organic relation to us, susceptible to our grasping and continual reframing as it remains wildly beyond and precedent to our cognition, volition, and so on, was a philosophical hurdle that Einstein could not surmount.

should such life exist and persist on earth and perhaps elsewhere in the universe amid a seemingly overwhelming, unmanageable, chaotic predilection to no-life? Barth's thought echoes this rhetorical question: God's existence just is the relentless giving of life amid death.

The being of God is not *abstractly* "event," but the *concrete* effect of transforming children of the dark into his offspring, into creatures who think, speak, and act according to the light of the Word. His existence today is in *this* event, which is triune-ly one with the event of creation, whereby he brought being out of non-being, and reconciliation, whereby he brought life out of death.

Correspondingly, the being of humankind is not *abstractly* "event," but the *concrete* coming-to-be before God. Our being today is in *this* event, of thinking and speaking and acting in the biorhythms of the Word, of obedience to the Father rather than self-compromising disobedience, of resurrection hope for life and goodness rather than grave despair of evil and mortality, of being redeemed.

God's triumph and our corresponding redemption, however, are not a *synthetic* outcome, which is to say, it is not as if God's victory over non-being, death, and human rebellion is the (Hegelian) synthesis of God's creating, fidelity-to-Self-and-creature, and eternity, on the one hand, and our uncreating, infidelity-to-God-and-self, and temporality, on the other. Triumph and redemption are not the assimilation of rebellion into God's life-act, transforming him into a kind of higher "God-form," but uncompromised refusal of that rebellion. They remain *dialectically* related to our rebellious non-being. That is because they are simply the continuation of the same reality in which God has always existed relative to what he is not: his actualistic living *as Lord*.

God will have his existence as he has always had it, namely, in the *exercise* of his power among and over all that is alien to him, and in this the *giving* of his power to that which cannot and will not receive it. We must understand the time of creation and the time of redemption in terms of reconciliation; the past and future obtain meaning and direction in terms of the present reality of God bringing forth children of light from among the darkness. We can only comprehend who God was and will be, and who we were and will become, in view of his Lordship here and now. This is the comprehensive determination of Easter time.

God exists and is known as God in the power of translation, his making flesh and assuming it and his living thus, and in this, fully corresponding to it, his making thought and speech and assuming them as the condition of our living thus. We only know God as God in this happening:

> The divinely effected existence of these believers is the answer to the question whether the world can hold out and close itself to the Word. The divinely effected existence of believers replies that the world cannot do so, that the Word is mightier than the world. But only the existence of believers, and this only as divinely effected, makes this reply. There is no answer at all alongside this wholly "actual" answer.[10]

God is God in the power of his turning to us—this is revealed and accomplished in the exercise of that power. It takes place in the wholly actual event of faith. It does not stand outside this event either as its distant origin or distant outcome but willingly takes place in and with this event. The origin and outcome of revelation are comprehended only in the moment of revealedness, in the instant that God exists and is known as Lord, that in exercise of his power over what he is not he gives to that reality a share in his life, in his power to turn outside himself, so that it may see him and love him.

Thus, if we are to know God according to his revelation and not according to the darkness of human self-contradiction, then we cannot abstract to a time before time or a time after time, to a time of creation or a time of the eschaton, that is not grounded, framed, and informed by the time of reconciliation. God has his eternal existence in the concrete effect of making believers *out of nonbelievers*, of making the living *from among the dead*, of bringing forth children *out of the depths of nothing*:[11]

---

10. Barth, *Witness to the Word*, 70

11. It is not possible to think of God as a living being without delimitation of being. (If "in eternity" there is nothing but God, then there is nothing but God!) But this is a positive and not a negative delimitation, which is to say, it is a form of self-realization in self-constraint, of achieving maximal living, so to speak, in and through maximal life-giving. Concretely, God has his being and is known as God in the moment that he creates and sustains dimension for another and lives in relation to this other. Beyond and behind this moment, we cannot think. We act as if we can think of a realm beyond and behind God-with-us, as if temporality is a mere interlude in an inert and all-encompassing eternity, but that is the consummate invention of human religious imagination. It takes but a mustard-seed quantity of introspection to realize that such a realm and such a god are nothing but the inversion of temporality and creatureliness with an exception made to accommodate the world and its inhabitants. It is the manufacture of a very inconsistent deity, for there is no living alongside or in opposition to a truly infinite god so conceived; the only living of such a god is this god's living—no sequence, no this then that, no "time" before creation, "time" of creation, and "time" after creation, for there is no time at all! To sequence eternity and grant humanity a segment in this sequence is already to project temporality onto god, all the while declaring god's a-temporality. By contrast, for us really to live and move and have

There were and are those who indeed live in the world like all the rest but who receive him, who believe in his name, and who in so doing show that in principle the darkness, the hostility of the cosmos, is opposed and defeated. They do not do this by their own strength or deed, but because their existence when they do so has its origin totally and directly in God himself and nothing else.[12]

God's opposition to and defeat of darkness and cosmic nothingness take place and are known strictly in those who are of this darkness, who live in the world, yet receive him. It is in just this active reception, this divinely effected being, that God is known as God. Barth here thinks of being in terms of temporal actualization, for these children of the light do not receive the Word on their own count, but *when*, which is to say, in the moment that they *are made* to receive him. Their reception of the light comes with the light and only happens directly in it. Thus, all being is contingent upon the prior act of God opposing non-being and overcoming it.

God has his being in the act of refusing death and non-being, this in himself and in repetition externally, in which self-consistent repetition the world comes to be. So far our account of God according to his Word: God is the event of existence in opposition to nonexistence, which happens and is known in the moment that entities in the world accept the Lordship of Jesus Christ. There is no reality (of God or humanity) outside of this event, only falsehood or cloaking of reality under the illicit darkness of personal lordship.

Humanity correspondingly has its being in the event of knowing (*ginōskein*) and believing (*pisteuein*) the Word of God, which persistently comes to it.[13] Of ourselves, or better, as creatures of darkness (for strictly speaking

---

being in God, not as God, demands a *consistent* self-limitation on God's part. It demands a deity who has his living in the forfeiture of his living that he might give life. It demands Father, Son, and Spirit, respectively, existing and known in the coordinated event of revelation, revealer, and revealedness.

12. Barth, *Witness to the Word*, 69.

13. By incorporating *knowledge* into his exegesis of 1:12, Barth reflects the fact that *ginōskein* and *pisteuein* form a hendiadys in John (cf. 6:69; 11:22-25; 14:5-14 [cognate in John is the relationship between seeing and believing: 2:23; 9:38; 20:29; see also 1 John 2–3 concerning knowledge and obedience]). The two terms convey a singular meaning: to know God is to trust and obey him, and to trust and obey *God* (and not an abstract projection of deity) is to know him in Christ Jesus. "Whether *ginōskein* is put above or below *pisteuein* in John is hard to say. Perhaps both are true. Knowing is the basic act of discovery which always precedes faith as an attitude or *habitus*, but which always follows it too, both opening it up and also crowning it" (ibid., 71).

there is no "of ourselves"), we do not know and believe in his name. Knowing and believing come with God's coming to the dark. They presuppose receiving (*lambanein*). "*Ginōskein* is enlightenment, *pisteuein* is brightness, and *lambanein* is the aptness of the subject for both these experiences, which cannot be distinguished chronologically. *Hosoi elabon auton* thus signifies an *event*."[14] Knowledge entails clarity, and both assume aptitude for what is revealed. Being is the occurrence of this aptitude, or the receiving of receptivity, we might say. It is the event of "those," entities made definite by the right, by being given the power to become children of God.

The power truly to live, truly to command and obey, truly to rule and to serve, is an entirely given and derived power. It is the *exousia* by which God lives, commands, and serves. It is the reverberation of his self-repetition, by which the world exists, in the thought, speech, and acts of his people, that is, *in*, but not *of*, the world's existence:

> The Word gives them a new essential character, his own character. Their action becomes a grasping of the Word, their attitude a Yes to it. Their *exousia* to be God's children lies in this gift, this self-giving of the Word. . . . It is not at all that they are already there as *lambanontes* and *pisteuontes*, and for this reason can become God's children. They are *not* there! *Skotia* is there and not the *exousia* for this existence. The cosmos is there, *anthrōpoi* are there, *unfaithful idioi*, who do not understand themselves as such, are there. Into this non-being the light comes—Let there be light, and there was light [Gen. 1:3]!—the *exousia*, the right to be children of God.[15]

It is not the case that humans exist and may or may not come to stand in relation to God as children by virtue of an extant disposition toward or away from him. Darkness exists. It must receive the light if it is to become a recipient of the light, if it is *to be*. We must be given the potency, the right and authority to be. Human being is the happening of this potency, this *possibility* attendant upon God's *reality* in the event of the Word.

"The possibility [of being God's children] is given solely by the Word itself. *The Word* convinces, converts, forces, and decides. The Word is subject

---

14. Barth, *Witness to the Word*, 71. (italics in original).
15. Ibid., 74.

and not object in this action. *Gratitude* is the last and deepest thing with which such people can grasp their existence."[16] Genuine human existence is postlude not prelude or interlude. It is doxology; when and where there is praise to God for life, then and there is life, for then and there is the Word by which all things exist.

God has his being in giving life. It is as simple as that, and as complex! The giving by which God exists and is known is present-tense. It is the constancy of his initiative, decision, and act, the steady exercise of his unrivaled power, which happens and is recognized in the actual lives he brings about. Thus more fully, God has his being in the *event* of giving life, in and with the beings that he makes to be. There is no God behind or beyond this event.

Thus, there is no Spirit behind or beyond the Word. And there is no Word behind or beyond the Spirit. It is, once more, only in the wholly actual event of faith that God exists and is known. There are two sides to the real dialectic by which Christianity stands or falls, neither to be subsumed into the other. God has his being in coming to humanity, which happens in bringing humanity to be before him. There is the action of God *in* its reception, the exercise of his power *in* its bestowing, the revelation of God *in* its revealedness. "The revelation of redemptive life demands that people be open, that they be ready for perception; the light that shines demands an eye that sees, the spoken Word demands receptivity, reason."[17]

We can and, if we are not wrongly to assume a native capacity for him, we *must* think and speak of God in terms of the Spirit's life and work. But we must first think and speak of the Spirit's life and work in terms of the Word's life and work, for the actuality by which God exists is revealed here and not elsewhere, here and not in any disconnected experience of "spirit" or whatever. The Spirit simply is the reverberation of God's external self-repetition in the Word, his being in the world, coming to his own, refusing their refusal of him, which takes place in the thought, speech, and acts of his people. He is the condition and form of receptivity to God by which God speaks forth life, by which God is Immanuel. He is the power and action of the Word, by which God exists and is known as God. As Spirit *of the Word*, God exists and is known in the time of his acts, in his history with humankind.

And again, we exist authentically and are known in truth only in this Spirit, only in the defining life–act of God. Only in the reality of God as he establishes

16. Ibid., 75.
17. Ibid., 71.

it in Christ Jesus here and now do we have any grasp of who we are and who we might be:

> Those who receive and believe in v. 12 confront their own existence
> as such as a miracle, a creation of God, from their own standpoint
> a new birth, the beginning of a new existence. The truth of their
> existence, which has been initiated for them by the Word which
> per se convinces, converts, and compels, is a miracle, a creation, a
> new birth. It is so in relation to the existence of the cosmos that is
> covered by darkness, to their own existence insofar as it belongs to
> this cosmos. In no way can they know that they are established and
> exist as receivers and believers except of God.[18]

The realization of genuine humanity takes place in the event of faith, in the miracle of the Word to convince, convert, and compel responsive obedience. Taking place in and conforming to this event is one's knowledge of it; recognition of oneself as addressed by God, coming to awareness of oneself as his child is simply part of the work of the Word. It transpires in and with the reverberative power of the Word, its actual authority over living consciousness, its power to reorient our thought and speech even at the level of self-understanding and awareness. It is the action of the Word, or more exactly, the life and work of the Holy Spirit.

The Spirit of God is the reality of God in his life-act precisely as a life-act that involves us. Precisely as the being of God in the work of re-creation, the Spirit frames the world; he sets it on its foundations in that he makes us to be citizens of *God's time*. He rewires our neural circuitry such that we know all things in and through the Word—as coming from the Word, being governed and sustained by the Word, and returning to the Word. As we find no other basis for existence than God's Word—and this is the significance of John's emphatic refusal of any other ground of being (in blood, flesh, or will)—we discover our every possibility in God's reality:

> This is the last and supreme thing that John has to say about the
> work of the Word in its *erchesthai eis ton kosmon* in v. 9; with the

---

18. Ibid., 82–83.

authority that only God can have it presents to us the completed fact that we are of God and only of God. It sweeps all other foundations from under our feet and sets us on this one alone. It robs us of all the security of self-contemplation that does not consist of seeing ourselves as put in our place by God. It gives the *exousia* to burn all our ships behind us, to raise no more claim to genius, to know that we are secure on the far side of every natural self-understanding.[19]

"Reality" and "Possibilty" in CD I.2

This book's guiding theme is comprised of two components. The first concerns Karl Barth's directive that contemporary theology should orient around the Holy Spirit. I have argued that Barth's coaxing cannot be taken as justification to dismiss, ignore, or otherwise move beyond his own focus on Christ Jesus. To read him as intending such a thing would entail sacrificing one of the greatest achievements of his life's work, namely, his triumph over the liberal tradition in which he had been trained and its ingrained tendency to confuse the human spirit with the Spirit of God. If Barth's gains are to be appreciated in an adequate Third Article theology, then the Holy Spirit must be thought and spoken of in terms of God's self-determinative life-act. He must not be known in abstraction from God's Word, God's revelation *as God* in direct confrontation with the hollow "revelation" of the transcendence of Man. The Spirit must have his life and work in making Christ known as Lord, in being the power and authority of God's revelation today as ever. He must be here and now what he has always been: Spirit of the Word.

Indeed, if we take Barth not to be encouraging dismissal of his core gains over liberal theology, but rather directing us to a more properly triune account of the Spirit in unity and distinction from the Father and the Son, then we can identify in Barth's own work a pneumatocentric complement to his christocentrism. We can return to an earlier phase of his development—phase 3 in McCormack's periodization—in order to lay out a framework for understanding the Spirit from which we can then think and speak constructively of God and humankind. We can distinguish certain features of thought, which are of such significance for Barth that they animate and reappear throughout his life's work and may similarly animate and shape our own.

19. Ibid., 84.

Specifically, we see that at the heart of Barth's understanding of God is the *Realdialektik* of God's engagement with space-time. God's assuming flesh in Jesus of Nazareth is of structural import for our thinking and speaking, because it is determinative of who God is as God. God has his being in the event of coming to humanity without forfeiting his deity in so doing. In fact, God has his deity just in the Lordship of this event. Here and now, wherever and whenever he is present as being *among* non-being, light *among* darkness, life *among* death, he exists in unrivaled freedom and authority—bounded and limited neither by eternity nor by time, neither by some ontological need of deity for transcendence nor by some ontological need of humanity for immanence, but self-determining in the eternal act of coming to time, of being God-with-us.

Second, then, this book presents a constructive proposal; it functions as the prologue to a larger theology of the Third Article. By demonstrating that the Spirit must be understood in terms of the real dialectic of the Word, that we must also think and speak of the Spirit as God coming to space-time without losing his deity in so doing—that the Spirit has his identity in continuation of God's life-act in Christ, or we might say, in a parallel life-act of assuming the specific thought and speech that he generates and shapes in witness to the gospel—it builds a foundation on which to conduct further thought and speech of God. The Spirit is God inverberate, not—and this point cannot be overstressed—*not* an additional revelation alongside God incarnate but differentiated continuation of God's revelation in the Word made flesh. He is the living contemporary of the Word by being divine contemporaneousness, God here and now, the power and authority of Christ Jesus today as he was in 1–30 c.e. and has always been.

The Spirit is God a third time, the Redeemer who makes real and brings to culmination God's Lordship over non-being, darkness, and death. For instance, he is, as we began to discuss in the last chapter, the *Creator* in that he makes *time* to be the theater in which God summons entities to life before him, as well as the "as-which" of God's covenant history. God remains Lord over time as he assumes time in the Spirit, having his life in and with the cadences of loving union, which he generates "in the beginning" and sustains in ongoing rejection of human rebellion.

Working to identify this pneumatocentric complement to Barth's christocentrism, we have considered several relevant writings from his corpus. We have been guided throughout by detailed interaction with Barth's commentary on the Gospel of John, specifically, his work on the prologue of John 1:1-18. This important but largely neglected material from Barth's third phase has again and again turned our attention to the living contemporaneity of the Word. God's Word is not just a past speaking but the dynamic life-act by which God wills to be God. It is his ongoing Lordship, which as such engages creation across time. He really comes to exist again as Lord here and now as he always has been. This livingness of God, his coming again to what he is not and making his all-determinative dwelling among us, is the life and work of the Holy Spirit. The Spirit is Spirit of the Word as he builds the kingdom of Christ Jesus across space-time, bringing all things under his reign.

Penultimate to works of Barth's third developmental phase (that is, exhibiting the *an-enhypostatic* orientation of that period while still operating within the earlier dialectic of time-eternity) are lectures on "The Need and Promise of Christian Proclamation" and "The Word of God as the Task of Theology." These works taught us that thought and speech of God in Christian proclamation and theological reflection must take place *a posteriori*, after the fact of the Word and in conformity to the Word, if they are to be true. If our ongoing thought and speech of God are accurately to reflect the life and action of God, then they must reiterate the dialectic of judgment and grace, God's loud "No!" in condemnation of human sin and his louder "Yes!" in forgiveness of that sin. They must confess their utter inadequacy and relativity as fallen and shortsighted human productions, and their redeemed adequacy and stability in the *promise* of God. They must find their content again, each day anew, in the reality of God's persistent coming to humankind, which is to say, in the movement—the generative summons and sustaining breath—of the Spirit of the Word. This Spirit wills not to have a life and work independent of this movement, but again, in assuming the witness to the Word that he generates and sustains.

This *reality* of God, to be Lord over non-being, darkness, and death in the persistent life-act of speaking all things into existence and holding them in being by the inverberate modulations of his eternal Word, determines all *possibility*—God's and ours. That and what God might be are given in Christ Jesus. An adequate Christian eschatology, as Barth showed us in the Göttingen Dogmatics, is governed by the same Lordship of Christ taking place and experienced in history. It is defined by the same, consummate refusal of every force of nonexistence. The God of tomorrow is the same God of yesterday and today; the Spirit who hovered over the chaotic abyss, who regenerates our dead minds and hearts by illuminating them with the light of the Word, this Spirit will raise our bodies from the dead and enable authentic, responsive, moment-by-moment loving union with God. He will not suddenly be the Spirit of atemporality, but the re-creator of time in and through his assumption of time.

This is not "merely theological" speculation. Time is susceptible to reformation. Einstein helped us to recognize both the objectivity and subjectivity of time—that it becomes what it is. Time is a co-determined modality. It exists both as measure of the events of our world and as byproduct of those events, given in the relationships of motion and observation that fill space in every instance. Thus, the heralding of time's remaking is not some alien incursion into the land of the physical sciences by an overreaching, overinvasive concept of deity.

Quite the contrary, as Barth showed in CD III.2, it is an overreaching, overinvasive humanism that brackets time off from God. The Christian God exists as Lord of time; this, again, in the coordinated action of assuming the time that he makes. God's reality simply is this action and is thus a *historical* reality. God's determinative life-act is not a timeless datum, but an event, which as such entails a "coming-from," a "happening-among," and a "heading-toward." God's reality involves a definite past, present, and future, which, while taking place simultaneously in God's living, nevertheless define his living in willful, covenant relationship with sequential creation. There is no God above or beyond the God of time. God "will be" this God. He will have a future, and it will be determined by his gracious engagement with us in the present.

CD III.2 provides a nice illustration of the way that a defining construct emerging in Barth's third phase—the irreversible direction from God's reality to all possibility—continues to inform his thought through the fourth and final period of his development, and thus why we cannot simply work off of assumed breaks in Barth's thinking to build a pneumatocentric theology, but must attend closely to instructive continuities. We have not, however, fully addressed the emergence of the "reality/possibility" schematic in phase 3 and thus will now return to what has to be considered the ultimate work of this time period, CD I.2 (1938).

The second part-volume of *Church Dogmatics* is the production of an exceptional theologian in magisterial command of his material. Barth was fifty-two years old when it was published, entering the middle portion of his vocational life and at the height of his intellectual powers. He had a clear sense of the direction that his doctrinal work would take, with two unsatisfactory attempts behind him, as we have seen, and the first part-volume of the new approach appearing six years earlier. Subsequent texts would arrive in rapid succession; the next three part-volumes would be made public within seven years of CD I.2, so that collectively between 1938 and 1945, Barth would publish more than twenty-five hundred pages of systematic theology, not to mention the essays that he authored and talks that he gave during this time, as well as the staggering letter correspondence that he kept.[20]

CD I.2 demands special consideration given the central importance of its subject matter and its thematic connection to Barth's earlier work. The entire part-volume is dedicated to the threefold form of the Word of God, which Barth introduced in Göttingen and we addressed in chapter 2. It comprises three lengthy chapters on Revelation, Scripture, and Proclamation.

A couple of items emerge immediately in comparing Barth's treatments of the Word in the Göttingen and Basel Dogmatics. First, the latter is considerably more expansive. It is approximately three times longer than the former, and it covers a wider range of relevant material.

In fact, the second thing that surfaces in setting the two treatments side by side is the inclusion of a major subsection on the Holy Spirit. Barth subdivides the chapter on Revelation into two parts. One deals with "The Incarnation of the Word"; the other with "The Outpouring of the Holy Spirit." God's determinative life-act, his self-revelation, is a coordinated movement. His coming to time consists *both* of his assuming flesh in Christ Jesus *and* the giving of his Spirit, of his being an object before us, but not just any object. God stands before us in Christ *as Lord*, as the object that makes all others to be and to be known in truth. God's revelation also consists of his generating the perceptual framework by which we may see him in Christ, thus in bringing about and assuming continued thought and speech that bear obedient witness to him. This comprehensive act of revelation simply is God's reality.

Barth's treatment of these ideas in CD I.2 is more thorough and consistent. Significantly, Barth changes the breakdown of subtopics concerning

20. For letters that have been collected and published from this period, see the following volumes of Barth's *Gesamtausgabe*: vol. 1, *Barth–Bultmann Briefwechsel 1911–1966*; vol. 15, *Offene Briefe 1945–1968*; vol. 33, *Barth–Brunner Briefwechsel 1916–1966*; vol. 36, *Offene Briefe 1935–1942*; and vol. 43, *Barth–Wilhelm Adolph Visser't Hooft Briefwechsel 1930–1968*. For the sermons that Barth gave, see vol. 26, *Predigten 1935–1952*. Future volumes will contain additional material from this time frame, including lectures and smaller writings (thus far the *Gesamtausgabe* contains works of this kind up to 1930), as well as letters exchanged with individuals not mentioned here. (A somewhat dated but still helpful overview of the plans for the collected works can be found at the Princeton Seminary library page, Center for Barth Studies: Hans-Anton Drewes, "The Future of the Complete Edition," trans. Matthias Gockel, https://www.ptsem.edu/library/barth/default.aspx?menu1_id=8457&id=10851). Meanwhile, see the bibliographies in the *Festschriften: Antwort: Karl Barth zum siebzigsten Geburtstag, am 10 Mai 1956* (Zurich: EVZ-Verlag, 1956); and *Parrhesia: Karl Barth zum achtzigsten Geburtstag, am 10 Mai 1966*, ed. Eberhard Busch et al. (Zurich: EVZ-Verlag, 1966). See also the comprehensive online bibliography offered jointly by institutions supporting Barth research internationally at barth.mediafiler.org/barth/index_Eng.htm.

Incarnation and Spirit as well as the order in which he handles these subtopics, in order better to reflect the claims he had been making about revelation. In Göttingen, Barth moved from "The Possibility of Incarnation," to the "The Historicity of the Incarnation," to "The Reality of the Incarnation," and then to "Incarnation and Revelation."[21] In Basel, he is clearer that one can speak of the possibility of Incarnation only in the light of the reality of Incarnation, which is to say, that the possibility of God's becoming man is given in his actually becoming man, not any theoretical account we might give of "deity" and "humanity." It is given in God *himself*, hence the possibility of Incarnation just is the real birth, life, death, and resurrection of Christ Jesus. Jesus Christ is "the objective *reality* of revelation" in the opening subsection of CD I.2, and *therefore* "the objective *possibility* of revelation" in the ensuing subsection.[22]

In other words, Barth reverses the order of treatment from Göttingen—now moving from *reality* to *possibility*—to better reflect the claim that, as we noted, he was already making then: that we can only think and speak of God's life-act in full encounter with that life-act. And Barth clarifies that what we are encountering in that life-act is the actual existence of God, his self-determination, which defines all subsequent possibility, that and what he can be and that and what we can be before him.

In Jesus Christ, God reveals himself to humankind, specifically as the God who *can* reveal himself, who is not subject to the limits of deity or humanity, who is not lost in eternity or time but who is eternal God in history, Immanuel, God with us. "The incarnation of the eternal Word, Jesus Christ, is God's revelation. In the reality of this event God proves that he is free to be our God."[23] God shows us his unique freedom as God in the exercise of that freedom. He is not constrained by notions of autonomy on the one side; he is not "God" because he is free from all things, existing in perfect *aseity*. And he is not constrained by notions of human incapacity on the other side; he is not "God" by making himself a datum that we can understand. His accommodation is not to our native capacities of experience and reason, but in remaking our capacities as he addresses them. God is God in a third kind of freedom, beholden neither to independence nor to human need, but living in moment-by-moment self-determination, exercising unlimited right to limit himself, reigning in submission, remaining Lord in the form of a servant. That is his self-determinative reality:

21. Barth, *Göttingen Dogmatics*, 131–67.
22. CD I.2, 1–44 (italics added).
23. Ibid., 1.

God is not prevented either by His own deity or by our humanity and sinfulness from being our God and having intercourse with us as with His own. On the contrary, he is free for us and in us. That is the central content of the doctrine of Christ and of the doctrine of the Holy Spirit. Christology and Pneumatology are one in being the knowledge and praise of the grace of God. But the grace of God is just His freedom, unhindered either by Himself or by us.[24]

The revelation of God is the event in which God causes himself to stand before us and causes us to stand before him. God has his existence in this event; his God-ness is just his freedom to move himself toward us and to turn us to him. He is Lord in this coordinated action, neither unable to move toward us because of his eternity nor unable to turn us to him because of our temporality. He reigns over eternity and time by being unconstrained by either in the event of revelation. He lives and reigns this way in the life and work of Christ and the Spirit.

The life and work of Christ are bound up with the life and work of the Spirit and vice versa. God's standing before us and his making us to stand before him are *together* his grace. Confession of Christ is knowledge of grace. Confession of the Spirit is obedient thankfulness for grace. The one confesses God's objectivity, his freedom for us, the second his subjectivity, his freedom in us. The one acknowledges God's making himself perceptible as a human; the second, his making humanity to perceive him as God.

This means that God's objectivity, as we saw in chapter 1, is a subject-determining objectivity. It is not that in Christ God just stands before us as an object in space-time. No, he stands as Lord of space-time (invisible in his visibility) and so transforms us, refusing our sense of self-priority and placing us after him. Thus, we cannot really separate God's objectivity from his subjectivity. We cannot distance his standing before us from his turning us to stand before him. We cannot separate the Word from the Spirit as if they were two distinct beings. They are one being differentiated only as to their relations of opposition.

The Word is God's address to us, which address involves us. God's speech situates us as his own and denies us any kind of self-sustaining existence apart from him. So the Word is only God's Word in the factual happening of Christ's power and authority. The Spirit is God's address in us, the power and authority of the Word, the content and shape of perception that is responsive to the Word, a manner of observing all things as being from the Word and reflecting

24. Ibid., 2–3.

upon them in the light of the Word. So the Spirit is only God's Spirit in the factual happening of Christ's standing before us.

But we say all of this only in encounter with the enfleshed Word. There is reciprocity between Word and Spirit, yet direction from the Word to the Spirit. Our understanding of God in his revelation is structured after the enfleshing of the Word and not after some kind of intuitive or extrasensory encounter with "spirit."

We think and speak of God's freedom *for us* and *in us* strictly on the basis of encounter with the first, God's objectivity or freedom *for us*, and not the second, God's subjectivity or freedom *in us*. The first never takes place independently of the second, but the first remains the basis for our understanding of the second, not vice versa. We think and speak of the life and work of the Spirit in terms of the Incarnation, not the other way around lest we lose the Spirit in our subjectivity and en-Word the flesh.

God's unique freedom in Word and Spirit is comprehended according to the real dialectic of the Incarnation. It is here, in this singular reality, that we encounter God having his being with us, that he reveals himself as delimited neither by deity nor by humanity, but is Lord over both. How do we know that God can stand before us? How do we know that he can move in us? The answer to both questions, the basis of both Christology and Pneumatology, is the same: Jesus Christ. The event of God's being is given in this reality. The reality of the Spirit is thus shaped after the reality of the incarnate Word. He is, again, the eternal event of Inverberation. We will come to the reality and possibility of the Spirit later, which is to say, we will consider how the Spirit is both the subjective reality and possibility of revelation in due course.

First, what does Barth have to say about the reality of the Word? How is the Word the objective reality of revelation? Or, more exactly, "How does the encounter of His revelation with man become real in the freedom of God?"[25] That is the question that Barth contends must be asked and answered above all others.

The question itself is complex. By "encounter of God's revelation with man," Barth is referring to the concrete happening in which God actually meets the human being. He is speaking of that factual confrontation, when and where God exists as God, delimited by neither deity nor humanity but having his being in and with the creature. This happening is obviously enough a matter of God's freedom. It is an event that has to be "real in the freedom of God," which is to say, it has to be an unfeigned, bona fide moment in the life of God.

25. Ibid., 3.

Otherwise, in what sense would God's confrontation with humankind actually amount to *revelation*? If God's being in and with the creature was not authentic to God's life, if it was in any way extraneous to him, alien to the freedom in which he moves as God, then in what sense would it convey actual knowledge of God? Unless God's movement to and among the creature genuinely defines the reality of God, unless it is real in his freedom, then there is no revelation in the act of revelation.

Our question, then, is *how* encounter with God's revelation is real in the freedom of God. How is it that God is God in the event of confrontation with Man? The answer, as I have been indicating, is not that God is God according to some capacity in Man, in human being and doing. God is not the living Lord only when his Lordship meets some organ of the divine within the human. God is God in the event of confrontation with Man *by God*. God's God-ness consists of the fact that he *decisively wills* to reveal himself in and with Man, that he is not unable to will this, but is free to do so. God is God in the event of confrontation with Man by being God in this event, which is to say, God is God in the event of confrontation with Man by the truth of the Incarnation:

> The approach to Christology is affected by the realization that first we have to put the question of fact, and then the question of interpretation. Or (because interpretation is involved in the question of fact, and nothing but fact is involved in the question of interpretation) we must first understand the reality of Jesus Christ as such, and then by reading from the tablet of this reality, understand the possibility involved in it, the freedom of God, established and maintained in it, to reveal Himself precisely in this reality and not otherwise, and so the unique possibility which we have to respect as divine necessity.[26]

The first question that has to be asked about revelation concerns the fact of revelation, not theoretical possibility. It concerns, again, how revelation is *real* in the life of God, not how it is possible. And the answer to that question *is* the reality of revelation. Theology reads from the tablet of the God-Man, understanding God's freedom in the light of his decisive action in Christ Jesus. It begins with revelation even in its attempt to understand revelation.

26. Ibid., 7–8.

Barth is not bashful about the circularity inherent in such a method. He simply is thinking through the ultimate basis for true thought and speech of God. That basis has to be God. Even when theology undertakes to adjudicate the nature and content of "revelation," it must find itself within the movement of revelation. It cannot suddenly occupy a point outside of God's own thought and speech, as if now, with regard to this topic, reason or experience might be an adequate means of knowing God, as if how God is God in his confrontation with Man might be adjudicated outside of that confrontation.

To know how God is God in his act of revelation, we begin with that act, with Jesus Christ, lest we supply our life-acts in his place. "This name is God's revelation, or to be more exact, the definition of revelation arising out of revelation itself, taken from it and answering to it."[27] We begin with the *fact* that God is God in this Man, that he has his deity in this flesh.[28]

The objective reality of God's revelation consists of "the twofold statement, that God's Son is called Jesus of Nazareth, and that Jesus of Nazareth is God's Son."[29] If we are restricted by God in our every comprehension of God, if our every concept of what constitutes God's God-ness is given in the exercise of that God-ness, in God's factually being God, then we are bound to confession that God is God in the coexistent unity of full deity and full humanity. Our thinking is bound to confession of the name, "Jesus Christ."

This name itself has authoritative dominion over human thinking and speaking as the name to which God's covenant history refers. For Barth, we know God entirely in "Jesus" the "Christ," which is to say, in a dialectical process of acknowledging the genuine humanity of God alongside the genuine divinity. The very name enforces this way of thinking; it turns our attention, on the one hand, to the man of Nazareth called "Jesus" and, on the other, to the Word of this flesh, the one whose origins are of old (Micah 5:2), the "Christ":

What we hear about the name Jesus Christ is witness about God's Son who became a man, about the man who was God's Son, one related to the other, but not in such a way that the first ceases to be the first or the second to be the second, nor in such a way that the

---

27. Ibid., 10.

28. Barth understands the best of classical and medieval theology to have operated under this procedure. "*Credo ut intelligam* means that in view of the fact that in faith God's objective truth has met and mastered me, I am determined under the instruction of this truth alone to give an account of the encounter in thought and speech" (CD I.2, 9).

29. CD I.2, 15.

first and second dissolve into a higher third. Our task is to hear the second in the first, the first in the second, and, therefore, in a process of thinking and not in a system, to hear the one in both.[30]

The dialectic of human thought and speech of God is not a system but a living process of cognition given in the real dialectic of God's being God in *Jesus Christ*. It is not, therefore, a Hegelian dialectic, where thesis is subsumed into antithesis, say, the deity of God is subsumed into the humanity, forming a higher synthesis from which we might construct a new understanding of "God." No, the highest thought and word that can be had and said of God are his self-thinking and speaking in the Word made flesh. The Incarnation is not a jumping-off point whereby we might surpass revelation. It is not the means by which we may gleefully and triumphantly set revelation aside—rejoice! God has made himself human that we might think and speak of divinity in terms of personal transcendence, in the experience of struggle and victory, *Sturm und Drang, Geist und Volk*—but the substance of revelation, its exclusive, special content and form.

If we think of *Geist*, Spirit, we must do so according to God's defining objectivity. This is such an important point for Third Article theology that its making warrants the risk of overrepetition. We never graduate from the Son to the Spirit; never are we justified in thinking and speaking of God in abstraction from the incarnate Word, even in behalf of the Spirit, for God's reality is given in the incarnate Word. "God's freedom for us men is a fact in Jesus Christ. . . . The first and last thing to be said about the bearer of this name is that He is very God and very Man. In this unity He is the objective reality of divine revelation."[31] We do not know what we are thinking and saying of God's freedom, of what it means for God to be God, if we do not start from the objective fact of the God-Man.

In the unity of the God-Man, God exists as God. He is who he is; his revelation is real in his freedom to be this God. That reality, then, is the basis of God's possibility. God's revelation with humanity not only takes place in his freedom, but also, reciprocally, it shapes his freedom. How God might be God is given in the way that God is God. God's freedom is not an abstract postulate, not an outcome of a given system of logic or a feature of a given experience in the world. It is, rather, his real power and authority to be God with what is

30. Ibid., 24–25.
31. Ibid., 25.

not God, to retain the majesty of his eternal existence in the servanthood of his temporal history.

As indicated, Barth transitions in CD I.2 from "Jesus Christ the Objective Reality of Revelation" to "Jesus Christ the Objective Possibility of Revelation." In the latter subsection, Barth asks a parallel question to the one that guided his thinking in the former: "How in God's freedom is it possible for His revelation to encounter man? How far can the reality of Jesus Christ, i.e., the unity of God and man indicated by this Name, be God's revelation to man?"[32]

One can answer this question, again, only on the basis of the fact that revelation has occurred, and so only in the terms of that reality. It is possible for God's revelation to encounter man, for Jesus Christ really to reveal God to us, only because God's revelation has encountered man, only because Jesus Christ has revealed God to us. Only because God has been this God do we now confess that he can be this God.

If this was not the case, if we were not constrained in our thought and speech by the event of God being God with us, thinking and speaking exclusively from Immanuel outward, then we would be imparting some alien potency on to God, constraining him according to possibilities constructed, inevitably, in our vision of the feasible, achievable, doable. We would wind up explaining "revelation" as an activity and content that met up with a given understanding of the world scientifically, historically, philosophically, or psychologically. The great majority of "God's" being would be beyond this understanding, so that the *deus revelitas* would always be overshadowed by (and not dialectically related to) the *deus absconditus*, the knowability of God by the hiddenness of God. But that would obviously amount to restricting God's freedom by our capacities, making him to be free for us only insofar as he operates within our constructs.

It is just this order of thinking from ourselves to God that revelation, precisely in its objectivity, corrects. God is not hidden to us only in those areas that he operates beyond our capacities for experiencing divinity, but in every area of our lives, for revelation shows us that we have *no* capacity for divinity. Thus, God is manifest among us not in those areas that we have a capacity to see and know him, since these are none, but in each place and moment that he determines to have a capacity for us:

Revelation itself is needed for knowing that God is hidden and man blind. Revelation and it alone really and finally separates God and man by bringing them together. For by bringing them together it informs man about God and about himself, it reveals God as the Lord of eternity, as the Creator, Reconciler and Redeemer, and characterizes man a creature, as a sinner, as one devoted to death. It does that by telling him that God is free for us, that God has created and sustains him, that He forgives sin, that He saves him from death. But it tells him that this God (no other) is free for this man (no other).[33]

We cannot think and speak of how God might stand before us by taking an inventory of ourselves and our world and then locating him partly in those areas that afford empirical verification, rational explanation, or experiential validation, yet mostly in those crooks of our being and cosmos where mystery reigns. God, if he is really to be the free Lord, is not captive either to our abilities or to our inabilities, to our knowledge or ignorance, to those areas where comprehension is sure or to those areas of existence that presently lack for adequate explanation. Were this the case, then the death of God would in fact be imminent, if not already realized, as modern atheism impatiently proclaims, by the steady march of science, philosophy, history, and so on into the territories and fortresses of mystery in which the greater part of God had been imprisoned by the pious. (It may prove to be the case that piety should thank critical scientists, philosophers, historians, and so on, not for killing God but for liberating him from its principalities and powers.)

More to the point, God is hidden by God in his revelation. This is the paradox of the Incarnation; God veils himself in his unveiling. He takes on the flesh of a servant and discloses himself, just in this flesh, as Lord of all flesh. The boundary between time and eternity, humanity and divinity, is not fixed by temporal human being, but by the eternal God precisely in coming to the temporal human. In this act, God shows who and what he can be. He discloses the truth that he is not bound to eternity or time, to deity or humanity, but is Lord over his God-ness and our human-ness. And in this, he affixes a once-for-all line that we may not cross. Now, just here, he shows that he is no God that we have comprehended or can comprehend, that he is not the confirmation of our humanity or the fitting referent to our mysteries, but that our every comprehension of his God-ness and our human-ness is given by him. He shows that we are in grave need of him; that we possess no being of our own, that we

33. Ibid., 29.

rebel against our very source of being, and that we are bound for death. But he shows us this by giving us being, by forgiving our sin, and by raising us from the dead, that is, by being God in Jesus Christ. The mystery of God and the knowledge of God are given together in the revelation of God.

God's every possibility is given in the reality of the incarnate Word:

> To the question how far the reality of Jesus Christ can be God's revelation for us, the only fundamental answer is: As far as the reality of Jesus Christ requires for the revelation of God to us. What we need, what is necessary for this, follows from what Jesus Christ can do. He can do exactly what we need. And what He can do is all that we need. The possibility of revelation is actually to be read off from its reality in Jesus Christ.[34]

Christ Jesus sets the parameters of who God can be and who we are and can be before him. Just in his factual existence, he is the answer to the question of how in his revelation God is free for us, or as Barth formulates it, how our encounter with revelation is both real and possible in the freedom of God. He is the unlimited limit of God's being and ours. He is the condition by which God exists relative to what is not God, to non-being, darkness, and death; he is the beginning and end of God's God-ness and our humanity.

Christ is the break and the bridge, *God* as God for us. The eschatological boundary between time and eternity is not a border arbitrarily set by time at its linear end. It is rather an infinite and qualitative break set by God moment by moment in the act of revelation, in his coming to time. It is Jesus Christ. Although not yet comprehensively realized, the eschaton is already happening as an experience in God's self-determinative life-act; it is given with the *reality* of God in Christ Jesus as the event horizon of his every *possibility*. There simply is not a way of thinking and speaking of God except in response to Christ Jesus, no spirit of the eschaton that is not one with God's reality in the time of Christ.

Time, which is the modality according to which we think and speak of God—the cadence of our words and the distance separating and defining our acts of perception—is given by God in his revelation as the condition of our knowing him. "Time" is not a given construct in which humanity passes existence, in opposition to "eternity" as an equally given construct in which

34. Ibid., 31.

God exists. God establishes the sphere of his existence and that of humanity, along with the boundary separating them, in each instant that he exists as God among humanity, that he crosses the boundary. We only know the constitution of the boundary between eternity and time—that it exists and how it might exist—as God reveals it to us in coming to man; that and how he is not man, that and how he is hidden, is given with his being man, revealed.

We cannot assume a particular time concept as basic to human existence, the negation of which forms our eternity concept. Eternity is not mere negation of time, as God is not the mere negation of Man. We do not delimit his possibility by making it to be the inverse of our possibility. God is God in establishing his own possibility in and with his lived reality in Jesus Christ. In each instant of his existence, God is free for man, and as such, he is, again, Lord of time.

Jesus Christ is the comprehensive, objective possibility of revelation. Barth follows this subsection by treating "The Time of Revelation."[35] He begins this section rejecting both a classical account of time in Augustine and a modern account in Martin Heidegger.[36] The shared failure of these otherwise distinct understandings of time is that each figure "regards time definitively and unequivocally as a self-determination of man's existence as a creature."[37] For Augustine, "time" is simply the given distention of a human soul; the room of a soul's movement in the external world. It is composed of expectation and recollection, but one's own. It is not expectation and recollection of the incarnate Word, not a movement determined primarily by God and only secondarily by the human in relation to God, but of one's distinct past and future. Time is made by humanity in the acts of anticipation and memory. Hence for Augustine, "it would be an intolerable anthropomorphism for God Himself to have to possess time and have time for us, by time becoming a determination of Himself in his revelation."[38]

35. CD I.2, 45–121. I focus here on the first portion, "God's Time and Our Time" (45–70). Barth extends his thesis concerning "revelation time" (God's time for us alongside created time and fallen time) to show how this new time moves from a past ("The Time of Expectation," 70–101) to a future ("The Time of Recollection," 101–21). The former is the prophetic time of the Old Testament; the latter, the apostolic time of the New Testament. The one looks to the coming of Christ; the second bears witness to his arrival. Our time in confrontation with God's revelation, our fallen time is met with this movement. God's revelation restructures our horizon of possibility after his own as we think and speak according to the prophetic and apostolic testimony to Christ. We discussed how this is so in the previous chapter; see especially my treatment of CD III.2.

36. See Augustine, *Confessions*, XI; Heidegger, *Sein und Zeit*.

37. CD I.2, 46.

38. Ibid.

For Heidegger, too, time comes to be with human being. A little more precisely, time is the modality by which the existential agent realizes her true being—the means by which there are such things as *Angst*, resolve, and achievement. Each of these states of being-there presupposes a preliminary and posterior, a present that is always a moving from a past to a future. Time is thus the condition of possibility, the framing of *Dasein*. Hence, "that there should be for us anything like God's time might in the framework of Heidegger's thought be little more than a quite superfluous metaphor."[39]

Barth's problem with Augustine and Heidegger is not that they offer subjective accounts of time. We noted in the last chapter that Barth leaves ample room for human determination of time and, reciprocally, of time's determination of the human. But for Barth, time is *co*-determined by human existence. Primarily, time is determined by *God's* existence, and exists itself ultimately (and reciprocally) in determination of God's existence. (To say that God gives a share of the power of his life to another is not only to say that he causes an "other" to exist, but also that he causes that other to exist in such a way as to exercise a kind of determinative effect on his life. Just that is God's unique freedom, just that his power and authority as God, just that the possibility of God's being God according to his reality in Christ Jesus, just that the contemporaneity of God by the Spirit of Christ Jesus.)

In Christ Jesus, God has time for us. His eternity is not atemporality. "If we are to understand revelation time . . . it must be regarded as a proper reality, as accessible to God as is human existence. A time concept which denies this cannot be of service to us."[40] We cannot construct an account of time out of given humanity, to which God is immune, or which is superfluous to his deity, such that his revelation to humanity constitutes an invasion into time by a timeless entity. It is in this concrete revelation, in his coming to humanity in the man Jesus, that God is God, and so he is God in assuming time as he assumes flesh. "'The Word became flesh' also means 'the Word became time,'" Barth writes.[41] God reigns over time as he lives temporally, as he takes time into his living and reigning.

A time concept given by God in his decisive life-act divides time into three spheres. There is created time, the state and operation of God's primal address to non-being and darkness in which he brings about life and light and relates to it. There is fallen time, the state and operation of human rebellion and inclination to non-being and darkness. And there is revelation time, the state

39. Ibid.
40. Ibid.
41. Ibid., 50.

and operation of God's being-for-us, of his refusing our predilection to non-being and darkness and reconciling us to himself:

> Between our time and God-created time as between our existence and the existence created by God there lies the Fall. "Our" time, as Augustine and Heidegger in their own ways quite correctly inform us, is the time produced by us, i.e., by fallen man. . . God-created time remains a time hidden and withdrawn from us. If God's revelation has a time also, if God has time for us, if we really (really in a theologically relevant sense) know and possess time, it must be a different time, a third time, created alongside of our time and the time originally created by God.[42]

Humanity does in fact have its being in time, as Augustine and Heidegger rightly observed. But its time is the movement from nothing to nothing, from the abyss of non-being to the darkness of death. If humanity is to enjoy actual, authentic being and life, to move from non-being to the fullness of being and from death to life in abundance, then it would have to be constituted in a new time. It would have to live and move in the life and action of the Reconciler.

So, God has "time for us." Barth intends a double entendre by this phrase. Obviously enough, in his revelation God makes time for us in the conventional sense. He places himself in proximity to us and patiently waits on us. But in having time for us, Barth also means that God lives on our behalf. He creates a new time, the time of our restoration to him, by his coming to us and being with us. "God's revelation is the event of Jesus Christ. We do not understand it as God's revelation, if we do not state unreservedly that it took place in 'our' time. But, conversely, if we understand it as God's revelation, we have to say that this event had its own time."[43] God stands before us in the sequences of the world we know, but as we have been saying, he does so as Lord over this world. He shows us a world that we have never known in and with this world; he shines the light of the world's redemption in the dark cadences of human thought and speech. He is God in *time*, yes, but *God* in time, the maker of a new time in each instant that he encounters us in fallen time.

42. Ibid., 47.
43. Ibid., 49.

God's life in Christ Jesus is a substitutionary *life* in every sense. It is God's living for us (with us and in our behalf), making the thought structures, speech-acts, and overall cadences of being that in our rebellion we have unmade, confronting us with this new way of being, thus at once showing us the old in the new and overcoming it. God is God just in doing this; he is God in his determinative revelation:

> We must emphasize the fact that God has time for us because . . . he reveals Himself, i.e., proceeds out of a veiling and unveils Himself. . . . The veil of which we must speak in this context is general time, the old time, our time, so far as He assumes it in order to make it—and this is the unveiling—His own time, the new time. . . . Neither the old nor the new time exists abstractly and solely as such; they exist because the new time which already exists triumphs over the old which therefore still exists also. This triumph, this act of victory in which the victor already exists and the vanquished likewise still exist, this transition from the Old Testament to the New Testament, from the old aeon that ends with the cross of Christ to the new one that begins with His resurrection—this transition is revelation, is the light of fulfilled time.[44]

Even that we have time for rebellion against God takes place in God coming to us; old time happens only in the event of God taking it to himself as his veil, which he does *not* to affirm the essential nothingness of that time, but to put it off, to unveil his proper time in fulfillment of fallen time. Even that we have time for distorted notions of self is given in the fact that God has time for us, that he lives his being in the life-act of Jesus Christ.

God has time for humanity because he self-determinatively reveals himself to humanity. Time is part and parcel of his existence because it is the veil of his unveiling, the history in which his eternal grace and truth are made known. More exactly, it is the old history giving way to the *new* history (and thus the newness of history itself); the time of life, the happening of victory over death. God's being is in this victory; he lives his being in self-consistent, fully actualized refusal of non-being, darkness, and death in that he comes to time but as its Lord and Maker.

44. Ibid., 56.

God's history with man in Christ Jesus is of ontological import because of the sequential motion, the temporality it entails; it places all being, God's included in motion from old to new. God wills to have and so does have his existence as light coming to darkness. In turn, we have no living, no authentic temporality and no true being outside of this divine life-act, external to the reciprocal movement from darkness into the light. Our genuine existence simply is this transition (*transition*, not yet accomplishment):

> Time, and, with the time of revelation itself, the time also of the person making the statement, has found its Master; it has come to be mastered time. He who makes this statement has ceased to have any other time as such. . . . In his own time he is aware of this fulfilled time, and in this awareness he has become contemporary with it, a partner in this time and so a time-partner or contemporary of Jesus Christ, of the prophets and apostles. . . . If we are contemporaries of Christ because of His act of lordship in revelation, then as contemporaries of His apostles in recollection of Him we can only look back upon this time of ours as the lost, i.e., already essentially past time of the old aeon, really only in its passing. Nevertheless, so far as it continues as such still to be our time, what else can our business be in this time than with the prophets to await Him?[45]

We come to stand as creatures before God in awareness of his standing before us, which is to say, in his mastery over our time, and therefore being, that takes place in contemporaneous encounter with Christ Jesus, in the event of faith and obedience. We become contemporaries of the enfleshed Word as we move within the testimony of the prophets and apostles. As our thinking and speaking are brought into conformity with theirs, as we concretely *anticipate* Christ by *recollecting* his life, ministry, death, and resurrection, we transition from life defined by the horizon of mortality—the movement from dust to dust—to life determined by the limitless sustenance of grace—from life to the plenitude and fulfillment of life.

We do not hastily leap out of our fallen time into the time of fulfillment. No, we exist in the transition from the one to the other in correspondence to the victory in which God exists. We live already as citizens of the Kingdom of

45. Ibid., 59.

Light, yet still under the tyranny of night. We reiterate in the biorhythms of our being the victory over death by life as persons who live proleptically, *toward* resurrection, but resurrection from *death*. We promote life and reflect the light as *mortal* citizens of this present darkness. Yet again, we really do promote life and reflect the light; this, when and where we live in obedient conformity to the life and light of God in Christ Jesus. "The grace and mercy of God, which become effective in that He has time for us, i.e., His own time for us, answer to the long-suffering of God whereby He leaves us time, and our time at that, to adopt an attitude to this condescension, time, that is, to believe and repent."[46]

Authentic humanity, the determinative life-act of the creature in conformity to the life-act of the Creator, takes place in the act of *believing*, in *repenting* of our sin and grasping again in ever-new concepts, words, and actions the forgiveness of that sin. We do not realize our true being by presumptuously grabbing after eternity as the negation or inversion of temporality; it is lazy science fiction that sets as the goal of humanity the permanence of its *now*, or that thinks of "heaven" as the infinitizing of finite human life. Precisely the opposite, genuine humanity is realized in repentance of all the ways that we would make and sustain our own living and create divine existence out of that living.

In short, divine reality is determinative of all divine and human possibility. That direction is Barth's first non-negotiable in opposition to his liberal forebears, who operated in the reverse. This direction, second, is given exclusively in Christ Jesus. He alone determines the shape, structure, and content of "God" and "Man." All reality, God's included, is given in him. Time itself, the revelation time by which God moves to us and the fallen time that is known only in this move, the very constructs according to which humanity has any right cognition of divinity and humanity, is given in Christ. There is therefore no possibility for thinking and speaking of the Holy Spirit as God among humanity except as the Spirit of Christ.

The time of God in Christ Jesus is determinative of his life in the Holy Spirit in that it makes that life to be the concrete action of creating faith in Christ, bringing humanity to authentic existence by rendering it obedient to his Lordship; of generating ongoing thought and speech that recollect Christ's life and anticipate his coming again; of creating and sustaining time-partners or contemporaries of Jesus. We cannot think and speak of the Spirit himself in any other way without necessarily thinking and speaking of God's life in

46. Ibid., 68.

another way, a thesis that lacks any basis other than in the old aeon, in the self-compromising, self-contradictory abyss of human self-contrivance.

Barth can move to consider the subtopics of "The Holy Spirit the Subjective Reality of Revelation" and "The Holy Spirit the Subjective Possibility of Revelation" only after treating the Incarnation. We must continue to follow him in this path.

"What is the meaning of revelation as the presence of God Himself, so far as it is not only an event proceeding from God but also an event that reaches man[?] . . . The object of this question we call 'the subjective reality of revelation.'"[47] God's revelation really does encounter the human. God's freedom for us involves the reality that we become free for him, that we actually and truly hear and obey. But again, this corresponding reality is given in the prior reality of Christ Jesus. To understand our freedom, both how it is real and possible for us to hear God's voice and live in a manner that is appropriate to it, we cannot start with given notions of human freedom. We may no more presume "autonomous choice" to be the necessary agency of humanity qua humanity any more than we were allowed to do so of deity. God's revelation does not encounter us only when we permit it, only when out of an artificially assumed self-actualization we say "yes" to God. As if we could! As if we possess independent existence opposite God out of which we might decide independently of his Word!

"If we remain objective and so pursue our thinking in this area, one thing can and must be regarded as fixed *a priori*. This freedom of man's can only be a freedom created by God in the act of his revelation and given to man. In the last resort, it can only be God's own freedom."[48] Even considering the *subjective* reality of revelation, Barth expects us to remain *objective*! He expects that our thinking and speaking of the freedom of the human to respond to God, the coordinate life-act in which we come to enjoy true humanity, are given *by God* in revelation. It is neither more nor less than reiteration of God's own life-act, enjoyment of his own freedom, the gift of his life to us.

This is a decisive claim for Pneumatology. If the Holy Spirit is the subjective reality of revelation, and that reality is neither more nor less than God's own freedom in the life-act of Christ Jesus, which is given to the human, then the Spirit can be neither more nor less than reiteration of that life-act in the corresponding life-act of human thought and speech concerning Christ Jesus. There is simply no basis for us to think and speak of the Holy Spirit except

47. Ibid., 204.
48. Ibid., 204–5.

within the real dialectic of God's own thought and speech given to us, which is to say, except within the living revolution of the Spirit's life *precisely as content and reiteration of the Word*:

> Subjective revelation can consist only in the fact that objective revelation, the one truth which cannot be added to or bypassed, comes to man and is recognized and acknowledged by man. And that is the work of the Holy Spirit. About that work there is nothing specific that we can say. We can speak about it only by sheer repetition, that is, be repeating what is told us objectively, that "God was in Christ reconciling the world unto himself."[49]

All we can say of the defining life-act of the Spirit is what we must say of Christ Jesus, that in him God is Lord over non-being, darkness, and death. We can make this claim—it is possible that these words can be effectively formulated—only because it first was said to us. The subjective reality of revelation is given in the objective; the content of the life and work of the Spirit is given in the life and work of the Word. It is only by Christ being made real to us that we know ourselves before God in this history and so co-determinatively set ourselves to participate in its motion. That is to say, paradoxically, it is only by the Spirit's movement in *us* (Christ being made real to us) that we think and speak of the Spirit as the Spirit of *God* and not of ourselves, as the coming of God to us, really *us* today as he came (was made real to) them in the past. The Spirit can only be Spirit of the *Word*.

He is God a third time precisely in being the contemporary reiteration of the defining life-act of God in the Word—his self-consistent refusal of every force of nonexistence. The Spirit's life-act is one with the life-act of the Word. Thus Barth says, in a citation that should be underscored by anyone wishing to conduct pneumatocentric theology after Barth: "He is not a Spirit side by side with the Word. He is the Spirit of the Word itself who brings to our ears the Word and nothing but the Word. Subjective revelation can only be the repetition, the impress, the sealing of objective revelation upon us; or, from our point of view, our own discovery, acknowledgement, and affirmation of it."[50]

---

49. Ibid., 239.

50. Ibid. I noted in chapter 2 that a statement like this admits of two interpretations in light of Barth's later call to Spirit-centered theology. One is to take it as "typically Barthian christocentrism," which his

To regret, lament, or be uneasy about the fact that the Spirit is exclusively Spirit of the Word, that there is no basis on which to think and speak of the Spirit except the life-act of Christ Jesus, that the Spirit is the contemporary power and authority of the Word, which is to say, the ongoing freedom of God made known and exercised, exercised and made known in Christ, is to miss the core reality of the Christian faith. It is a pitiful distortion of the gospel when Jesus becomes decentered; a vacant, impotent, anthropocentric, counterfeit message emerges whenever and wherever a "spirit-center" is sought for theology that is not one with its essential Christ-center.

We do not lose the Spirit in following Barth, but seek him where he may be found. We encounter the Spirit in the same act of revelation that determines God's existence in the beginning and in 1–30 c.e., in the same elective self-determination to be God-with-us. We encounter him in the corresponding act of making us to be-with-God, to stand before him in faith and obedience:

> As distinct from objective proclamation we are not here abandoned to quite a different field of inquiry. . . . The fact and form of the coming of God's Word to man so that man becomes a hearer and a

late-in-life summons to pneumatocentric theology intends for us to abandon, overcome, or correct. In that case, we might think of the Word as "Word of the Spirit." Reconciliation would be understood in light of redemption, and Christ in light of God's sustaining breath. We would, in short, be granted license to conduct Spirit-Christology in a manner corrective of Barth's Filial-Pneumatology. Yet again, I think that this is a misinterpretation of Barth's designs. First, he gave no indication that this was the way forward; indeed, as noted in chapter 1, his response to the perils of anthropocentric theology would seem to suggest that he intended for the corrective objectivity of God in Christ to remain in force in any pneumatocentric turn. Second, Barth is doing far more than just following a material principle to its logical conclusions. He is identifying a theological method given in encounter with God's real dialectic in the Word incarnate. Working within an alternative encounter would necessitate some sort of undialectical process of thought and speech. But once more, to abandon Barth on this point, on the central significance of the Incarnation not only for our material content of "God" but also for our method of thinking and speaking, is to abandon the most essential feature of his decisive critique of liberal theology—the directive objectivity of God coming to Man—and in this, to sacrifice the gains of that critique. Since Barth gave no indication that this is what he intended, and in fact suggested just the opposite, I prefer another reading of his early work in the light of his provocative call to the Spirit. Barth is directing us to a kind of Spirit-centered thought and speech that retains the objectivity of his postliberal move. McCormack helps us to see where we might look for resources to construct that kind of theology: the pneumatocentric dialectic of Barth's third developmental phase. If we focus here, above all in CD I.2, we find that we do not need to abandon or correct Barth, for he has at least the foundation of a robust Pneumatology. The Spirit is fully his own totality in the contemporaneity of the Word, in a parallel life-act of coming to be with us, or in concrete, differentiated repetition of the life-act of the Word, the life-act of Inverberation.

doer of it, the fact that Jesus Christ the Son of God acquires many brothers and His eternal Father many children . . . these very facts constitute an integral part of the biblical testimony to revelation and of revelation itself. . . . We can say, not only that "*God* with us" is a fact, but also, and included in the former statement, that "God with *us*" is a fact. . . . Not God alone, but God and man together constitute the Word of God attested in Scripture.[51]

The subjective reality of revelation is not a line of inquiry that admits of an alternative theological method or way of thinking and speaking to that of the objective reality of revelation. No, the same dialectic in which revelation is objectively real in God's freedom applies, in fact structures our thought and speech on the subjective side. We are free in God and with God; only here, only now, in factual encounter with God's revelation. Apart from this we are in bondage to ourselves. We are free only in coming to God, in the act of the Spirit turning us to hear the Word.

The Spirit brought the thought and speech of the prophets and apostles, after which our own thought and speech take shape, into conformity with the Word of God. In fact, it is in the ongoing act of making the prophetic and apostolic testimony true, one with the Word, that our thinking and speaking are grasped, taken up, and set into cadence after-Word. We encounter the Spirit—or, God's revelation is subjectively real in our freedom—to the extent that we are correspondingly made to think of reality and formulate it in terms of the Word testified to in Scripture. The Spirit is the power and authority of the Word, encountered in the biblical witness to the Word.

The Spirit is known in no place and moment except the animation of those lives summoned by Christ Jesus and placed in obedience to him. The Spirit is known in the life of the *church*.

Barth's treatment of the subjective reality of revelation is comprised mostly of a discussion of the church. I am convinced that the road to Barth's reconciliation with Schleiermacher starts here, with the *ecclesia*.[52] What has to be shown is how the church is the first instance of true humanity, that in the Christian faith we do not start with an abstract anthropology within which the church constitutes a special, curious collection of individuals whose piety

---

51. CD I.2, 207.

52. I intend for my next book to present an account of the covenant that builds on the central themes of this prologue, as a necessary first dogma of creation.

determines that they live in dependence on God, but with those who are freed for God by God, the children of God in whose light humanity at large stands as the object of God's love. It must be shown that these children are themselves an event, that their freedom is a secondary happening in conformity with the prior event of God's Word, thus that the church never constitutes a static repository of the Word or of authentic humanity. The church is simply the first instance of receptivity or aptitude for the Word in the world; in this sense only is it "the light of the world" and "a city on a hill" (Matt. 5:14).

The church is simply the event of the Word's hearing, which draws all people to Christ, declaration of and response to the gospel of Christ under the generative influence and guiding tutelage of the Holy Spirit. My sense is that Barth intended for us to begin here, with a proper ecclesiology, as we think and speak of God in terms of the Spirit:

> What is the Church. . . ? The decisive answer . . . must certainly be to the effect that it involves the outpouring of the Holy Spirit, i.e., it involves the fact that, after He has become man in Christ for us, God also adopts us, in such a way that He Himself makes us ready to listen to the Word, that He Himself intercedes with us for Himself, that He Himself makes the speaking and hearing of His Word possible among us. Therefore the decisive answer to the question of the existence of the Church must certainly be to indicate the mystery of Pentecost, the gift which men who themselves are not Christ now receive in their entire humanity for Christ's sake, the gift of existing from Christ's standpoint for Christ and unto Christ, "the power to become the sons of God" (Jn. 1:12).[53]

The outpouring of the Spirit refers to the work of God making humanity ready to hear the Word, making us free for God just in this hearing. The Spirit's life and action are in the event of causing humanity to exist from the standpoint of Christ, of living in his light and life. We become children of God as we partake of *Christ's* pedigree.

This partaking, once more, is ontologically real insofar as it is a temporal event. Humanity enjoys true being, the very freedom of God for life, insofar as it exists in an actual, tangible transition out of death and darkness. Humanity partakes of Christ's pedigree, exists as offspring of the Father, where and when

---

53. CD I.2, 223.

it participates in Christ's victory over every force of nonexistence. *Where* and *when*—the event of the church is a space-time occurrence:

> By God's election and calling, by his hearing of the Word, by the witness of the Holy Spirit, this man is distinguished non only invisibly and inwardly, but also and in spite of all that remains invisible and inward in the reality of the revelation which comes to him, very visibly and outwardly. He stands at a definite place in history, which is not by accident, but by a most definite necessity, is this particular place and not another.[54]

As noted in chapter 2, Barth adjusts the Reformation concentration on the invisibility of the true church to focus on its event-character. Even in its inward and invisible form, the church is not a given. The church is always and everywhere the occurrence of corporate faith in Christ Jesus, the summons by God into being out of non-being in the hearing of the Word by the power of the Spirit. It is therefore outward and visible, a historical reality, a coming-to-be before God in response to his standing before us.

Yet in this, also as noted, Barth retains the Reformation interest in locating the church in God's life-act. Even as outward and visible, the church does not possess its own being. It is, again, a coming-to-be *in* the living Spirit of the Word. "The existence of the Church involves a repetition of the incarnation of the Word of God in the person of Jesus Christ in that area of the rest of humanity which is distinct from the person of Jesus Christ."[55] The church is a "repetition of the incarnation" in that we encounter God with humanity in a concrete history. We encounter God assuming time among humanity distinct from Christ Jesus, but in Christ, which is to say, in patterns of thought, speech, and behavior that are visible for their obedience to Christ, which therefore repeat the transition from old time to new time.

"The repetition is quite heterogeneous," Barth continues. "Yet for all its heterogeneity it is homogeneous too (although the uniqueness of the objective revelation forbids us to call it a continuation, prolongation, extension or the like).[56] The "body of Christ," which is the biblical metaphor that Barth is

---

54. Ibid., 209.
55. Ibid., 215.
56. Ibid.

working from in this context, is not to be conflated into the bodily history of 1–30 c.e. We might think of the Spirit's life as repetition of the life of the Word, but the church is not the Spirit anymore than the flesh of Jesus was the Word. Rather, in its distinct, heterogeneous way the church repeats in our time the reality of the historical flesh of Jesus of Nazareth in that it, too, is *anhypostatic*. "This life of the children of God is always a life for Christ's sake. . . . We might say that it corresponds to the *anhypostasis* of Christ's human nature. By its inmost nature, the Church is forbidden to want independence of Christ Jesus."[57]

The church boasts no autonomous authority, no right to exist in itself. Quite the opposite, the reality of the church strictly is the life of *absolute dependence* on God in Christ, actualized moment by moment by the Holy Spirit. It is the event of *finding* no basis for thought and speech of God or humanity outside the totality of Christ's all-determinative life and work.

Just as the flesh of Christ existed only *enhypostasis, in* the hypostasis of the Word, so also the church exists *in* the hypostasis of the Spirit, specifically as Spirit of the Word. The subjective reality of revelation is the event in which people are brought to exist in biorhythmic dependence on God in Christ Jesus, that their thought and speech are called forth in reverberative echo of the prophetic and apostolic testimony to Christ, making them really to be contemporaries of Christ.

The visibility of the church just is the event of repentance and belief in Christ in the testimony of his time partners, in which testimony we come to be his time partners. This event is no individualistic act of cognitive assent for Barth. It is a time-defining actuality in that it engages persons in relationship, in the back and forth of interpersonal commerce linguistically and in perceptible activity. "By belonging to Christ we belong to all who belong to Him—not secondarily but a priori, not by the existence of Christian virtue, but according to our nature, i.e., for Christ's sake, and therefore not by accident or disposition or choice, but in the strictest possible sense, by necessity."[58]

In the church, as partakers of God's time for us, we have time for the other; not only in the conventional sense but also in the sense of giving our lives to the other, of repeating in our lives the self-sacrificial love of God in his life-act. We do this not by arbitrary choice but by "nature;" our *being* turns us to the other when "being" is not a static thingness but the event of coming-to-be in the Spirit of the Word. The Spirit is our necessity and our promise or possibility, who we might be tomorrow, which is to say, the means and manner

57. Ibid., 216.
58. Ibid., 217,

of the particular ideas, words, and acts by which we can live in freedom for the other. It is simply the reality of the Spirit, the freedom of God given to us, to forbear, to take another's burdens to ourselves as our own, and to point their gaze upward to a new horizon, to proclaim hope in a world too proud to know of its own despair, yet eerily conscious of it nonetheless. "By this all men will know that you are my disciples, if you love one another" (John 13:35) is not "spiritual" truth if we mean *non-sensate ideal*. It is the truth of the Spirit as a *visible reality* corresponding to the objective, visible reality of the incarnate Word:

> Therefore the work of the Spirit is nothing other than the work of Jesus Christ. . . . By the Spirit He separates them out from the world and gathers them to the hope of their eternal inheritance. In this way He creates His Church. By the Spirit He calls to Himself prophets, i.e., pupils and teachers of revelation. By the Spirit all men go in body to death to meet resurrection. . . . And just because He is Christ's Spirit, the work of Christ is never done without Him. Nor is it done except by Him. The grace of our Lord Jesus Christ does not exist except in the fellowship of the Holy Spirit (2 Cor. 13:14), and the love of God is not poured out into our hearts except by the Holy Spirit (Rom. 5:8).[59]

The Spirit draws all people to Christ. That is his self-determinative work. There is no other work, no other reason or experience, in which Christ is known as Christ. Jesus is Lord and Savior, the grace of God, only in the Holy Spirit. Yet that means there is no other work, no other reason or experience, in which the Holy Spirit is known per se. He is the means of grace, God's continuing presence in and with humanity, insofar as he is the means and manner of the knowledge of God in Christ Jesus. The Spirit is the freedom of God in us, God's freedom given to us and so our freedom to stand before God, to the extent that he is the reality of the Word among us.

Human freedom for God is the *miracle* of the Spirit of the Word, namely, the act of God free of constraint by himself or by us to make his life with us and so to make our lives with him. It is the outpouring or giving of God himself, framed and understood in Christ, now a third time, that is, reiterated in the

59. Ibid., 241.

Spirit. It is the active movement of God, shaped and perceived in Christ, now in us, that is, real in the active movement of that humanity perceived as Christ's offspring. The children of God are the *anhypostatic* nature assumed by the Spirit, the thought and speech of testimony to Christ by which God is with us in the Spirit. Encountering God in the Spirit takes place only in this active operation of the Spirit to make Christ Lord in our time, of our time.

God's revelation is *possible* only in human freedom, something that is grasped and reverberated in our actual thought and speech, insofar as the Word's power and authority are given in and with the *reality* of God's freedom, insofar as the Spirit is one with God's incarnate life:

> Easter and Whitsunday are—and not merely within our knowledge—two different things. So, too, are the objective state and subjective process, Word and Spirit, divine command and human reception. But when we inquire into the possibility of the second, we can only reach back to the first and say that it is there that its whole possibility is to be found. The Holy Spirit is the Spirit of God, because He is the Spirit of the Word.[60]

The Spirit is the subjective possibility of revelation insofar as he reinstantiates the freedom of God as God-with-us actualized and made known in Christ Jesus. There is no other way in which we may encounter God than in this way, the Incarnation, and therefore there is no other way in which we may think and speak of the Spirit of God than as Spirit of the Word.[61]

Christ Jesus is not auxiliary to the life of God but determinative. Therefore, there is no other center from which we might think and speak of God unless we are to posit a different God. There is no other movement within which we might think and speak of God than his gracious movement to us, unless we are to move from ourselves to him and manufacture a manmade deity.[62] The totality of human thought and speech of God is given in Jesus Christ

60. Ibid., 248.

61. Ibid., 249: "If we want truly and properly to investigate the subjective possibility of revelation, and therefore to understand the Holy Spirit and His work, we must never look at subjective realities in which he might presumably or actually be seen and experienced. We must look rather at the place from which He comes and at what He brings. We must look at the contents of God's hand stretched out to us in Him. We must look at the love of God shed abroad in our hearts by Him. We must look to the objective possibility of our communion with Christ. In other words, we must look at Christ Himself."

because the totality of God is being given in his revelation. There is no other possibility of revelation in God or in humanity than the reality of God in the act of revelation.

In seeking another center for theology we can really only seek a basis and process for thought and speech that are one with the real dialectic of God in his enfleshed Word. There can be no subjective possibility of revelation, no thought and speech of God in our time, that is not one with the objective reality of revelation in the *time* of Christ Jesus. There can be no pneumatocentric theology that is not given in and structured after christocentric theology.

CONCLUSION

The Spirit of God must be Spirit of the Word inasmuch as "God" is defined and made known in the life-act of Jesus Christ. The reality of God is given in this life-act and so is divine possibility. Not only what God *is* but also that and what "God" *can be* as *God* are determined and revealed in the incarnate Word. The freedom and authority in which God might again be God-with-us are set forth here and not elsewhere.

But the freedom and authority must really be *set forth*, God really must *meet* humanity again as God if God really is to be known and confessed. If the reality of God did not at once constitute human reality and possibility, if his freedom and power did not involve the creature, did not summon an audience and fit that audience to see and hear, did not convey to that audience a share in that freedom and power, then there would be no God so far as we know. If the objectivity of God in his revelation did not correspond to the subjectivity, then there would be no revelation.

Thus, there is no Spirit without the Word and no Word without the Spirit even as the Spirit is Spirit of the Word. Indeed, exactly as the Spirit is Spirit of the Word, exactly as the Spirit is the subjective reality and possibility of *revelation*, there is reciprocity, a relation of opposition between Word and Spirit, for only in this, when and where the human subject is made fit for revelation, is there the Word of *God*. Only as the Spirit generates and maintains witness to

---

62. Ibid., 248–49: "We can never more mistake the work of the Holy Spirit, and discredit it in our own eyes or others', than by making it the object of an independent investigation. For when we do that . . . the possibilities which we will certainly consider have nothing whatever to do with the great possibility that we might receive revelation. There can be no doubt that our feet are already on the road either to skepticism or to a mild or even violent fanaticism."

Christ Jesus is there Christ Jesus here and now, God as object before us in his God-ness, his freedom and power to be God-with-us.

The Spirit just is this freedom and power of God in the actualistic occurrence of faith, of obedient witness to Christ Jesus. Here, now, in this witness, God is again God-with-us, as the source and norm of our every thought and speech, as Spirit, but as Spirit of Jesus Christ.

Only as the Spirit of Christ, then, can the Spirit be Sprit of the church; only as the freedom and authority by which witness to Christ takes place is he the Spirit of that witness in collective, space-time form. The Spirit must moment by moment will to have his existence as God wills to be in Christ: in the veil of creaturely media, but as the source and norm of that media, as the Lord unveiled in and by it. Only as the Spirit exercises this will of God again are there people of God, is there free and potent witness to Christ Jesus.

To think and speak of God in terms of the Spirit is thus to think and speak of him in terms of the event of this free and potent witness. It is to think and speak of him as the actualization and preservation of this witness, by which there is further witness, which is to say, by which further thought and speech of God take place, by which take place further obedience and faith.

From such a center, one might, in turn, think of humanity and creation at large as the object of God's freedom and power. One might think and speak of them as the target of his love. One might, in turn, think and speak of reconciliation with this God as the freedom and power of God to refuse the stubborn rebellion of human being, to make it real and known as it is overcome, that is, as faith and obedience in Christ are cultivated. And one might, in turn, think and speak of redemption as the consummation of this freedom and power in the full measure of Christian faith and obedience. One *might* think and speak in such ways. "If the Lord wills, we will live and do this or that" (Jas. 4:15).

5

The Spirit of Election and Obedience

The goal of human life is not death, but resurrection.
-Karl Barth[1]

I have been making the argument that one cannot think and speak of the Holy Spirit apart from Christ Jesus without forfeiting the corrective objectivity of God's revelation. And because God has his being in this revelation, to think and speak of the Spirit on some basis other than the Word is to theologize about a no-god, an idol of human manufacturing. It is God's nature to be God in Christ, to take up humanity in the veil of fallen time and to unveil himself as Redeemer who has time *for* us.

That means that the very triunity of God is logically constituted in the enfleshed Word. There is no logical means of thinking and speaking triunely of God apart from the life-act of Christ. I have said that God is Creator, Reconciler, and Redeemer in that he exists in active refusal of non-being, darkness, and death, which active refusal is made known and manifested in Christ Jesus.

It remains to be shown, then, that God in fact does logically have his triunity in the event of the Word, thus that the Spirit is to be understood in the light of this event. That twofold demonstration is the aim of this chapter. It shows that Christ (not another) is the subject of God's eternal self-election, therefore that he is the logical ground of the Trinity, and that the Spirit can only be the eternal Exegesis corresponding to the Exegete. It shows also that Jesus is the object of God's election, therefore that the Holy Spirit is the reiteration of Word's humility and glory in the life-act of the community. He is God's breath not in a mystical sense but as vocalization of the Word, the tremolo as well as rhythm, meter, mood, and tempo of the Word, the time of the

1. Barth, cited by John T. Elson, "Witness to an Ancient Truth," *Time,* April 20, 1962, cover.

Word in confrontation with fallen time, the ideation, inflection, and substance of the Word proclaimed and heard, heard and proclaimed today. He is God inverberate.

BARTH'S EXEGESIS OF JOHN 1:14-17

KAI HO LOGOS SARX EGENETO KAI ESKĒNŌSEN EN HĒMIN, KAI ETHEASAMETHA TĒN DOXAN AUTOU, DOXAN HŌS MONOGENOUS PARA PATROS, PLĒRĒS CHARITOS KAI ALĒTHEIAS.

And the Word became flesh, and dwelt among us, and we saw his glory, glory as of the only begotten from the Father, full of grace and truth.

"The divine, creative, redeeming, revealing Word, whose sovereign being and action vv. 1-13 depicted, has left his throne, comes down to the level where creatures are . . . and himself becomes an object."[2] Barth relentlessly draws attention to the objectivity of God in Christ Jesus. The point of v. 14, and with it the entire prologue inasmuch as "the content of the verse is naturally decisive,"[3] is not that the Word came to an already-existing subject as a prearranged correlate to that subject, a thing to be had according to human subjectivity, but that *in coming*—precisely in this active-verb manner of subsisting—God the Word confronts human being as *object*.

The significance of *sarx egeneto* ("became flesh") is not that God clothed himself in skin, that he rendered himself visible and thinkable by native human capacities. Rather, as we have been saying, he is visible and thinkable *as God* in his enfleshing, invisible and unthinkable. His objectivity remakes our subjectivity to perceive him in truth. That is so *when* and *where* God's objectivity consists not in a fixed product of his activity, but in the event where the product—the incarnate Christ—is perceived as pure activity; when and where (in the space-time actuality) that God is revealed as factual, operative Lord over

---

2. Barth, *Witness to the Word: A Commentary on John 1. Lectures at Münster in 1925 and at Bonn in 1933*, ed. Walther Fürst, trans. Geoffrey W. Bromiley (Grand Rapids: Eerdmans, 1986), 86.

3. Ibid., 85.

all that he is and is not, when and where he confronts every rival power and conception and overcomes them. Thus, "the stress [in interpreting *sarx egeneto*] lies on the coincidence of Word and flesh which John states to be the mode of the coming.⁴

The point of v. 14 and of the entire prologue of John is that God is objectively, self-determinatively God in the uniquely decisive event of *coming* to humanity. This is his freedom as God, or again, the constitution of his deity—to be God *in* concrete refusal of eternity on one side and time on the other, to rule over eternity and time by *moving* from the one to the other.

This means that God is not God in coming to humanity abstractly considered. Rather, he is God in coming to fallen humanity, humanity in rebellion against him:

> That the Word became a man is not the primary issue. Nor is it the point that the Word assumed human nature in general, although this is also included. . . . John speaks explicitly of becoming flesh, of assuming the nature of Adam, of the servant form which is proper to human nature under the sign of the fall and in the sphere of darkness, of the fallen and corrupt human nature which needs to be sanctified and redeemed.⁵

Barth's language is highly nuanced here. He is not saying that the Son of God straightforwardly assumes sinful nature. Rather, God assumes "the servant form which is proper to human nature under the sign of the fall." God takes up the contradiction proper to humanity in rebellion against its Maker, but as the Maker, and so in order to unmake the contradiction. He does not forfeit himself in coming to us by taking up our sinful nature, but remains Lord over us by correcting that nature. "One may rightly say that the flesh is sanctified when assumed by the Word. . . . We must indeed state that because the one who is person in it is a divine and absolutely sinless person, it may be called, with Paul in Rom. 8:3, the *homoiōma sarkos hamartias*, but not *sarx hamartias*."⁶

God sends his Son in the *likeness* of sinful flesh but not *as* sinful flesh, sanctifying and redeeming humanity in coming to us, taking up sin in order to

4. Ibid., 87.
5. Ibid., 88.
6. Ibid., 92.

cancel it. It is critical for Barth that God really does come to *sinful* humanity, then, for it is in his act of canceling the sin that would overcome him that he is known as God. "The antithesis, the distance, the abstraction that is created by the fact of darkness, of *ouk egnō* (v. 10), or *ouk elabon* (v. 11), is overcome . . . by a third inconceivable thing, namely, that the Word is there as others are, in the midst of the darkness."[7]

As the Word is made the concrete flesh of Adam, as God moves to that which neither knows nor receives him, he is made known and received. The distance between God and man is clearly settled and at once unsettled, overcome by God in his concrete acting as Lord over deity and humanity.

In short, there is no God specifically or deity generally that is not revealed in the event of sovereign rule that is Jesus Christ. God is God not in the activity of coming or moving per se, but in *this* activity, in *this* coming and moving, *this sarx*. Thus, we cannot give account of the Spirit of God apart from this act of this coming to this flesh. This is the logical center from which all thought and speech of God must derive, including pneumatocentric thought and speech, lest we suggest that the event of Incarnation is not in reality revealing, that there is actually some other deity yet to be made known apart from the Word Jesus Christ.

God wills to be God in Christ Jesus and not elsewhere if the event of Incarnation in fact constitutes the true reality of God and not merely an interesting interlude in an otherwise more or less different divinity to which we have no access, but for which we readily assume access. The work and person of the Spirit must be known in respect of this subject-determining objectivity if he is not to be turned over to that specific, alternative source for a knowledge of God against which the Incarnation is directed, namely, the dark subjectivity of Adamic human nature. God confronts and corrects our nature here, now, in this one; thus, the Spirit must be the Spirit of God's here and now, of that confrontation, of the contemporaneous coming and movement of God a third time to the darkness, of assuming its constituents not in themselves but in sanctification and redemption. He is the reiteration of divine Lordship, the real dialectic of divine freedom to move out of eternity to time without forfeiting eternity and without obliterating time, but in remaking time by setting it in relation to eternity, restructuring the sequences, consequences, cadences, and cycles of our being–there not by lifting us out of the here and now, but by coming to us *in* the here and now, *in* our life-acts, our thoughts, our *verba*, and pointing them to the new horizon of life beyond death.

7. Ibid., 89.

Again, if it was otherwise, if there was another center on which to think and speak of God, then the Incarnation would not really *reveal* God, and reveal *God*. It would mean that we have encountered a godlike object in Jesus, a man who resembles humanity from a distance, but only from a distance because of his moral excellence, superior piety, and so on, who is not in his very being the judgment and forgiveness of Adam's seed, the cancellation of our self-contradiction by its assumption. But for John (and Barth), Christ is the determinative objectivity of God because he is, in his being, the pure act of divine sovereignty over every force of darkness.

In Christ we are dealing with full God among full humanity, or, once more, with God who is God, who has the fullness of his deity, in being Lord over rebellious humankind. He is God again as God has always been, God as he was, is, and will be. Barth therefore goes on to interpret *eskēnōsen en hēmin* ("dwelt among us") in reference to the tabernacle. "What is now called the *skēnoun* of the Logos *en hēmin* is indeed fulfillment in relation to the Old Testament *skēnē*."[8] The dwelling of the Word among us in the flesh of Jesus is the realization of God's presence among his people, the full and total deity of the one true God with full and total humanity.

Indeed, as the fulfillment of God's tabernacle presence, the *skēnoun* of the Word is temporary. "It is only promise, only the provisional and transitory *skēnoun* of a visit in comparison with the future *skēnoun*."[9] Barth prefers to translate this term as "lodging" to indicate that, "the Logos . . . has not come to dwell here."[10] Without this delimitation, God's objectivity becomes fixed and is not really *God's* objectivity. He is no longer known by faith, by obedient receptivity of his address but by ritual mastery. This was the constant threat of the Israelite cultus, which was met again and again with God's withdrawal. So, too, for us. God remains in charge of his giving. In Christ, he comes to lift our gazes upward and to turn our thinking and speaking forward, to a future presence, and not to level or flatten our perception by an eternal present.

In Christ, we have beheld the glory of God, *etheasametha tēn doxan autou*. "Who are the 'we' of the *en hēmin*? Not the same as the ensuing 'we' of the *etheasametha*, who apparently form a smaller and more specific circle."[11] Among the darkness in which the light shines, there are those who receive and reflect it. In the visible flesh of Jesus there are those who perceive the invisible

8. Ibid., 94.
9. Ibid.
10. Ibid.
11. Ibid., 95.

glory of Almighty God. "We have here a 'we' of majesty in which the first generation, or whoever is authorized to speak for it, speaks to the generations that follow. In distinction from the many among whom the Logos lodged, this 'we' *perceived*."[12]

With the coming of the Word among humankind there is a generative act, a rebirth and renewal, a corresponding coming to being in the event of perception. A first generation is called out of the darkness and given *exousia* to be God's children, authorized to think and speak of God, as he has objectively encountered them, to successive generations, indeed, to take part in the generation of successive generations in and through their thought and speech. With the coming of the Word come witnesses to the Word, both primary and secondary.

With the coming of the Word comes the Spirit of the Word in the event of the church. The act of generation just is the self-determinative life-act of God, which life-act is given in the Word and reiterated a third time in the Spirit. With the coming of the Word there is the power to perceive God, there is the *act* of the Word and its *effect*, the generation (verb) of witnesses and the generation (noun) of witnesses. The Spirit is both this act and this effect, both the generative work of giving the perception to see God's glory and assumption of that perception, the taking up of thoughts and words testifying to Christ to make them in fact bear the grace and truth of God. This assumption is itself thought and spoken after the manner of Christ's assuming flesh—the *enhypostasis* of an *anhypostatic* modality—sanctification and redemption of rebellious human being in this witness to this flesh.

The Spirit has his agential identity in generating the first generation of witness to Christ and taking up their thought and words, and in continued execution of this generation and assumption in the thoughts and words of successive generations animated and informed by the witness of the prophets and apostles. As Spirit of the Word and only as Spirit of the Word is the Holy Spirit the Spirit of the church. As the ongoing, contemporary source and means of the church, the inspiration of the prophetic and apostolic testimony on which the church is founded and the illumination of hearts and minds to perceive the Word in these words—really the Word, really the glory of God in the flesh of Christ—the Spirit reiterates the presence of God among authentic humanity realized in Christ.

Thus, the *future* presence of God to which we are directed in the Spirit cannot be an alien presence relative to what we experience today, to what

12. Ibid., 96–97.

the apostles experienced in 1–30 c.e., to what the Old Testament witnesses experienced in the tabernacle. It has to be fulfillment of the promise that is Christ Jesus just as Christ Jesus is fulfillment of the promise of the tabernacle. It has to be the continuation of God's Lordship in its actual exercise; it has to be God's victory over every force of non-being, darkness, and death known and experienced *as victory* and not as given stasis. It cannot be the annihilation of time by an atemporality in which God statically exists "in us" and we statically exist "in him." It must rather be consummation of the initiative, decision, and act of God in faultless execution of a corresponding initiative, decision, and act on the part of the creature.

The elective will of God to be this God, to reign sovereignly over all that he is not, must be concretely met with a corresponding will of the creature to be a child of this God, making his Lordship complete when and where the seeds of his reign yield a full harvest—the full measure of God's children and the fullness of God in the lives of these his children. By the Spirit of the Word and as the life of the Spirit of the Word, the church will be the first instance of authentic being, taking its part in the generation of continued instances of such being unto the achievement of this measure. This achievement remains the work of God and only the co-work or cooperation of his children in that they are only his children in receipt of his prior work moment by moment, only God's in dependent unity with his Spirit. The fullness of the life of God in the life of the church is yet future for the church, too. God's future presence simply is his reign over his people without quantitative or qualitative remainder; this, so long as we understand the life and work of the Spirit of God in terms of God's self-determinative life and work in the incarnate Word of John 1:14.

IŌANNĒS MARTYREI PERI AUTOU KAI KEKRAGEN LEGŌN, HOUTOS ĒN HON
EIPON, HO OPISŌ MOU ERCHOMENOS EMPROSTHEN MOU GEGONEN, HOTI
PRŌTOS MOU ĒN.

> *John testified about him and cried out,*
> *saying, "This was He of whom I said, 'He*
> *who comes after me has a higher rank than*
> *I, for He existed before me.'"*

The witness to Christ in which humanity glimpses authentic being, the witness of the church, is given tangible form in the witness of the Baptist. Here, as in vv. 6-8, reference to this John, while interruptive, is not without significance for the overall meaning of the prologue to the Gospel of John. All true witness to Christ (and thus all true being as children of God) takes shape after the Baptist:

If we understood vv. 6-8 correctly in the context of the first part, John is there a witness to the light that shines, to its coming into the world, to the glimmering and dawn that precede the sunrise, to Advent. He is so, not for himself alone, but for all that comes under the concept of witness, and hence for the author of the Gospel too. Every word that is said about John the Baptist, John the prophet, is said about John the Apostle as well. The apostles, too, are *anthrōpoi apestalmenoi para theou*, but they, too, are only witnesses *peri tou phōtos*.[13]

Barth understands the character of evangelistic testimony to Jesus to be given its theme and structure in the testimony of John the Baptist. Even more, what it means to be a witness per se is determined by the work and word of John. Only with him are the evangelists also people sent by God, those who bear witness to the light, for in John is it determined that all witnesses are only such by *coming into* the light. In John it is perceived and proclaimed that human thought and speech must be taken up in correspondence to God's own thought and speech, that God must be primary and humanity secondary, that we must

13. Ibid., 102.

stand (and therefore must be made to stand) in utter need of God for every right comprehension of him and of ourselves.

Barth stresses just these matters in his treatment of the Baptist in v. 15. First, he again strikes the note of divine objectivity. Prophetic and apostolic witness to God finds no origin other than in the Word become flesh. Whereas in vv. 6-8 John is introduced as a witness to the light "coming into the world" (v. 9), in v. 15 he appears as one who has seen the light, who looks back upon the Word made flesh (v. 14). And it is this recollection that is actually the basis of John's anticipation:

> The presupposition of Advent is Christmas. And so, strangely, we have to say that the presupposition of the prophet is the apostle. V. 14 speaks about the presupposition, about the light itself, the sunrise, Christmas, the apostles. With the *ho logos sarx egeneto* we have seen how far the revelation to which the witness refers is possible and actual, how far with the fact of the object of witness the witness itself receives its *ratio*.[14]

Witness to God in Christ receives its geometry and algebra, accounting of its shape and operation—not only its shape and operation, but also the rationale for this shape and operation—in Christ himself. As we have been discussing, his reality is the condition of all possibility, the determination of who God is and can be in every act of cognition as well as product, and now as we turn to the witness, he is no less the determination of who we are and can be.

Prophetic testimony derives from its object, not from the subject of the prophet; witness to God in Christ derives from the reality of Christ and not from the compromised reality of the human speaker. Witnesses are only witnesses, only persons whose thought and speech actually, truly reflect the divine reality, insofar as they have been encountered by that reality, found by it such that they may, in turn, find their entire reason for being in it. Their genuine subjectivity must be grounded in God's objectivity; prophecy in apostolate.[15] Their initiative, decisions, and acts must first be drawn up into

---

14. Ibid., 102–3.

15. Ibid., 103: "If the Baptist truly stands there among the prophets, he has to stand here among the apostles too."

proximity with the initiative, decision, and act of God in Christ if they are genuinely to testify about God.

The witness finds its true being, its character as witness as well as testimonial content and shape, in Christ. This is the significance of John's saying, "He who comes after me has a higher rank than I, for He existed before me." For Barth, John the Baptist is put into ontological place by the object of his witness. He exists in subordination and contingency relative to the Word that he declares:

> I am already overtaken, set aside; the appearance is already a mere appearance, it was never the truth; the fact that this person came after me never meant that I was before him in dignity and authority. I already stand in his shadow even if in your judgment he and all others stand in mine. The only point is that you should see this too, that I should show him to you, this specific person in face of whom no doubt can arise as to who is subordinate.[16]

The Baptist and all witnesses are subordinate to the content of their collective witness because they, like all things, exist only through the Word to which they testify (*panta di' autou egeneto*, v. 3). One can only be a prophet by first being encountered by the Word made flesh, by finding oneself in subordination to this event even as a participant in it, in being called and sent by it. "What makes the prophet a prophet, a witness to the light that comes into the world, is that he *has* the concept of *prōtos autou*, the divine Word which is superior to him from all eternity and thus which makes it possible for him to be a prophet from all eternity."[17]

The revelation of God in Christ brings to the darkness the necessary self-awareness of its absolute dependency for being upon God, setting it into authentic reality in the very event of divine objectivity, in the event of God's coming. Here, now, the human finds herself in the factual subordination of all existence to divine reality, and as such, only in actually receiving and having the concept of divine first-ness, thinking and speaking in this order, does she in actuality think rightly and speak rightly of God and creation.

16. Ibid., 106.
17. Ibid., 107–8.

Second, then, the objectivity of God in Christ entails a compulsion; the generation of witnesses to the coming of God in the event of Christ Jesus is simply basic to this event. "Face to face with the incarnate Word, he must now say his word, his human word, about himself and his relation to that Word."[18] Thought and speech of God come necessarily with the happening of God's own thought and speech, indeed as reiteration of that thought and speech.

It is not just that God *spoke* in Christ Jesus. He *speaks*. The enfleshed Word is not an autonomous object, but the objectivity of God in and with the human subject that it assumes, sanctifies, and redeems:

> Note the present tense *martyrei*. Face to face with readers and hearers of the Gospel the Baptist still has to say what he says. And note the urgency: *martyrei kai kekragen legōn*. How emphatic that is. Someone has *spoken* here. Why? Because God's Word has been spoken. This Word evokes human words to testify to it, and they are there. *By whom* are they spoken? By the Baptist, yes, but again, the text has it, by John.[19]

The Baptist has to speak—he must cry out—for he is taken up by the Word as the means of the Word's continuing expression. His words are evoked by the Word as testimony to the Word. In his testimony to Christ, to the event of God's coming as God's self-determination, God speaks. He continues to reveal himself in this testimony to his revelation, assuming it in a manner parallel to his assumption of the flesh of Jesus.

Thus the apostle is born. John the Evangelist is a witness in conformity to the witness of the Baptist, which is to say, in the act that he looks to the Baptist's witness and makes it his own. In turning to this witness, calling upon it as authoritative thought and speech, the Gospel of John participates in the witness itself. "The witness, like the Revealer himself, speaks as a present and contemporary figure to the readers and hearers. The author calls upon him to give his witness as if he were alongside him. His witness is to the incarnate Word, and it is thus to the same object as the author's own apostolic witness. Hence the *matyrei* denotes an *actus continuus*."[20]

18. Ibid., 103.
19. Ibid., 104.
20. Ibid., 104–5.

Testimony to God in Christ is a continuing act. It is an event given determinative shape and content in the witness of John the Baptist, in his compelled declaration of divine superiority in the objectivity of the enfleshed Word, reverberated among the apostolic testimony to this same objectivity. "Thus the Bible arises, God's authoritative Word, as the *witness* to revelation."[21]

In the witness to revelation, revelation itself takes place; God's authoritative Word is spoken among the darkness, and, as such, God is again God. Here and now, in the prophetic and apostolic testimony to Christ Jesus, the coming of God takes place as determinative object in space-time.

The key, then, is to recognize that the coming of God in Christ is an ongoing act. It is once for all in the sense that its historical reality in 1–30 C.E. is the precedent, the *prōtos autou* according to which any thought and speech of God's coming (and being) must derive and take shape. This coming in this flesh is the objectivity of God. But as a subject-determining objectivity, it is an objectivity that happens again; in the sensate declaration of God in Christ by the prophets and apostles, the determinative priority of God takes place for successive generations.

This act-nature of the Word is critical because it makes the event of the Word an *invitation*. The Word summons thoughts and words by its very existence. Thus, the proclamation of Christ by the church after the thoughts and words of the prophets and apostles is also an instance of the Word, a secondary instance just as is the collective Word of the prophets and apostles, a witness to the Word that becomes the Word like the Bible. More exactly, the very coming to thoughts and words of Christ Jesus, the calling of them up from among the darkness and making them to be sanctified vessels of the Word is itself the Word *in* its subject-determining objectivity. It is the act and power of the Word. It is, as I have been arguing, the life and work of the Holy Spirit.

The movement on the part of those who have no natural basis for it to act, to thought and speech of God in Christ, just is the event of God a third time. We are not God in this event, but God is God over us and in us. It is reiteration of his Lordship in the calling and forming of testimony to the light by the dark who neither knows nor receives the light. God is God *in* this act; *in* the *verberation* of the witness who has no intrinsic capacity for him, who is made to perceive her utter incapacity for him and speak it forth right here and now (and so become a witness), where and when he exercises a capacity for her; God is God again as he was in Christ Jesus, in the beginning and forever will be.

21. Ibid., 110.

*HOTI EK TOU PLĒRŌMATOS AUTOU HĒMEIS PANTES ELABOMEN KAI CHARIN
ANTI CHARITOS;*

*For of his fullness we all have received, and
grace upon grace.*

Against the preponderance of modern exegetes, but with the majority of
ancient interpreters, Barth takes vv. 16–17 to be a continuation of the Baptist's
speech begun in v. 15. He does so because only such a reading differentiates the
Baptist and all successive witnesses from the Word even as the Word is spoken
and heard in, and in fact makes itself to be one with, their witness. Reading
these verses as a return to the voice of the evangelist represents "a failure to
understand the representative position of the Baptist, especially in the prologue,
where it is appropriate that not merely in his own person, but as the conductor
of the Christian community in general and the apostolic and prophetic witness
in particular, he should show how they have come to be what they are."[22]

It is in the Baptist's address that the evangelist's address comes to be what
it is, indeed that the evangelist comes to be who he is—a witness to the Word
called and sent by the Word, an apostle. This is so, once again, in that the
evangelist does not stand outside the testimony of the Baptist, but finds himself
within that testimony as a continuation of it:

> History is not *narrated* here; it is *contemplated*, summarized, surveyed,
> and interpreted: this was the relation of the Baptist to the Christ. .
> . . He stands over against him not as himself a revealer, not as the
> founder of a religion, not as the head of his own church, but in
> exactly the same way as do the disciples, the apostles, the author of
> the Gospel, and the Christian community at large.[23]

John the Evangelist cannot stand outside the Baptist and in fact be the
evangelist; he cannot narrate the testimony of the Baptist as if it made no claim
upon him and be an apostle of the Word. He can only reiterate in his own

22. Ibid., 113.
23. Ibid, 113–14.

thinking and speaking the contemplation, summary, survey, and interpretation that characterize the Baptist's thought and speech in relation to Christ Jesus, finding himself in the same relation, summoned and placed in the same subordination that is true of the one crying in the wilderness.

Understood as a continuation of the Baptist's testimony, v. 16 underscores the factual priority of God and utter, subordinate dependency of the creature, which is established in the unassailable objectivity of God in vv. 14-15. As the content of this John's testimony (not as John the Evangelist's narration over against the Baptist), the declaration that "we all have received of his fullness" is an act that places all of us, all who hear these words, opposite Christ, reinforcing his singularity as the condition of our true being. "The uniqueness of Christ as the place where salvation is to be found, is the point of the first clause in v. 16, the first reason why the Baptist pronounces his *houtos ēn* in v. 15 and calls this one the *prōtos*, which is the equivalent of the *monogenēs*, the bearer of *doxa*, the Logos."[24]

The first point made by v. 16, specifically as a statement from the Baptist's lips, is that Christ is without peer. This one (*houtos ēn*) is above all (*prōtos*), the one and only (*monogenēs*), the distinctive glory (*doxa*) of the Father. We *all* stand across from him in subordination and contingency.

That surfaces the second point made by v. 16: when we take part in the Baptist's encounter with Christ, we come to our true being, specifically, *as* his subordinates. "As we receive in this way, from a source which is not only a special one but the only available source in which we can find *plērōma*, we are what we are. And because we received thus, we say: *houtos ēn*."[25] As we receive in the way of the Baptist, as Christ's superordination is made real in this testimony, we come to be what we are, children of the subject of that testimony. We, too, are compelled to declare *this one* as the first, highest, the one and only, *our* Lord and Maker.

In other words, the event of God's objectivity in the witness to Christ is a circular, or better, *spiraling* event contingent upon Christ's uniquely, actually *being* the fullness of God in the witness of his apostles and prophets. Objectivity does not take place outside this witness, but in and with the witness, as the *act* of witnessing in the manner and of the content of the first witness, of John the Baptist. It is a posteriori confession of the uniqueness of Christ, which uniqueness takes place again in that confession, so that the ongoing act of confession is summoned and shaped after encounter with that uniqueness:

24. Ibid., 114.
25. Ibid., 115.

Because he is for the *hēmeis* not just *one* source of *plērōma*, we say: *houtos ēn*. This is why he is for them the *prōtos*. This is why the Baptist is subordinate. This is the reason for the unconditional respect with which the Evangelist approaches his work. The exclusiveness of what meets them in this person demands and establishes the exclusiveness of this person and therefore of their attitude to this person.[26]

The exclusiveness of what comes to the witness in the event of Christ establishes anew the actual exclusiveness of Christ—he is who he is, as we have been saying, *in* the *coming*—and in this renewed exclusivity is established the hearing of subordination to Christ instantiated in the Baptist, reiterated in the evangelist, reverberated in the church. This reverberative *act* and *power* as a unified totality is the "fullness" of Christ. (It is, once more, the Spirit of Christ.) Of what does it consist?

"What touched us, what we took, what was given to us in all its greatness and strangeness, was grace, life wonderfully breaking into the world of death, redemption. There were no vacillations, no more or less, no this way and that. With the exclusiveness of the whence is the exclusiveness of the what, of what is received."[27] Barth sides with the history of exegesis that reads *charin anti charitos* ("grace upon grace" or "grace unto grace") not as a transition (from, say, the law to the gospel or the Old Testament to the New Testament) but as an idiomatic expression connoting *abundance of grace*. What we, *hēmeis*, have received in Christ is nothing less than the plenitude of life that *is* God's own life.

We received not only the gift of life as a thing to possess opposite God, and perhaps again in rebellion against him, but the *giver* of life himself, for we received *Christ*. Grace is not a thing given by God but the very existence of God, his active opposition to non-being, darkness, and death. Redemption is not a thing that a metaphysical God does; it is who he is as the historical God, Christ Jesus. This we receive in subordinately receiving Christ. Once again, "with the exclusiveness of the whence is the exclusiveness of the what."

What we are in the event of encounter with Christ is an empty vessel of Christ, a creature without creatureliness in itself, but nevertheless an entity, an

26. Ibid., 115–16.
27. Ibid., 119.

object in itself, a recipient of God's address, *anthrōpos* made by God for God. We are agents of Christ in the manner of the Baptist and the evangelist, secondary media of the Word. We are this as our thoughts and words are summoned to their expression of Christ, and so become yet again a moment, a place of the redemptive life-act of God.

I cannot stress enough that we are *not* this *in ourselves*, for the moment that we posit a kind of metaphysical self in receipt of God, we have made ourselves agents of divinity, gods; we have lived the rebellion of Adam and contradicted our very existence. We are recipients of God only in Christ by God the Spirit. He is the generative compulsion and shaping influence of the ideas and language that make us to be who we are, of our witness to Christ and therefore of our beings as witnesses to Christ. Strictly speaking, he is more basic to us than "we" are to "ourselves." Strictly speaking, it is in his life that we have life; it is in the life-act of God a third time that human witness is made real and possible, thus that humans are made real and possible as witnesses.

HOTI HO NOMOS DIA MŌÜSEŌS EDOTHĒ, HĒ CHARIS KAI HĒ ALĒTHEIA DIA IĒSOU CHRISTOU EGENETO.

> *For the Law was given through Moses; grace and truth were realized through Jesus Christ.*

With vv. 15 and 16, v. 17 sets even those who are called and enlightened by God in a relationship of subordination to him. It makes the would-be witness a witness only in this relationship. "'The Law was given by Moses' means that Moses did what Moses could do in his place and on his level as a mediator of revelation. But in his place, in his sphere, he is on the human side over against God, a mediator of revelation only insofar as he is first a recipient. Without any criticism of Moses or his Law, an order is thus established in the sense of v. 15."[28]

Barth does not read v. 17 as any sort of deprecation of Moses or the law of the Old Testament, which would entail a corresponding glorification of those who stand in Moses' position in the New Testament, the apostles. Rather, Moses is cited as an example for all witnesses to Christ (as beings whose existence

28. Ibid., 123.

simply is in the act of witnessing), in that even Moses is located alongside
the Baptist. "There are authorized and enlightened people. . . . Are they all
to be put in the shade with John the Baptist, or John the Baptist with them?
The answer is an unambiguous Yes. Yes, *charis kai alētheia dia Iēsou Christou,
ekeinos exēgēsato*."[29] Grace and truth come through Christ alone; alone, that one
exegeted (*ekeinos exēgēsato*) the Father. All others simply bear witness to Christ's
grace and truth as the Exegete, this insofar as they, with Moses, the Baptist, and
the Evangelist, encounter his Exegesis, insofar as this Word is known to them
in the words of Moses, the Baptist, and the Evangelist, and in turn, is made
known by them through constructive reiteration of the Mosaic, Baptistic, and
Evangelistic witness.

In this verse, too, accent is placed not on the witness per se, but on the
relation established between Witnessed and witnesses and on the uniqueness of
Christ by which that relation is established. Accent is placed not on those who
stand in the place of Moses but on him who stands in the place of God. "Exactly
in the place where Yahweh stood, there stands here the one to whom the *houtos
ēn* of v. 15 applies. Exactly in the function in which Yahweh acted there, he
acts here. Through him grace and truth come, or come about, or come on the
scene."[30] Barth understands John always to be emphasizing the central insight,
to which so many other insights accrue, that Christ Jesus stands before us as
YHWH stood before the ancient Israelites, as the LORD of all creation known
as such in the history of self-determinative acts among a specific people. He is
today the same God who has his being in covenant history, the God of grace
and truth.

God is God in the event of redemptively coming to humankind.
Throughout his treatment of the prologue to John's Gospel, Barth has stressed
that God has his deity in the *act* of coming, in *living* sovereignty over every
force of rebellion, every power of non-being, darkness, and death. God's God-
ness is in a unique kind of freedom—not an abstractly conceived quality but a
factual reign—in active authority over all realms and principalities, over eternity
and time, deity and humanity. It is in *being* sovereign over these modalities;
determining his "self" in relation to the realm proper to him and the realm
proper to all that he is not, that "God" is comprehended.

That means that "humanity" is comprehended in correspondence to the act
of absolute sovereignty that defines God. That is, humanity is *humanity* only in
the *event* of absolute dependence. Only when and where a creature is made to

29. Ibid., 121.
30. Ibid., 124.

declare "God" precisely in and by her inadequacy for genuine divinity is she truly a *creature*, does she truly stand before *God* (and is not god unto herself), does she really have a basis, means, and goal. Only *then and there*–only as her creatureliness is of such a "time," only as the history of the life-acts that comprise her being is contemporary (co-tempo) with Christ's, as the series of her life-acts takes place before the boundary set and crossed by God in his Word, does she truly live. Only as everything that she might be is given in the grace and truth that *he is*, as her reality takes place within his reality, does she exist. Only as she is a witness to the boundary and its crossing, only as the Spirit makes it so–and in fact, only as the Spirit *as Spirit* exists in making it so–does she draw the breath of life.

It is to gain these insights that we have walked with Barth through his treatment of John's prologue. We must think of God and ourselves, of all reality and possibility, of all truth and time, of all being and becoming, in the terms set by the Evangelist. That is so as we try to think in terms of the Spirit. His are not different terms, but creative reiteration of the real dialectic established by God in Christ Jesus according to the testimony of the prophets and apostles. The Spirit is this God again, Immanuel, God-with-us today as he has always been. Our final chapter demonstrates this by showing that God is God-with-us in the eternal election whereby he assigns himself just this way of being.

THE DOCTRINE OF ELECTION AS PART OF THE DOCTRINE OF GOD IN CD II.2

God is God in the event of an I standing opposite a thou, which thou being brought about by the I is utterly dependent on the I in this event, yet which exists as the object relative to which the I wills to exist, and therefore as a bona fide thou. Again, "God" is *God* in this event; there is no deity apart from the I–thou relationship given in Jesus Christ.

That is, divinity is divinity in the Christ-event, whereby sovereignty is decisively exercised over humanity, but thereby in and with humanity. The divine I–thou is thus first of all the event of God on one side, and humanity on the other, brought together and revealed in Christ, such that neither God nor humanity can be thought and spoken in truth apart from Christ. Christ is the event in which God is God and humanity is humanity—the first relative to the second and the second to the first, not reciprocally but in the definite order from the first (on whom the second depends) to the second.

This means that the second, humanity, actually must come to know and have its self in subordination to the first. Humanity per se must take place in the agential act of standing in dependency upon God for God to be God in Christ. It must take on the biorhythmic humility of the Exegete relative to the Exegeted revealed in Christ if God really is to be God in this revelation. It really must be the happening of Exegesis, the occurrence of knowledge through obedient reception of the Word, for the Lordship that defines God in the event of revelation to be complete. The event of human submission to God in Christ is simply a share in the reality of God as he is revealed and known in the Word made flesh.

The act of human submission to God correlated to the act of God's coming to Man is the life and work of the Holy Spirit. Most basically, *he* is the Exegesis of the Word, the condition of knowledge through obedience, the generation and assumption of thought and speech that bear witness to the Word. The Spirit, as such, is once again the divine I in that he is the living rule of God over human being, and also a Thou relative to the Father and the Son in the event of the Word in that he is the instantiation of the Word's humiliation and glorification by the verberation of witness to the Word. He is instantiation a third time of the defining, divine life-act in which God is God by taking up non-being, darkness, and death as a veil, yet to reveal his authority over them in their sanctification and redemption, to unveil his glory and make it real among them. The Spirit *is* this real dialectic of divine Lordship here and now, in the life-act of the *ecclesia*.

But this can be true only according to two prior truths. First, the Spirit can be the real dialectic of God in the life-act of obedient knowledge only if God's very being, his triunity, is logically established in the life-act of his executed decision relative to humanity, such that there is no Spirit of God operating or known apart from the eternal will of God made actual in Christ, and if the content of this decision really is the dialectic of veiling and unveiling in creaturely modalities. In his doctrine of election, Barth helps to establish both truths.

Students of his thought have frequently observed that the single most constructive contribution that Barth made to the history of Christian dogma is his *Erwählungslehre*, his doctrine of election. We noted in chapter 1 that Bruce McCormack credits this doctrine as providing the catalyst to the fourth and final phase of Barth's development.[31] I will return to McCormack's argument in due course. For now, it is necessary to note that Barth's third phase reaches its climax

31. See chapter 1, n. 85.

and gives rise to the more historical foundation discussed in chapter 1 when, in the late 1930s, he places God's act of election in his treatment of the doctrine of God. God's very God-ness is logically established—given its substance and shape—in the eternal decision to be God in the historical life, ministry, death, and resurrection of Jesus Christ.

Rather than taking up election in its traditional locus, under soteriology, Barth dedicates just over five hundred pages to its analysis in his second part-volume on the doctrine of God.[32] He begins with a lengthy section on "The Problem of a Correct Doctrine of the Election of Grace," in which he demonstrates the troublesome tendency across Christian history to make God's predestining work strictly a matter of individual human salvation. Election is, of course, *also* about individual salvation,[33] but Barth contends that it is first and foremost a matter of divine decision and therefore existence.

The election of grace is above all God's will to move toward humanity and to exist with and for humanity:

> In a Christian doctrine of God, if God is to be exhaustively described and represented as the Subject who governs and determines everything else, there must be an advance beyond the immediate logical sense of the concept to the actual relationship in which God has placed Himself; a relationship outside of which God no longer wills to be and no longer is God, and within which alone He can be truly honoured and worshipped as God. . . . Jesus Christ is indeed God in his movement towards man.[34]

If the Christian theologian is to give a decidedly Christian account of God, then she must describe him entirely according to the event in which God makes himself the object of his own activity, taking up the creatureliness that he has made into a self-defining relationship (having, in other words, his deity in the act not simply of making the creature, but more basically, of making it *for him*). She must not think and speak of God's relationship with humanity as a mere concept or general construct, as something extrinsic to God, which God

---

32. CD II.2, §§32–35, pp. 3–506

33. This is the last thing that election concerns, although not an insignificant thing for that; see CD II.2 §35, "The Election of the Individual."

34. CD II.2, 7.

assumes for a season, for God wills the relationship in such a way as not to be God apart from it. God is *God* in the concrete reality of Jesus Christ. Christ is not only the act of God upon humanity, but also the self-determinative act of God in and upon his eternal self.

That means that Christ is not a second "moment" in the life of God. God cannot be exclusively known in the history of his movement to humanity if there was a time in God prior to or apart from this movement. There cannot be a primal history in which God deals with all that he is not, which is independent of his history in Christ Jesus, for in that case Christ would no longer be the revelation of very God. He might constitute an intimate and hopeful intermission in the life of an otherwise aloof and angry deity, or something more in keeping with the character of the Father to whom he prays, a flower that comes with spring's bloom, but *only* with a season that is much more than flowers blooming. Who knows? God in his primal time would remain an unknown factor in any event.

Who God is even in the beginning is given and made known entirely in Christ Jesus. There is no willing in God that is inconsistent with or more than his willing in the enfleshed Word. That means that election, the exercise of divine will relative to the creature, is above all the exercise of divine will relative to God's self. Without losing sight of the creaturely factor in Jesus of Nazareth, but before thinking and speaking of that factor, we must think and speak of the divine decision to be God in Jesus, with humanity from all eternity. The doctrine of election is, properly considered, the focal point of the doctrine of God:

> It is undoubtedly the case . . . that the election does in some sense
> denote the basis of all the relationships between God and man,
> between God in His very earliest movement towards man and man
> in his very earliest determination by this divine movement. It is in
> the decision in favour of this movement, in God's self-determination
> and the resultant determination of man, in the basic relationship
> which is enclosed and fulfilled within Himself, that God is who He is.
> The primal relationship belongs, therefore, to the doctrine of God.[35]

---

35. Ibid., 52.

Because there is no God behind or beyond the God who is God in relationship with his creature, the doctrine of election ought to be hopeful and uplifting. Against the ignominious uncertainty traditionally associated with the church's teaching about predestination, Barth contends that election is "the sum of the Gospel."[36] It is the "glad tidings" that God, in the fullness of his being as God, exists for humanity, in an attitude and relation of grace. Election "does not proclaim in the same breath both good and evil, both help and destruction, both life and death. . . . The Yes cannot be heard unless the No is also heard. But the No is said for the sake of the Yes and not for its own sake."[37]

Whereas traditional (Augustinian and especially Calvinist) doctrines of predestination have focused equally on salvation and damnation, Barth contends that an adequate, Christ-oriented discussion of election must err on the side of the former. Salvation is known only in the light of judgment and condemnation. The divine "No" to human rebellion must remain in force in any discussion of God's predestining decree. However, if that singular decree is rightly taught, then it must be stated that God's judgment against sin does not stand as a balancing weight against his decree to salvation, but takes place in order to highlight God's self-determination to be the God of grace and mercy.

In opposition both to the traditional tendency to locate election within a mysterious, primal time of God's dealings with the creature and to obscure the grace of God in his movement toward humanity with an equally threatening word of damnation, Barth argues that the doctrine should be formulated in such a way as to *reveal* God precisely in his gracious existence as Christ Jesus.[38] It should neither spring from undefined mystery nor make the quantity or quality of saved humanity into undefined mystery, but should quintessentially express the good news of God's eternal movement toward humanity in Christ *as* the defining life-act of God and the *hopeful* determination of all humanity.

For Barth, it is not enough to say that God elects and humanity is elected, for neither side of this equation—neither God nor man—is a known quantity in that statement. In point of fact, Jesus Christ is the electing God and Jesus Christ is the elected human. Barth follows his opening discussion concerning the

36. Ibid., 12.
37. Ibid., 13.
38. See CD II.2, 146: "The history of the dogma is shot through with a great struggle for the affirmation of the fact that in the mystery of election we have to do with light and not darkness. . . . But this affirmation could not and cannot be made . . . as long as it is not admitted that in the eternal predestination of God we have to do on both sides with only one name and one person, the same name and the same person, Jesus Christ. Unless this is done . . . the assertion of the obscurity itself becomes the last and decisive word on the whole subject."

proper orientation of the doctrine of election with a section on "The Election of Jesus Christ." This section begins with easily one of the most provocative sets of observations made in the whole of the *Church Dogmatics*, a subsection on "Jesus Christ, Electing and Elected."[39]

Our two claims in this chapter hang on each of these two points—that Jesus Christ is electing God and Jesus Christ is elected Man—respectively. That God's triunity is logically grounded in his self-determination to be God in Christ Jesus (hence that the Spirit must be the Word's eternal Exegesis) hangs on the fact that Jesus Christ is the Subject of election. And that God's being in Christ consists of the dialectic of veiling and unveiling, or more narrowly in this context, of judgment and redemption (hence that the Spirit must be reiteration of this dialectic), hangs on the fact Jesus Christ is the Object of election. We must therefore look at each truth in turn.

In the first place, if God is God only in his movement toward humanity, if there is no primal moment in the life of God independent of this movement, and if Jesus Christ just is this movement, then Jesus Christ is the electing God. "We must obviously—and above all—ascribe to him the active determination of electing."[40] The decision of God to be God in relationship with the creature is a known commodity. It can be named, observed, comprehended in its distinct majesty, it is Jesus Christ. The love out of which God elects his being as a being-for-us, the love in action that determines God's very life and existence, is defined in this unique Person.

Christ is not merely the expression of God's charity, which is essentially unknown, or the dispenser of "divine benevolence," whatever it entails. He is the love of God in which God lives and moves and has his being:

> Jesus Christ is not merely one object of the divine good-pleasure side by side with others. . . . For in the first instance He Himself is this good-pleasure, the will of God in action. He is not merely the standard or instrument of the divine freedom. He is Himself primarily and properly the divine freedom itself in its operation *ad extra*. He is not merely the revelation of the mystery of God. He is the thing concealed within this mystery, and the revelation of it is the revelation of Himself and not of something else.[41]

39. CD. II.2, §33.1, 94–145.
40. Ibid., 103.
41. Ibid., 104.

We know who God is even in his primordial self-existence because we know Jesus Christ. He reveals not that God is mystery, as we more or less already suspected, but that the mystery of God is just his freedom to be this God, in communion with us in spite of our rebellion, in the triumph of grace over judgment.

Jesus Christ is the determination of divine being as being-for-us from all eternity. There is no other God even in pre-temporal election than this God, therefore no other basis on which to think and speak of God than this basis. He is the definition of the love in which God lives, and out of which God elects. We cannot seek another center on which to think and speak of God without compromising this truth, without returning the eternal will of God to the land of unknowable secrecy. We cannot formulate an account of God (in terms of the Spirit) that does not begin and end with the determinative life-act of love in Christ.

Thus, we cannot think of the very trinitarian nature of God apart from his primal self-election in Christ. The Trinity itself is comprehended in the light of God's most basic decision to be this God:

> So much depends upon our acknowledgment of the Son, of the Son of God, as the Subject of this predestination, because it is only in the Son that it is revealed to us as the predestination of God, and therefore of the Father and the Holy Spirit, because it is only as we believe in the Son that we can believe in the Father and the Holy Spirit, and therefore in the one divine election.[42]

That election is first and foremost *God's* election—that, on the one hand, it is the coordinated decision of the entire Godhead and, more strongly, that, on the other hand, it is the determination of the Godhead, marking out the agential character of the Father and Spirit as well as the Son—this is given in acknowledgment of the Son to be the eternal Subject of predestination. Confessing that Jesus Christ is the electing God and that he fully reveals God in his distinct Person compels confession that God just is the God of election, that there is no other moment of God's God-ness than this moment, that the Father

42. Ibid., 105.

qua Father and Spirit qua Spirit are known only in the terms of this primal life-act.

At least, this is the direction that Barth's thought leads already in his treatment of election. Students have noted, however, that Barth is not consistent in logically grounding the Trinity in the elective act of God in Christ. Here we reconnect with McCormack.

In 2000, McCormack sparked something of a wildfire in Barth scholarship with the publication of a brief chapter in *The Cambridge Companion to Karl Barth* entitled, "Grace and Being: The Role of God's Gracious Election in Karl Barth's Theological Ontology."[43] Scope does not permit examination of the cottage industry of support and criticism that argument has produced. I have written elsewhere in defense of McCormack, which work the reader may consult for a fuller handling of his case, and for an introductory bibliography of salient responses.[44]

In brief, McCormack makes two interrelated claims. First, he qualifies the theoretical need for a pre-enfleshed Word. The "Word without flesh" or *logos asarkos* is an ancient doctrine deriving from fifth-century christological debate, when in the context of metaphysical philosophy it seemed necessary to posit the eternal subsistence of God above and before space-time creation. "God," if this term was to be meaningful in a basically Neoplatonic sense, was metaphysical, beyond the physical, and so the Word in its primal form was *a-sarx*, without flesh.

McCormack observes that, while the *logos asarkos* retains some conceptual necessity for Barth and for us, it is a secondary dogma. One must acknowledge the existence of the *logos asarkos* and distinguish between it and the *logos ensarkos* (the "Word enfleshed") because, "after all, the human nature (body and soul) of Jesus only came into existence at a particular point in time, in history. It was not eternal; the Logos did not bring it with him, so to speak."[45] For obvious reasons, vis-à-vis divine freedom, Barth did not wish to collapse history into eternity and read the human body and soul of Jesus of Nazareth into the Godhead without qualification.

43. Bruce McCormack, "Grace and Being: The Role of God's Gracious Election in Karl Barth's Theological Ontology," in *The Cambridge Companion to Karl Barth*, ed. John Webster (Cambridge: Cambridge University Press, 2000), 92–110.

44. Aaron T. Smith, "God's Self-Specification: His Being Is His Electing," in *Trinity and Election in Contemporary Theology*, ed. Michael Dempsey (Grand Rapids: Eerdmans, 2011), 201–25; reprinted from *Scottish Journal of Theology* 62, no. 1 (2009): 1–25.

45. McCormack, "Grace and Being," 96.

However, it must immediately be added that this *logos asarkos* is not an independent agent existing for itself, not an autonomous entity but a useful referent only in anticipation of *ensarkos*. The subject of election is, again, not an indeterminate *logos* but Christ, which means that the *logos asarkos* does not exist of itself:

> If now Barth wishes to speak of Jesus Christ (and not an abstractly conceived *Logos asarkos*) as the Subject of election, he must deny to the Logos a mode or state of being above and prior to the decision to be incarnate in time. . . . To say that "Jesus Christ" is the Subject of election is to say that there is no *Logos asarkos* in the absolute sense of a mode of existence in the second "person" of the Trinity which is independent of the determination for incarnation; no "eternal Son" if that Son is seen in abstraction from the gracious election in which God determined and determines never to be God apart from the human race.[46]

For McCormack (and for Barth), affirming the reality of a *logos asarkos* is necessary to preserve the distinction between time and eternity, but it should not be taken in an absolute sense to indicate an existence in God apart from the temporal existence of Jesus Christ. There is no abstract Son prior to his decision to be God incarnate in history.

How can this be so? How can the eternally existing Son be only relatively and not absolutely distinct from Jesus of Nazareth? How, in other words, can Christ Jesus be the ground of divine determination without reading human nature (body and soul) back into eternal divinity? McCormack answers with the modality of *anticipation*. "God is already in pre-temporal eternity—*by way of anticipation*—that which he would become in time. . . . The being of God in eternity, as a consequence of the primal decision of election, is a being which looks forward. It is a being in the mode of anticipation."[47] In a primordial

---

46. Ibid., 95, 100. In Barth's own words, "If it is true that God became man, then in this we have to recognize and respect His eternal will and purpose and resolve . . . behind which we do not have to reckon with any Son of God in Himself, with any *logos asarkos*, with any other Word of God than that which was made flesh. According to the free and gracious will of God the eternal Son of God is Jesus Christ as He lived and died and rose again in time, and none other. . . . We must not ignore [God's free decision] and imagine a 'Logos in itself' which does not have this content and form [Jesus Christ]" (CD IV.1, 52).

47. McCormack, "Grace and Being," 100 (emphasis in original).

choice, God elects not to be God other than as *directed*, toward humanity and therefore for humanity. God is eternally *self-determined*. The Son, as subject of a pre-temporal decision (that is, there never was a time when this decision was not), wills not to be other than incarnational, which is to say that he wills not to be in and for himself at all but always in and for humankind. In this way, the pre-incarnate *logos* does not exist in abstract independence, but in readiness for incarnation. By way of anticipation he already is, in his eternal being, what he would become in time: Jesus Christ.

This brings us to a second claim that McCormack makes regarding Barth's doctrine of election: God's triunity logically follows his elective will. If we say that there is no *logos asarkos* in any abstract sense, and that the Son is Jesus Christ and not some independent agent, then we must also say that the being of the God who chooses not to be other than with human flesh determines his existence as such by this choice:

> The denial of the existence of a *Logos asarkos* in any other sense than the concrete one of a being of the Logos as *incarnandus*, the affirmation that Jesus Christ is the second "person" of the Trinity and the concomitant rejection of free-floating talk of the "eternal Son" as a mythological abstraction—these commitments require that we see the triunity of God logically as a function of divine election. Expressed more exactly, the eternal act of Self-differentiation . . . is *given in* the eternal act in which God elects himself for the human race.[48]

If Jesus Christ *is* the Word or Son of God and not merely the temporal counterpart to an already existing (pre-enfleshed) Word or Son, then there is no triune being of God logically prior to the event in God in which Jesus Christ exists as God's self-determination. If the Son is Jesus Christ, then the Son both chooses and obtains his existence in the divine decision to be for humanity. The Father is, in turn, Father of the Son and the Spirit is Spirit of the Word.[49]

---

48. Ibid.," 103 (emphasis in original).

49. As Barth has it: "In no depth of the Godhead shall we encounter any other but Him [Jesus Christ]. There is no such thing as Godhead in itself. Godhead is always the Godhead of the Father, the Son and the Holy Spirit. But the Father is the Father of Jesus Christ and the Holy Spirit is the Spirit of the Father and the Spirit of Jesus Christ" (CD II.2, 115).

McCormack acknowledges that this argument stretches sequential human reasoning to its breaking point. "How can the second 'person' of the Trinity . . . participate in the decision which gives him his own distinctive mode of origination?"[50] It would seem impossible to assert that God's elective decision is prior to his triunity while at the same time insisting that a result of that decision, the Second Person of triune God, participated in it. He must exist before he could will himself into existence. Even to conceive of the possibility that divine election determines divine being requires McCormack to stress that this relationship is *logical* and not *chronological*. "We are not asking here about a chronological relation. Election is an *eternal* decision and as such resists our attempts to temporalize it; i.e., to think of it in such a way that a 'before' and an 'after' are introduced into the being of God in pre-temporal eternity. . . . The triunity of God cannot follow this decision in some kind of temporal sequence of events."[51]

It is necessary to consider election before being in light of Barth's claim that Jesus Christ is electing Subject. Nevertheless, this ordering is of a conceptual and not chronological sort. God's being did not exist first for itself and then for humanity, but eternally for humanity, which means that God's decision to be for his creature determined his modes of being or manners of subsisting. Still, we must remain clear that this priority of treatment is logical and does not suggest a before–after sequence. God's will and being are necessarily simultaneous, existing as they do among the same eternal Subject.

This developed conclusion—that divine will logically precedes being—is, as indicated, McCormack's and not Barth's. Barth himself never carried through the implications of his doctrine of election to this extent. "He should have," McCormack argues, "but he did not," and so McCormack sees his own work as comprising a "critical correction" to Barth's inconsistent, or at least incomplete, thinking.[52]

Once more, a full defense of McCormack is beyond the purview of this work. One element of such a defense, however, merits observation in this context.

If McCormack is incorrect, if Christ's self-election is not the logical ground of the triune being of God, then there must be some other logical basis on which God's life is grounded, some metaphysical principle perhaps, apart from this act, so that when we think and speak of God, we must think and speak of two acts, or a being then an act, or something along these lines. There is the

50. McCormack, "Grace and Being," 104.
51. Ibid., 101, 104 (emphasis in original).
52. Ibid., 101, 102.

one act or being of metaphysical stasis, we might say, in which God is who he is, fully triune *in se* and apart from creation. And there is a second act of metaphysical compromise, when and where God forfeits his eternal stasis for a season in order to interact with creation in Christ Jesus. But in that case, we have no choice except to return election to the mystery of divine will in metaphysical stasis out of which God acts, a will to which we have no access because it is of a being to which we have no access, a being who inscrutably decides to be differently for a while, but why, exactly for how long, and exactly for whom, we cannot say. Barth is clear that we absolutely cannot take this path:

> If this is not the case [that Jesus Christ is the eternally electing God], then in respect of the election, in respect of this primal and basic decision of God, we shall have to pass by Jesus Christ, asking of God the Father, or perhaps of the Holy Spirit, how there can be any disclosure of this decision at all. For where can it ever be disclosed to us except where it is executed? The result will be, of course, that we shall be driven to speculating about a *decretum absolutum* instead of grasping and affirming in God's electing the manifest grace of God.[53]

If Jesus Christ is not the electing God, then we have no knowledge of the actual, eternal, essential character of God as *grace*. We are driven back to the mystery of an absolute decree, away from the God encountered in grace, for apart from Christ we have no knowledge of that grace. Importantly for my argument: Barth presupposes that neither the Father nor the Spirit is alternatively available to us as an agent of divine disclosure vis-à-vis the truth of election, for again, we only know the Father and the Spirit in the light of the Son, and specifically, in the light of the Son's electing activity. The Father and Spirit come to us as meaningful parties in the divine life when and where that life is determined by the decision to be Lord over non-being, darkness, and death, which gracious decision is executed exclusively in Christ as its Subject.

In short, it is not possible to contend that Jesus Christ is the electing Subject *and as such* the revelation of God without also contending that he is the logical ground of God's very triune being. Balking at the latter commitment entails balking at the former; Jesus Christ becomes a mere outcome of a mysterious eternal choice, not a Party to that choice (its "execution") and therefore not

---

53. CD II.2, 105.

its revelation, if God is God above and prior to the enfleshed Word. On the other hand, affirming the former commitment (that Jesus Christ is the electing and revealing Subject) entails affirmation of the latter (that he is the logical ground of the Trinity); that Jesus Christ *is* the grace of God entails that he is the determination of the gratuity by which God creates and redeems, that the Creator and Redeemer willfully and comprehensively have their life-acts in the life-act of the Reconciler. Barth shows flashes of this recognition even if, as McCormack points out, he does so inconsistently.

If, with McCormack, we carry Barth's logic through, then the Spirit has his own distinctive mode of origination in and with the elective grace of the Son. There is no Spirit other than as agency of the Son's continuing decision, the power of divine self-determination according to which God is and remains God-for-us. If it is in the eternal event of Christ that the being of God is logically grounded, then it is in him that the knowledge of God according to which that being finds its exercise—the occurrence of grace in the happening of revelation—likewise takes its grounding.

As the Son is the Exegete, the Spirit is the Exegesis of God. He is the condition of the divine possibility by being the instantiation of divine reality in Christ; this, in that he is at once the source and perceptual influence of faith, the giver of the eyes and ears by which God is perceived in the grace of Christ and the focus, in both senses, of those eyes and ears. He is their finely tuned aperture, and he makes Christ to be their object. He does this by reiterating in our space-time the history of Christ Jesus in his.

The Spirit bends space-time around this history in the verberation of witness to Christ. He summons the muscular flexes and reflexes, tones and intones, orally and auditorily, by which the name Jesus is proclaimed and heard *as it is*—the eternal, self-determinative grace of very God. He calls forth the synaptic transmissions, the ideas according to which Christ is communicated and received as, again, the elective will of God to be Immanuel.

In this regard, the Spirit as the power of God elides into the Spirit as an agential identity in God. The Spirit just is instantiation of the elective will of God today, the event in which God not only determines to create but also to make that creation his own, which is realized only as event, that is, only where and when creation actually is made to be God's own, only in the place and moment that the reality of the Word triumphs over humanity's usurped, finite powers of self-contrivance. This should not bother us, for what is true of the Spirit in this respect is true also of the Son, and indeed of God. It is the case neither of God in his Persons nor of God in his being that we can definitively differentiate between the power and agential quality of God, for as we have been saying, God is who he is in the exercise of his power, his authority over every force of non-being, darkness, and death. God is God in the act of *being* Lord.

This brings us to the second element in Barth's treatment of election, and the second claim advanced in this chapter. Jesus Christ is the Object of election. As Spirit of the Word, the Holy Spirit is contemporary reiteration of the real dialectic of judgment and mercy grounded and made known in Christ's receptive obedience.

"Before time itself, in the pre-temporal eternity of God, the eternal divine decision as such has as its object and content the existence of this one created being, the man Jesus of Nazareth, and the work of this man in His life and death, His humiliation and exaltation, His obedience and merit."[54] The object and content of the primal decision in which God is God are the life of the human Jesus. God elects himself to this life in the Son, including its dishonor in scorn, his veiling in this flesh and its rejection, as well as glory in resurrection, his unveiling in the empty tomb and its adoration.

First and foremost God elects to himself his own history, his own humanity in the man of Nazareth. Humanity at large is, in turn, elected in this history, *in him.* "In that he (as God) wills Himself (as man), He also wills them. And so they are elect 'in Him,' in and with his own election."[55] The exercise of divine will in the enfleshed Word entails not only that Christ is the electing God, not only that he is the actor, but also that Jesus is the elected man, the acted upon for all humanity. Before anything is said of human being as the object of God's eternal decree, everything must be said of this human being as principal recipient of that decree in which others are included. Our election is understood only in the light and as the consequence of Jesus' election:

> In the predestination of the man Jesus we see what predestination is always and everywhere—the acceptance and reception of man only by the free grace of God. Even in the man Jesus there is . . . no prior and self-sufficient goodness, which can precede His election to divine sonship. Neither prayer nor the life of faith can command or compel His election. It is by the work of the Word of God, by the Holy Spirit, that He is conceived and born without sin, that He is what he is, the Son of God; by grace alone. And as He became Christ, so we become Christians. As he became our Head, so we become

54. Ibid., 116.
55. Ibid., 117.

His body and members. As He became the object of our faith, so we become believers in Him.[56]

Perceiving that Jesus is the principal object of election entails recognition that the elective act is an act of pure grace. Nothing "of himself" as a human qualifies Jesus to receive God's attention, no moral superiority, prayer life, or piety, but only the gratuitous generosity of God's will and decision. Jesus is not the sinless man because he lucked into the right pedigree; his flesh is made suitable for God by the Holy Spirit, sanctified, redeemed, made immaculate in its conception. So also our election entails no prior qualifying essence, duty, or work; it is a matter of the free grace of God.

To say that our election by God to stand as creatures before God takes place *in Christ* (see Eph. 1:4, 7, 9, 11, 13) means that as God acts upon Jesus, as he is made by God to be the true human and to intercede for us, our humanity is drawn into the grace of God and we come to be who we are. We note, first of all, the actualism of this drawing. "As he became Christ, so we become Christians." As Jesus receives the divine command and obediently carries it out, as he is the intervention between God and Man, the Messiah, the Christ before us as the object of our every hope, of faith in God as our Redeemer, so that faith happens; it becomes the real determination of our being. To say that we are elected in Christ means that we are being drawn into an active, moment-by-moment way of living, an obedience to him sourced in and shaped after his obedience to the Father. Just as the content of election consists of the obedience of Jesus, so also does it consist of our obedience to Jesus.

This is significant for our present inquiry in that it means that the work of the Holy Spirit cannot be other than the act of drawing us into the life of Christ, of making our election tangible and sure in him. It can only be the ongoing operation of grace by which God is God and we are his children:

It is in him that the eternal election becomes immediately and directly the promise of our own election as it is enacted in time, our calling, our summoning to faith, our assent to the divine intervention on our behalf, the revelation of ourselves as sons of God and of God as our Father, the communication of the Holy Spirit who is none

56. Ibid., 118.

other than the Spirit of this act of obedience, the Spirit of obedience itself, and for us the Spirit of adoption.[57]

It is in Jesus actually being the object of election that we come to be who we are, recipients of divine benevolence as the children of God. And it is in our becoming who we are that the Holy Spirit is made known. He is the guarantee of this happening in that he is the instantiation of Christ's obedience here and now.

We note then also the content of our being drawn into Christ: as he lives the history of obedience to God on our behalf, obedience even unto death on a cross (Phil. 2:8), taking upon himself the full measure of divine judgment against sin, despised of men and afflicted by God (Isa. 53:3-4), we become accepted by God, recipients of salvation.

"The election of the man Jesus means, then, that a wrath is kindled, a sentence pronounced and finally executed, a rejection actualized. It has been determined thus from all eternity."[58] That the way of human redemption should be through divine judgment is not a consequence of history taking an unforeseen turn; it is not "Plan B" from the perspective of God's eternal will, counsel, and decision. It is "Plan A." It is the determination of God's self-election in Christ—*in Christ*, such that the consequence of this election does not amount to punishment inflicted on an unwilling object, but rather, said punishment is chosen for that object by himself as Subject—that Jesus should bear God's rejection of darkness in his existence as God's glorious light.

As we discussed in chapter 1, sin accompanies obedience as a possibility in the creative act of God, a possibility not actualized by God in this reality, but by the creature as a genuine, living agent opposite God. The possibility lacks any basis as a possibility except in the co-determination of the creature by the exercise of its faculties as a living agent, which is to say, except as self-contradiction, utterly unwarranted negation of human possibility given by God to be-his-creature. (We are, once more, "without excuse.") Yet as a possibility in this negation, it must be dealt with:

For teleologically the election of the man Jesus carries within itself the election of a creation which is good according to the positive

57. Ibid., 106.
58. Ibid., 122.

will of God and of man as fashioned after the divine image and foreordained to the divine likeness (reflection). But this involves necessarily the rejection of Satan, the rebel angel who is the very sum and substance of the possibility which is not chosen by God (and which exists only in virtue of this negation); the very essence of the creature in its misunderstanding and misuse of its creation and destiny and in its desire to be as God, to be itself a god.[59]

The election of Christ entails the rejection of that which is contrary to the will of God in its every force and variety. Jesus is the perfect bearer of that which God rejects in two senses. First, he is pure embodiment of God's will, including that to which God says, "No." But as such, second, he assumes the rejection, the abandonment and forsakenness of that realm and way of being against which God's will is directed. The nothingness that is external to God's will meets him in its fullest force. It co-determines his history. He is the forsaken one, "despised and rejected of men" and "stricken by God" (Isa. 53:3, 4).

Jesus is the one sent by God to that which is not God, the *christos* over and against which the *antichristos* arises. "Satan (and the whole kingdom of evil, i.e., the demonic, which has its basis in him) is the shadow which accompanies the light of the election of Jesus Christ. . . . And in the divine counsel the shadow itself is necessary as the object of rejection."[60] Satan is the illusive possibility, which is no possibility in itself but which nevertheless exists within the divine counsel and so exists genuinely, to which humanity is drawn in exercise of its faculties as an agent opposite God. His is the false flash of human perception by which another world seems to open to us, in which we are maker and lord. "To the reality of [the shadow's] might and activity . . . testimony is given by the fall of man, in which man appropriates to himself the satanic desire. . . . Man in himself and as such has in his creaturely freedom no power to reject that which in His divine freedom God rejects."[61]

Human inclination of itself is to the nothingness of its self, to the fleeting movement between the nothing of our time before birth to the nothing of our time after death, waking and walking within the horizon of mortality that bounds our existence. That inclination is stirred each moment by the dark shadow cast over our being, by the seductive power to reject the gift of life and

59. Ibid.
60. Ibid.
61. Ibid.

light in favor of its theft, of usurping to our selves the divine prerogative and point of view—to be Lord and Giver of life—and in this to become an adversary of God. This power is made real and known in our active impotency to resist and reject the seduction to self, which is to say, our powerlessness to repeat the life-promoting obedience of Jesus before God.

God's eternal predestination in Christ Jesus entails not only positive determination but also critical negation, indeed, in the positive determination—in the gift of being, light, and life, which overflows from the God who just is this gift—is the critical negation, active opposition to non-being, darkness, and death. Non-being, darkness, and death are a collective possibility that can be realized and comprehended only in the self-determinative election of God in Christ, only as the effective "in and among which" of his creation, reconciliation, and redemption. Satan and all evil, the shadow of all creaturely existence, take place as groundless resistance to and refusal of God's life-giving will, which take place nevertheless as the substance of what he rejects, and therefore part of the stage on which he actively is the Lord and Giver of life. We do not, cannot instantiate rebellion against God as a thing in itself, which might overcome God, but only as a modality to which God firmly and definitively says "No!" in Christ.

In Christ, God says no to human rebellion, negates our negation of existence and dispels the shadow of Satan, by condemning them in himself. The wrath of God and his rejection of sin are directed not toward humanity in itself, which stands powerless before temptation and as such would be consumed by that wrath, but toward Jesus:

> In this one man Jesus, God puts at the head and in the place of all other men the One who has the same power as Himself to reject Satan and to maintain and not surrender the goodness of man's divine creation and destiny. . . . The rejection which all men incurred, the wrath of God under which all men lie, the death which all men must die, God in His love for men transfers from all eternity to Him in whom He loves and elects them, and whom He elects at their head and in their place.[62]

62. Ibid., 123.

The wrath that is kindled against creaturely disobedience is kindled in Christ as the divine Subject and directed toward Christ as the human Object of election. In other words, the first statement that must be made about humanity in the doctrine of election is that the true, sinless human, Jesus, is elected to become the one true sinner and so to endure the suffering and death of those mired in sin; this, from all eternity. Sin is not dealt with, once more, by a backup plan hatched and enacted after the fact but according to the divine will and counsel in the primal reality of God. It is afforded its possibility in that counsel as negation of the divine will, which in the same counsel is itself negated. God is God over the negation of being from first to last, as Creator, Reconciler, and Redeemer. But he is this Lordship (and triune activity) in Christ, which is to say, by the initiative, decision, and act to reject every force of non-being, darkness, and death, which self-election takes place by Christ as its Subject *and* Object.

God simply is God in being Lord; in the exercise of unlimited authority realized and made known in the decision and act of assuming what he is not, the negation of being in the triumph of Satan, and triumphing over it. He acts as Judge and Judged; in Christ he condemns the usurping instinct to nonexistence, in which judgment he nullifies that instinct and its consequences and *is* God. "The essence of the free grace of God consists in the fact that, in this same Jesus, God who is the Judge takes the place of the judged, and they are fully acquitted, therefore, from sin and its guilt and penalty. Thus, the wrath of God and the rejection of Satan and his kingdom no longer have any relevance for them."[63]

God is God, Lord of deity and humanity, in the execution of a twofold steadfastness:

On God's side, it is the steadfastness of grace even in the judgment to which He condemns the Elect. It is the constancy of love even in the fire of the wrath which consumes Him. It is the steadfastness of election even in the midst of the rejection which overtakes Him. And on the side of the Elect, it is the steadfastness of obedience to God, and of calling only upon Him, and of confidence in the righteousness of His will. It is in the unity of this steadfastness both divine and human that we shall find the peculiar secret of the election of the man Jesus.[64]

63. Ibid., 125.
64. Ibid.

God is God in eternal self-election to judgment, in the merciful condescension by which all that he is not in fact and potential is assumed from the very beginning, and as such, is overcome. God is therefore God in the active will to have glory in and through humility, which is to say, to be worshiped and obeyed in the veil of flesh and death by which he is unveiled as Lord over death. "The Word of the divine steadfastness is the resurrection of Jesus from the dead, His exaltation, His session at the right hand of the Father. By these events God confirms the fact that the Elect is the only-begotten Son of God who can suffer death but not be beholden to death, who by his death must destroy death."[65] God is revealed in the steadfastness of Christ Jesus as the Elect to suffer death, through which steadfastness unto death God defeats death. The possibility of rejecting the will of God afforded by the divine counsel is nullified by the selfsame counsel in that God realizes the possibility in himself and overcomes it. He takes up sin and judges it. He assumes sin's consequence, death, in Christ Jesus and raises him from the dead. He exalts him over all creaturely reality as Ruler at the Father's right hand.

He is God *in* this electing. His glory as God is in the active operation of grace, of giving life where there is only death, of shining light where there is only darkness, of creating being where there is strictly nothing. He is this in Christ as the object of election, as the assumption of death, darkness, and non-being and their rejection. He is this in the steadfastness, the obedience of Christ to this election, to this rejection by which the glory of God is made manifest.

The Spirit of this God, then, can only be continued reiteration of this obedience. He can only be the ongoing instantiation of God's refusal of every force of non-being in the specific act and form of judgment, on one side, in and through which his grace and mercy shine forth in victory, on the other. The Spirit's agential identity must be in just this dialectical event.

It is not insignificant that Barth follows his section on "Jesus Christ, Electing and Elected," with a section on "The Election of the Community" in which Israel, the covenant people of God, is presented as the recipient of divine judgment and the passing form of God's children, and the church is presented as the recipient of divine mercy and the coming form of those children.[66] It should be obvious that Barth intends for us to think and speak of the actualistic event of God's life taking place in this covenant history.

We think and speak of God in terms of the Spirit when and where we think and speak in terms of the reality of the covenant. Specifically, we think

65. Ibid.
66. Ibid., §34, 195–305.

and speak of God in terms of the Spirit when and where the judgment and mercy of God are made real in space-time, when Israel's Messiah comes and is rejected, through which rejection the church's Hope comes and is manifested. God is God in the event of the Spirit when and where he is God in the continuing event of Christ Jesus, when and where the history of Christ Jesus is real again, which history commandeers and reorients our own, so that God has his same history, his same victory through death over death, here and now.

Pneumatocentric theology can only be this theology: thought and speech proclaiming God's covenant history again today, his being in movement from the Old Covenant to the New *as a continuing event*. In this continuing movement, God is God and the Spirit is the Spirit. In this movement, which takes place in Christ as the election of God, we speak both *of* the Spirit and *by* the Spirit as Spirit of the Word. For in this movement we ourselves come to be; in the obedience of this testimony to Christ as the judgment and grace of God we are actors in that judgment and grace; we are partakers of God by his Spirit.

CONCLUSION

We know God only when and where he actually *is* God, when and where the authority defining his being, when and where the primal exercise of Lordship over what he is and is not, actually meets us; when and where primal, unrivaled Lordship comes to and reigns over the creature. There is no God, so far as we have any knowledge, above and prior to this meeting. God is God in the *event* of coming to humanity, in the exclusivity of that happening in which humanity finds itself placed before this Lord, as the object of his life-giving graciousness, and therefore in obedience to him. God is God in the event of Jesus Christ, who is this happening—both its electing Subject and obedient Object.

We can think and speak of God only in the event wherein we encounter him and find ourselves, as selves, in him. We can think and speak of God only in the factual happening of the relationship in which we are dependent on him for our every thought and speech—the relationship of witnessing to the Word, of holistic obedience to Christ Jesus.

This relationship is given by God in his self-election, both his side and ours. On the divine side is the event of self-determination, the initiative, decision, and act to be God in love for the creature, which collective initiative, decision, and act is known only in the execution of that love. It is realized and known in Christ Jesus. But that it should be realized and known, that Christ Jesus should exegete the Father of many children, we his children really must stand as his own in perception of his reality and ours, in recognition that we are in fact his children. The execution of the love of God must draw us up and into it as beloved of God; Exegesis must take place with the Exegete.

The Spirit of God is this Exegesis of God. He has his identity in the power of the Word to make offspring of the Father, to generate witnesses in and by the act of witnessing. He simply is the authority of God's revelation or, more precisely, the authority of God in his revelation, of God to be God in the execution of his love for the creature.

The love of God for the creature, then, is an eternal love. It reaches back to the primal reality of God's God-ness and as such entails his rejection of human depravity and rebellion already in the beginning. He negates the negation of the creature in its baseless will to self in the bosom of his divine being by taking up the consequence of that negation—the judgment of sin, which is death—and so negating *it*. He elects the creature's death and damnation to himself that he might give life—that he might be who he is, the Lord and Giver of life—and this in abundance.

The Holy Spirit has distinctive agential quality as Lord and Giver of life in reference to the elective obedience of the Word unto death. He is the reiteration of that obedience, the assumption of death's veil in order to unveil the glory of God in resurrection. He is this inasmuch as he is the generation and assumption of witness to Christ, to the cross, on the one hand, and to the empty tomb, on the other. In the obedience of this witness, the life-act of thought and speech generated and conformed to God's life-act in Christ, which is to say, the life-act of faith by which we become children of God as we were created to be, then and there is the Spirit of God.

Conclusion

If we are to think and speak of God in terms of Christ Jesus, then we confess that God is God in the event of *being* Lord, that is, in the happening of a unique sovereignty wherein neither abstract limitlessness (eternity) nor given limitation (creatureliness) constitutes a constraint on life, but rather, there is freedom to assume limitation while remaining limitless, freedom of eternity for time without forfeiture of distinction from time. Indeed, it is in eternity's coming to time that the distinction is perceived for what it is—an absolute distinction that can be crossed only by the Lord of eternity and time. In this, the reign of God and the revelation of God are bound together: God is Lord in the event that his unique sovereignty happens again, here and now, in the obedient perception of the creature whereby the distinction is made manifest, which is to say, in the event of *faith.*

The contemporary event of faith is the life-act of God being God as he has always been—having his deity in the eternal election of the Son for us, in the decree of creation to be the theater of divine sovereignty, now a third time in the transformation (regeneration) of the creature. The Spirit is God this third time. He is the selfsame God who has his being in the initiative, decision, and act of Lordship, in the factual execution of his absolute sufficiency, on the one side, which takes place in the experience of absolute creaturely dependence, on the other. Thus, contra Robert W. Jenson, exactly as the Spirit *of Christ,* the Spirit of this coordinated happening of authentic divinity and humanity, the Holy Spirit possesses distinct agential identity, but he does so in ontological unity with the Father and Son. He is Exegesis of the Exegete, God's Inverberation in the manner and according to the content of the Word's Incarnation.

The event of faith in which the Spirit is individuated as an agent in the Godhead is not a purely subjective event. On the contrary, it is the event of subject-determining objectivity shaped after the history of Christ's subject-determining objectivity. It is the space-time happening of God's unique, eternal Lordship, here-now in the *verba* of the church's proclamation of Christ according to the *verba* of the prophets and apostles and the reception of those *verba*, which is to say, in continued *generation and assumption* of the media by which God is revealed *as God*, in authority and power over himself and what he is not.

Obviously enough, for Inverberation to be an episode of subject-determining objectivity and not object-determining subjectivity (which reversal of direction I take to be at the heart of Barth's complaint against Schleiermacher and the bulk of liberal Protestantism after him) the content of the event must be the same as that of the Incarnation. The Spirit is the determinative presence of Christ Jesus, manifestation of the enfleshed Word to human perception with ontological potency to make disciples. He is the revelation of God today by which children are born not of natural descent, but of God, just as in 1–30 c.e. and in the beginning. The content of the Spirit is the content of the eternal Word precisely as God's *living* Word.

And the act of Inverberation must also be of the same character as Incarnation. It must continually be God's initiative, his election to this life, his generation of these words and his assumption of them, just as it was his initiative and decision to generate and assume the flesh of Jesus. The event of God being God in these words is of the same essence as his being God in this flesh. He is God with *us*, yes, but *God* with us. Our words are shown for their inadequacy precisely where and when they are made adequate to him, and it is experience of that inadequacy before true adequacy, utter dependency before authentic sufficiency, that of itself proclaims God in the power of his presence.

I would like to conclude this argument by consulting one final piece from Barth, in which we can see the book's claims encapsulated succinctly.

In October 1929, the federation of Reformed churches in Germany held its third biennial "theological week" in Elberfeld, a conference for pastors and students of theology, on the theme of the Holy Spirit. Barth gave a lecture for this conference, which we note took place in the heart of his third developmental phase, on "The Holy Spirit and the Christian Life."[1]

---

1. Barth, "Der heilige Geist und das Christliche Leben," in *Vorträge und kleinere Arbeiten 1925–1930*, Gesamtausgabe 24 (Zurich: Theologischer Verlag, 1994), 458–520; English translation: *The Holy Spirit and the Christian Life: The Theological Basis of Ethics*, trans. R. Birch Hoyle (Louisville: Westminster John Knox, 1993). The first two theological weeks covered the topics of "The Church" and "The Word of God" in 1925 and 1927, respectively (see "Der heilige Geist," 458). The 1929 conference dealt with the theme of the Spirit via three lines of inquiry. It was handled first in the context of the week's preaching seminar. It was also taken up in relation to the two historical movements of Pietism and German Idealism, the latter being handled by Barth's brother, Heinrich. Finally, it was covered in view of three systematic matters. The systematic subtopics included "The Holy Spirit and Justifying Belief (or the 'Faith of Justification'—*Rechtfertigungsglaube*)," "The Holy Spirit and the Church," and the topic Barth was invited to take, "The Holy Spirit and the Christian Life." Barth gave his lecture on Wednesday afternoon, October 9, to around one thousand eager auditors (ibid., 459). It was initially published with his brother Heinrich's lecture under the common title, *Zur Lehre vom heiligen Geist*, Zwischen den Zeiten 1 (Munich: Kaiser, 1930).

The trinitarian structure of the lecture is immediately obvious: Barth divided it into three parts, "The Holy Spirit as Creator," "The Holy Spirit as Reconciler," and "The Holy Spirit as Redeemer."[2] To think and speak of the Spirit is to think and speak of God in his fullness a third time, which is to say, as the Lord who brings being out of nothing, light to darkness, and life from death.

The Holy Spirit is God and not a cipher for human achievement or transcendence. This is the central thesis of Barth's understanding of the Spirit as *Creator*—that "between being Lord and being lorded over there exists an irreversibility such as excludes the idea of God as an object of whom, in Platonic fashion, we have a reminiscence."[3] The Spirit is known in the event of God's Lordship, in the actual happening of humanity's being lorded over, in the manifest relationship between Lord and lorded over. It is essential to the happening of this relationship that there is a distinct direction from the Lord to the lorded over. The lorded over do not make the Lord out of their position, but the other way around—they exist and are made known in the rule of the Lord, as the objects of his rule.

The Holy Spirit is this self-governing happening of divine Lordship. He is not a concept, a mystical quality, or a means given to humanity, which the human governs, cultivates, and pursues so that, by introspective rediscovery, she ascends to God. The Holy Spirit is not the mimetic soul, whereby the divine is reproduced in human perceiving and doing. Rather, the Spirit comes to be known in truth, as he is, in and by the same act of revelation in which God is known in truth, as he is:

> The sayings "God has made us for himself" and "man made in the image of God" are not to be taken as meaning an abiding and sure fact of revelation that we once and for all have made our own, but it is a process of revelation, which in the strictest sense, is first coming to us and to come, moment by moment, if, as we should, we have taken seriously what is meant by the *Deity* of the *Creator* Spirit.[4]

2. Barth, *Holy Spirit*, 3–17, 19–58, 59–70, respectively.
3. Ibid., 4–5.
4. Ibid., 5.

In thinking and speaking of the Spirit, we are thinking and speaking of the selfsame God who speaks (present tense) to humanity in his Word, such that our relationship to God, any point of contact in *spirit*, is given in revelation as *process* and not as *datum*. We do not take the divinity of the Holy Spirit seriously if we convert his identity into a cipher for our own realization. He is humanity's point of origin, our Creator, not a product of the creature, our creation.

But God *is* known as Creator, and therefore by the created specifically as the object of his work and will. When it is firmly established that the Spirit is not the created but the Creator, then it must be said that the Spirit has his life and work in and with the creature. "Man as he is, in his creaturely existence as man and as an individual, is opened, prepared, and made fit by God for God. 'By the *Spirit* for the Word' is what we mean when saying by *God* for God."[5] The life and work of the Spirit in his active Lordship as God is to fit the creature for the Word, to make God and creature alive and known to the creature in the life-act of Christ Jesus.

Barth places special accent on the event-character of the Spirit in this life and work. The Spirit is not a fixed thing anymore than God is a fixed thing; his self-governing activity of turning the creature to the Word is never to be taken for granted as a datum within the creature's range of comprehension but must continually come to the creature as a new phenomenon, rearranging her knowledge and understanding:

> Ability to take in God's Word, must be his [the creature's] own; yet it is not his own possession, but it must simply *be conveyed* to him all along. A sheer miracle must happen to him, a second miracle in addition to the miracle of his own existence, if his life shall be a true Christian life, which is a life within the hearing of God's Word. This miracle is the office of the Holy Spirit.[6]

The Spirit has his life and work in the act of miraculously conveying God's Word to the creature, not only the content of the Word, but also the openness to this content. The human does not ever possess a readiness for the Word in herself, but constantly receives it in the same way that she receives life from this God, in and by God's self-determinative life-act of grace.

5. Ibid., 7.
6. Ibid., 11.

God remains God in the event of being known by the creature. In fact, his deity is *in* this *remaining*, in the exercise of self-determination even as he makes himself co-determined by creaturely thought and speech. It is in moment-by-moment encounter with this self-determining Lordship among the lorded-over that the lorded-over hear God and perceive themselves relative to him. "In actual fact, we can only hear in the action itself, in the divine assurance within our own human lack of assurance, which corresponds to the fact that this hearing is the miracle of God."[7] Only as human need is established with the divine provision, as our lack of self-possession is made real alongside God's self-possession, do we know God as he is, as the one who loves us in the unrivaled freedom to give himself to us. The Holy Spirit is the miracle of this freedom:

> It can, and must, be said further that we are only able to hear as we *pray*: "I am a sojourner on earth, hide not thy commandments from me" (Ps. 119:19). Only in the miracle of the Holy Spirit are they not hidden from us. But who could, or also would, only pray for the revelation of those commandments, if they had not already become revealed to him while praying, in the miracle of the Holy Spirit?[8]

The event in which God exists and is known as God, the event of revelation among humanity, the miracle of the Holy Spirit, is a present-tense, spiraling affair. The revealedness of God among his creatures, our readiness for his Word, is the precondition of receiving his Word and having our lives in it. But it is in receipt of the Word, in its revelation of God and humanity, that we know who God is, where to seek him and wait upon him, which is to say, that our openness to the divine Lordship obtains its necessary content and shape.

One cannot subordinate one to the other—the subjectivity of revelation to the objectivity or vice versa—for God is God and the creature is the creature only in the happening of both. Only as God actually makes himself to stand before us and makes us to stand before him is he God; only as such, in this miracle, is he the Lord who freely loves, God-with-us, and thus do we become the lorded-over who freely return that love, humanity-with-God.

So far the Holy Spirit as Creator: it is in and by the Spirit that the self-determination of God and humankind happens again today. Barth stresses the

7. Ibid.
8. Ibid.

activeness of this happening not only because the creature lacks self-possession, such that apart from the livingness of grace we have no raison d'être, but also and more profoundly because, as fallen creatures, we live in hostile opposition to God. This is the central motif of his treatment of the Holy Spirit as Reconciler—that God actively refuses human rebellion.

"It is not his *difference* from the created spirit that constitutes the holiness of the Holy Spirit. It is holiness pregnant in its *opposition* to the forceful and radical perversion and sin of the created spirit."[9] The ontological distinction between Creator and created is critical if we are to understand the Spirit of God, but it is not most critical. More basic is the distinction between the holiness of God and the depravity of humanity. We know the Spirit as the *Holy* Spirit insofar as we encounter him in dynamic opposition to our sinful nature.

Even though it exists in utter ontological dependence on the Creator, humanity is not inclined to this existence. It must, once more, be brought again to this dependence. It is not disposed to live under his Lordship but to exercise self-lordship and, in fact, lordship over God. It is not disposed to hear the Word of God about himself and us, but to generate its own words about both. It is not given to faith but to unbelief. But as the Lordship of God over the creature, the Spirit is known in persistent opposition to the persistent perversion of human being. The "operation of the Spirit has to be seen in its radical and inevitable erection of a barrier against all that is our own action."[10]

Humanity is sinful. So much is this true of our nature that we cannot even recognize it to be true of our nature. "Sin, like righteousness, is as little a quality that would really attach to man and be understood, apart from God's revelation. He could not know that he is a sinner: this he can only believe."[11] It is therefore the life and work of the Spirit to make the reality of sin manifest to us that it might be overcome, obviously not by us, who are so mastered by it, but by God. In the Spirit, God not only erects a barrier between eternity and time, but also, and more essentially, between righteousness and unrighteousness, this, as he takes up our time and unrighteousness.

In his treatment of the Spirit as Reconciler, Barth is unabashedly a classically orthodox (over against modern liberal) Protestant theologian. This is an important observation, for if one would advocate for Barth's account of the Spirit as I do, he must embrace the conviction that historical Protestantism continues to make a relevant contribution to contemporary theological discourse. And of course, conversely, to reject Barth's account of the Spirit

9. Ibid., 19.
10. Ibid., 20.
11. Ibid., 27.

amounts to at least tacit rejection of Reformation theo-logic. Barth certainly updates the Reformers' thought, translating its metaphysical substructure into an actualistic, event-ontology, as we have been seeing, but he nevertheless strives, in effect, to be truer to their thought than they could have been in their context.

Barth recognizes that the character of sin in the Reformation doctrine is of such a radical degree that to be perceived, sin must be made real to us; God must take it up and show it to us right when and where he, only he, rejects it (for only he *can* reject it). To say that the human is dead in sin means that she cannot be made alive but in Christ, that this is as true now as ever, and therefore that the Spirit of God cannot be thought and spoken by sinful humanity apart from just this work. He must be, today as ever, God in the life-act of declaring "No" to humanity in its darkness that he might say "Yes" to humanity in him. Thus, the protest of Protestantism can be set aside only when and where the weight of that protest has actually been felt, when and where its commitment to the radical otherness *and* holiness of God relative to the human has been registered, and hence, when and where it is recognized that the Spirit of God can never be conflated into any human spirit—any aesthetic appreciation, moral fiber, fortitude, esprit.

For Barth, as for Luther and Calvin (over against even Augustine), sin is not merely disordered perception, moral infelicity, sickness, or weakness. It is not simply a wound or disease that can be cured. It is, rather, fatality, the night of humanity, the impenetrable darkness of being out of which no light shines, thus in which there is *no* order, morality, health, or strength that we might start from in order to mount an ascent to God. "Sin is not taken in deadly earnest when it is regarded as something that can be radically overcome by the enthusiasm of 'good intentions,' and then, by and by, can be removed by practical activity. You may cure a wound by such treatment by you cannot restore a dead man to life."[12]

The first thing that must be said about the Spirit as Reconciler is that he makes real and known to us the fact that humanity is *dead* in sin (Eph. 2:1; Col. 2:13). In this, he is the Spirit of Jesus Christ, the reiteration of the life-act in which God confronts humanity in its contradiction that he might overcome it. *He* might overcome it: as the Spirit of the Word, God establishes us in our incapacity that he might be our capacity, that he might bestow upon us the repentance, faith, and obedience by which we can and do live as his children:

---

12. Ibid., 23.

The significance of the Holy Spirit for the Christian life lies, in the light of the contrast between grace and sin, with especial pregnancy in the fact that he is the Spirit of *Jesus Christ*, of God's Son in the flesh who was crucified for us, or (what amounts to the same), the Spirit of the *Word* of the Father, spoken to us. If Jesus Christ, the Crucified, or if the Word of the Father is our reconciliation, then the meaning of this takes completely away any working of ours. And if the Holy Spirit is the Spirit of Christ, or of the Word, then he, for this reason, cannot be the unblest Spirit of our own working.[13]

That creaturely reconciliation with the Creator is a reality in Christ Jesus, that he is its shape and substance, dictates that the Spirit of Reconciliation can only be the Spirit of Christ. There can be no other Spirit or other basis upon which to think and speak of the Spirit than the work of God in reconciling humanity to himself effected and made known in Jesus. This is given in the essentially Protestant theo-logic whereby grace is not the perfection of sinful man but opposition to sinful man and his resurrection to new life. For Barth, the Spirit can only be the manifest happening of this real dialectic, for there is no other God that the sinner as such can know.

The Spirit cannot be the synthesis of humanity and deity. He cannot be the unblest spirit of human efforts at repentance, faith, and obedience, but the refusal of those efforts and the supply of each in its respective propriety. Indeed, the Spirit is our supply by first showing our need to us; he makes way for real repentance, faith, and obedience by showing the inadequacy of our own attempts at them.

Any moment that we actually live as Christ's, as Christians in faith and penitence, is determined by the prior act of God's power over us in the Spirit. Any moment that we actually hear the Word and stand before God takes place in response to the prior moment of the Spirit's life and work in us. "Only in the Holy Spirit . . . is it decided, with reference to our purest, best-intentioned action, whether it is perhaps, and remains, sin, or whether, by virtue of God's forgiveness taking a share in our action—a share we cannot apprehend—it might be well done, done in God."[14]

We can never freeze our action, even by retrospection, and adjudicate its worthiness relative to the will of God. Such adjudication is the office of the

---

13. Ibid., 25–26 (italics in original).
14. Ibid., 36.

Spirit alone. "The Holy Spirit is absolutely and alone the umpire with reference to what is or is not Christian life."[15] All we can do is live the obedience that we perceive in Christ by the Spirit, in each moment that we are made to perceive it, in full awareness of the imperfection of our living, but also in this, in full hope that *God* will declare that living right and good, that *he* will take it up and make it useful. All we can do is walk in faith *and* in the penitent prayer, "Lord, help my unbelief" (Mark 9:24)! That is the Christian life, life in the Spirit of Reconciliation.

God brings this life about in coordination with his life-act in Christ, this each day anew, as in and by the Spirit he makes Christ to be the determination of our reality. *In and by*—God has his being as Spirit when and where he once again exercises the Lordship made real and known in Christ. God is God the Spirit, or conversely, God the Spirit is God in the event that the ontological boundary between Creator and created and the moral boundary between righteousness and unrighteousness are affixed and overcome, or better, are affixed in their overcoming, in God's coming to our mortality and depravity in Christ according to which act we are made to look beyond that mortality and depravity.

This is the guiding premise of Barth's treatment of the Holy Spirit as Redeemer—that "the boundary lines between God and ourselves, but also the relation between him and us, are openly always set by this, that in his revelation he *promises* us something that is ultimate and future, something that is his characteristic purpose with us."[16] Quite simply, the Spirit of God is the event of making real and showing to humanity its inclination in sin to death and so placing it, for life now and forever, entirely in God. It is in actuating total creaturely dependence on the Reconciler and Creator by turning the creature's gaze, with death and depravity yet in view, beyond death and depravity to life in communion with God.

I indicated in chapter 1 that such actualism vis-à-vis the Spirit forms the bridge to Schleiermacher, which Barth saw from a distance in his late ruminations about a theology of the Third Article, in that it forms a bridge to thought and speech of *God* in connection with *human being*. Barth gives the same indication here:

> We can now say that the whole of Augustinianism—its doctrine of man's having been created by God and its doctrine of righteousness

---

15. Ibid., 37.
16. Ibid., 59.

as a quality infused into man, that is, justification by works (and in the last analysis these two doctrines are one and the same)—would be tolerable and feasible, if Augustine had but been interpreted as thinking in eschatological terms of thought.[17]

If we transfer the frame of reference within which so much Roman Catholic and liberal Protestant dogma correlate the divine and human in the Spirit to eschatology and thereby actualism, to the "already-but-not-yet" and therefore to the moment-by-moment act of God to establish his reign *as God* and our existence *as God's children*, then we might reconcile nature and grace, Catholicism and Protestantism, Barthian christocentrism and modern liberal piety. Then we might have a repetition in the creature of God's self-knowledge. Then we might have co-knowledge, *con-scientia* or "conscience." Then the Spirit of God might testify with our spirit that we are in fact God's offspring (Rom. 8:16).

"This child may, and can, and must say to himself what the Father says; even to this child is referred the great Schleiermacherian monstrosity—the 'God-consciousness.' God-consciousness within the self-consciousness of man is no longer a horror but utter truth."[18] Awareness of God as the singular Source and Substance of human being occurring within one's self-awareness as standing before the eschatological boundary, which self-awareness comes only from God crossing that boundary here and now in revelation, is an entirely legitimate form of the knowledge of God. The experience of dependency generated and shaped moment by moment *in this crossing* is an entirely legitimate experience; it is the event of God being God today, God the Spirit.

I conclude with this brief exposition of Barth's 1929 Elberfeld lecture because in it we find the whole of the present work's argument in summary form. First, the Holy Spirit is not the human spirit. The human spirit, or religion, or piety, or any cognate expression, is not the condition of our self-knowledge and our knowledge of God, but vice versa; God's Spirit is the condition of the knowledge of God and of humanity. The Spirit is the Spirit of objectivity and subjectivity.

Second, the knowledge of God given by God in his Spirit is a miracle each day anew. It is the self-determinative act in which he exists and is known and we are and are known. The relationship in which he exists as Lord and we

17. Ibid., 60.
18. Ibid., 65.

exist as lorded-over is established in this act, as is our knowledge of it, such that everything we would think and speak of God and ourselves is given in it. The Spirit is the Spirit of reality and possibility.

Third, the content of this act, of God's Lordship, is his consummate rejection of the sinful matrix in which and according to which humanity structures the world. His is the right perception of things, which confronts our perception and remakes it. His is the act of assuming space-time and reframing it according to the sequences and consequences of faith, hope, and love. The Spirit is Spirit of truth and time.

Fourth, the Holy Spirit, then, is none other than the Spirit of the Word Jesus Christ. The Spirit's life and identity are as reiteration of the life-act made real and revealed in Christ. He is the real dialectic of God's "No" to sin and "Yes" to us, happening in the proclamation of Christ, which is to say, happening in the power of the Word to make disciples. The Spirit is the Spirit of being and becoming.

Fifth, as the Spirit of the Word, the Spirit establishes and steps over the eschatological boundary between God and humanity when and where he casts a definite people's gaze beyond the horizon of mortality, which horizon they must yet cross. As Spirit of the Word, the Spirit is the Spirit of the church, when "the church" is neither more nor less than the active coming of God's creation to hope. The Spirit is the Spirit of election and obedience.

These ideas can be found, as they have been here, across the third of four periods of Barth's theological development, as defined by Bruce McCormack. We can surface them in his exegetical understanding of the Word in the prologue to the Gospel of John. We find them as guiding premises in his first attempt at dogmatics in Göttingen. They animate the logic of his grand achievement in CD I.2. They are not restricted to such works, in that lectures taking place near the end of phase 2 already seed their claims, and Barth harvests those claims in later works like CD II.2 on election and III.2 on time. It is probably best, then, to understand pneumatocentric dialectic as characteristic of Barth's thinking between 1924 and 1939, while dawning just before and shining beyond those years.

Still, the road to reconciliation with Schleiermacher, to which Barth pointed late in life, runs through this earlier thinking. It does so inasmuch as this earlier thinking prizes the actualism of God's encounter with the creature. God has his God-ness moment by moment in coming to humanity, in refusing the nothingness of our self-priority and reestablishing his rule in the event of faith. To the extent that a doctrine of the church, then, can retain this actualistic dialectic, this happening of God a third time as he has always been—in and with the object of his creative, reconciling, and redeeming will—there is hope for redeeming the anthropocentrism of Barth's liberal forebear. The obvious first thing that must be done in a theology of the Third Article, which hears Barth's call, is to think and speak of the covenant people as the place and moment, the space-time happening of God's sovereignty and human dependency, and in this, as the collective, first instance of authentic humanity.

Index of Names

Ables, Travis, 49–52
Apostle Paul, 15–16, 23–30, 39n51,
  59n95, 201–2
Aristotle, 129n37
Athanasius, 66
Augustine, 4–5, 50, 73, 128, 159n6,
  181–83, 220, 245, 248
Ayres, Lewis, 4n8

Balthasar, Hans Urs von, 52n81
Barnes, Michel René, 4n8
Barth, Heinrich, 240n1
Bultmann, Rudolf, 117–18
Busch, Eberhard, 19n10

Calvin, John, 73, 159n6, 220, 245

de Régnon, Théodore, 4n8
Del Colle, Ralph, ix
Denecke, Axel, 38–39, 39n50

Edwards, Jonathan, 129n37, 139n57
Einstein, Albert, ix, 12, 66n9, 110, 124,
  128–43, 153, 160n9, 170
Ellul, Jacques, 110, 124–28, 139–41, 143,
  153

Fr. Phil Rossi, S.J., ix

Gadamer, Hans–Georg, 110n3
Galileo, 130
Gockel, Matthias, 55–56, 56n85

Habermas, Jürgen, 110n3
Harnack, Adolf von, 13, 37n47, 159n6
Hector, Kevin W., 11n17
Hegel, Georg Wilhelm Friedrich,
  50n77, 129–30, 130n38, 161, 177

Heidegger, Martin, 113n6, 129–30,
  130n38, 138, 181 83
Herrmann, Wilhelm, 13
Hills, Julian, ix

Irenaeus, 145n73

Jammer, Max, 130n38
Jaspers, Karl, 110 n. 3
Jenson, Robert W., 2–10, 239
John the Baptist, 67, 114–20, 206–16
Jülicher, Adolf, 13

Kant, Immanuel, 24n16, 110n3, 129–30,
  130n38, 134n46, 137n54
Kierkegaard, Søren, 15–16, 124
Kutter, Hermann, 13

Langdon, Adrian, 145n73
Lee, Sang Hyun, 129n37
Leo I, 120–21
Lessing, Gotthold Ephraim, ix
Long, Stephen D., 52n81
Luther, Martin, 50n77, 73, 245

Mach, Ernst, 129–30, 130n38
Marcion, 77n36
Mary Mother of Jesus, 121
Maury, Pierre, 56n85
McCormack, Bruce, ix, 6n13, 24n16,
  50n77, 52n81, 54–59, 60n95, 108n2,
  167–68, 189n50, 217–18, 223–28,
  249
Migliore, Daniel, 94n69
Miner, Robert, 110n3
Moltmann, Jürgen, 51n80, 51–52,
  52n81
Morrison, Roy D. II, 130n38
Moses, 34–35, 214–15

Index of Subjects

absolute dependence, 19, 93, 119, 239, 244; dialectical event of, 23, 36, 53, 151; and human being, 61-62, 71, 191-94, 208, 212-17, 240, 247-49; and sin, 27-30

an-enhypostasia, 54-59, 75-76, 108n2, 121; and church, 193-205

Barthian neglect of the Spirit, alleged, 2-12, 51-54, 56n86, 167-68, 189n50; see also christocentrism

beginning, the, 70, 73, 77, 99; and the being of God, 63-68, 94, 102-5, 109, 115-16, 122-23, 156-57, 168, 190, 219-28, 235 37, 239-40; see also election, event ontology

christocentrism, 18-19, 51-59, 167-68, 189n50, 192-96, 248-50

church, 1, 8-10, 12; and divine address, 14, 38n49, 38-39, 39n50, 39-46, 81-86, 107n1, 210-14; and Inverberation, 92, 103-4, 121, 156, 193-205, 239-40, 249-50; time of, 78-79, 148-53; see also *an-enhypostasia*, space-time

dialectic, 6-12, 17-21; Barth's theological development, 49-60; and divine lordship, 190-96, 202, 217-36, 249-50; preaching and theology, 38n50, 38-39n51, 37-49, 85-92, 169-78, 189n50; prophetic and apostolic offices, 34-35, 115-20, 206-16; and time, 129-37; and truth, 111-14, 138-42; see also absolute dependence, lordship of God, space-time, truth

eschatology, 55-56, 83, 95-104, 108n2, 141n61, 169, 180-81, 248-50

event ontology: God, 1-2, 11-12, 18-24, 35-36, 44-48, 61-62, 66, 70-71, 82-89, 92-93, 104-5, 150-51, 158, 161-70, 172-73, 175, 201-4, 215-16, 225-28, 235-37, 239-41; humanity, 8-12, 26-27, 50n77, 43-54, 59n95, 61-62, 74-79, 89-91, 102-5, 107n1, 122-23, 129-39, 144-51, 155-56, 161-70, 172-73, 181, 184-94, 204, 208, 213-17, 239, 249-50; and divine self-limitation, 162-63, 163n11; and subject-object interface, 110-16, 139-41; and Word's establishment of time-eternity boundary, 6-8, 10, 31-35, 37-48, 60-62, 64-68, 75-76, 81-83, 85-89, 92 93, 104-5, 150-51, 163-67, 193-94, 207-13, 245-47; inspiration, 10, 68, 204; and illumination, 31-35, 52, 68, 73, 76, 85-90, 93-94, 122-23, 169, 204

Inverberation, ixn1, 7-8, 20-22, 48, 102, 108, 110, 120, 128, 179, 199-200; and Incarnation, 35, 44-45, 58-60, 63, 82-83, 114, 120-21, 155-56, 178, 184, 189n50, 239-40; see also *an-enhypostasia*, church

Liberal Protestantism, 10, 13-18, 23, 37n47, 38n49, 50n78, 51-54, 59-61, 99, 167-68, 186-87, 189n50, 240, 244, 248-50

lordship of God, over God's self, 66, 100-4, 150-51, 158, 168-69, 175,

CPSIA information can be obtained
at www.ICGtesting.com
Printed in the USA
LVHW081951300122
709793LV00007B/262